The Database Dictionary

The DATA BASED ADVISOR® Series
Lance A. Leventhal, Ph. D., Series Director

The Database Dictionary

dBASE®, R:BASE®, Oracle®, Ingres®,
DB2®, FoxBASE®, Clipper®, SQL®

Ellen Thro

Microtrend™ Books

ISBN 0-915391-34-1

Library of Congress Catalog Card Number: 89-43501

Microtrend™ Books
Slawson Communications, Inc.
165 Vallecitos de Oro
San Marcos, CA 92069-1436

Edited by Lance A. Leventhal, Ph.D., San Diego, CA
Front Cover design by Lori Maida
Interior design by Sandy Mewshaw, Slawson Communications, Inc.

Printed in the United States
10 9 8 7 6 5 4 3 2 1

TRADEMARK LIST

The following are either trademarks or registered trademarks of their manufacturers, developers, or suppliers:

Actor (The Whitewater Group)
Ada (U.S. Department of Defense)
Ada Program Support Environment (U.S. Department of Defense)
ADABAS (Software AG of North America, Inc.)
Advanced Program-to-Program Communications, APPC (IBM)
AIX (IBM)
ARC/INFO (Environmental Systems Research Institute, ESRI)
Clipper (Nantucket Corp.)
Codabar (Welch Allyn, Inc.)
Code 39 (Intermec, Inc.)
CodeView (Microsoft Corp.)
Color Graphics Adapter, CGA (IBM)
C++ (AT&T, Inc.)
Crosstalk (Crosstalk Communications)
DATACOM/DB (Applied Data Research, Inc.)
Datamanager (MSP)
DB/DC Data Dictionary (IBM)
DB2 (IBM)
dBASE (Ashton-Tate)
DBMS-11 (Digital Equipment Corp.)
dBXL (WordTech Systems, Inc.)
DMS 1100 (Unisys)
Earth One GIS (C.H. Guernsey & Co.)
Eiffel (Interactive Software Engineering, Inc.)
Enterprise Systems Architecture, ESA (IBM)
Excel (Microsoft Corp.)
Focus (Information Builders, Inc.)
FoxBASE (Fox Software)
FoxPro (Fox Software)
Framework (Ashton-Tate)
GemStone (Servio Logic Development Corp.)
GURU (Micro Data Base Systems, Inc.)
HyperCard (Apple Computer, Inc.)
HyperText (Apple Computer, Inc.)
Hyperties (Cognetics, Inc.)
IBM (IBM)

IBM PC (IBM)
IDMS (Cullinet)
IDMS/R (Cullinet)
IFPS (Execucom)
IMS (IBM)
Ingres (Relational Technology)
Integrated Data Dictionary (Cullinet)
Integrated Database Management System (Cullinet)
Integrated Database Management System/Relational (Cullinet)
IST/RAMP (International Security Technology, Inc.)
Knowledge Engineering Environment, KEE (IntelliCorp)
KnowledgeMan/2 (Micro Data Base Systems)
Knowledge Tool (IBM)
Linotronic (Linotype Corp.)
Lotus 1-2-3 (Lotus Development Corp.)
Macintosh (Apple Computer, Inc.)
Microsoft BASIC (Microsoft Corp.)
MicroVAX (Digital Equipment Corp.)
Model 204 (Computer Corporation of America)
Monochrome Display Adapter, MDA (IBM)
MS-DOS (Microsoft Corp)
MVS (IBM)
MVS/ESA (IBM)
MVS/XA (IBM)
NetBIOS (IBM)
NetWare (Novell Corp.)
Nomad2 (Dun & Bradstreet Computing Services)
1-2-3 (Lotus Development Corp.)
Oracle (Oracle Corp.)
OS/2 (IBM)
PageMaker (Aldus Corp.)
Paradox (Borland International)
PC-DOS (IBM)
PostScript (Adobe Systems, Inc.)
Presentation Manager (IBM)
ProKey (RoseSoft)
PS/2 (IBM)
QuickC (Microsoft Corp.)
Quicksilver (WordTech Systems, Inc.)
R* (IBM)

R:BASE (Microrim, Inc.)
RIM (Boeing Corp.)
RSA (RSA Data Technology, Inc.)
SAA (IBM)
Scalable Processor Architecture, SPARC (Sun Microsystems)
SDLC (IBM)
SideKick (Borland International)
Smalltalk-80 (ParcPlace Systems, Inc.)
Smalltalk V (Digitalk, Inc.)
SNA (IBM)
SPARC (Sun Microsystems)
SQLBase (Gupta Technologies)
SQL/DS (IBM)
SQL*Forms (Oracle Corp.)
SQL*PLUS (Oracle Corp.)
SQL Server (Ashton-Tate, Microsoft Corp., and Sybase)
Starburst (IBM)
SuperKey (Borland International)
Symphony (Lotus Development Corp.)
Systems Application Architecture, SAA (IBM)
Systems Network Architecture, SNA (IBM)
Telenet (US Sprint)
Tom Rettig's Library (Tom Rettig Associates)
Turbo C (Borland International)
Turbo Debugger (Borland International)
Turbo Pascal (Borland International)
UNIX (AT&T, Inc.)
VAX (Digital Equipment Corp.)
Ventura Publisher (Xerox Corp.)
Video Graphics Adapter or Video Graphics Array, VGA (IBM)
VINES (Banyan Systems)
Virtual Networking Software (Banyan Systems)
VMS (Digital Equipment Corp.)
VSAM (IBM)
VTAM (IBM)
Windows (Microsoft Corp.)
Word (Microsoft Corp.)
WordPerfect (WordPerfect Corp.)
WordStar (WordStar International)
XENIX (Microsoft Corp.)

Universal Product Code symbol copyright © Uniform Code Council, Inc. The reader should not attempt to utilize this copyrighted material for commercial purposes or to reproduce the symbol for commercial purposes. The Uniform Code Council will not assume any responsibility or incur any liability by virtue of misprinting the copy.

Illustrations for the terms bar code, entity/relationship (ER) Model, and Warnier-Orr diagram reprinted with permission from *Data Based Advisor*. ©Copyright 1989 Data Based Solutions, Inc.

Contents

Contents ix

Acknowledgements xi

Preface xiii

A 1

B 21

C 39

D 67

E 95

F 109

G 125

H 133

I 143

J 159

K 163

L 167

M 181

N 199

O 209

P 219

Q 243

R 247

S 261

T 291

U 307

V 313

W 319

X 325

Y 327

Z 329

Appendix A – Common Mathematical, Logical, and Other Symbols 331

Appendix B – Computer Database Landmarks 333

Appendix C – Standards 337

Appendix D – British Usages 343

Appendix E – Multilingual Equivalents of English Database Terms 345

Appendix F – Sources of Information 349

Appendix G – Misspellings and Correct Spellings . . 353

Appendix H – dBASE Commands and Meanings . . 357

Appendix I – Abbreviations and Acronyms 367

Appendix J – Structured Query Language (SQL) Commands 373

ACKNOWLEDGMENTS

While I was in college, I became an admirer of the 18th century author Samuel Johnson, who compiled the first great English dictionary. So it gives me special satisfaction to acknowledge his inspiration and to think that in some measure I am following his example. Johnson also provided the all-time disclaimer. When a reader asked how he could possibly have defined a word as he had, Johnson boomed back, "Ignorance, Madam, sheer ignorance!" I hope I shall not have occasion to use it.

The constantly changing and growing English language, coupled with the rapidly evolving field of computer databases, presents a lexicographer with a twofold task. One must both provide precise definitions and also record contemporary and changing usage of standard terms and newly coined ones. To accomplish this, I consulted sources ranging from standard textbooks and proceedings of scholarly meetings to articles in trade and popular computer magazines. Two books require special acknowledgment for contributing to my broader understanding of database theory and use: Shaku Atré, *Database: Structured Techniques for Design, Performance, and Management* (New York: John Wiley, 1980; 2nd ed., 1988) and C.J. Date, *An Introduction to Database Systems*, 4th ed. (Reading, MA: Addison-Wesley, 1986).

I am especially pleased to thank the General Editor of this book series, Dr. Lance A. Leventhal, for his heroic work in helping me conceptualize *The Database Dictionary*, define its scope, and bring comprehensive meaning to each term. His encouragement, sense of humor, maddening ability to be right, and inexhaustible supply of blue pencils enabled me to navigate the lexical trees.

I would also like to thank my production editor, Sandy Mewshaw, Mike Kelly for converting the disks, the staffs of Slawson Communications and *Data Based Advisor*, and the technical reviewer, Professor Joan Pierson of James Madison University (Harrisonburg, VA).

PREFACE

WHY THIS BOOK?

SQL. QBE. Recursive. Audit trail. Inference engine. Binary tree. Object oriented.

Two of these terms are new features of Ashton-Tate's dBASE IV. Two come from computer science, the rest from accounting, artificial intelligence, and information management. But they are all part of the world of databases. Other related terms come from communications, computer security, graphics, data processing, and software engineering. If you work with databases, you will need to know the meaning of terms from all these sources.

Why?

Here are some practical reasons. If you are an accountant, you will need to learn computer terms. A programmer, on the other hand, may need to learn accounting terms for a particular application. Both may need help understanding terms used to describe local area networks and security methods.

To use software manuals effectively, database designers and users need to understand terms related to data structures and file handling. Graphics and operating systems both have their own vocabularies, as does artificial intelligence (or expert systems).

Even the term "database" may need defining, since there are several types, each with its own terminology. Specialized programming environments exist – dBASE, DB2, Oracle, SQL, and UNIX, for example – and most databases also can link to general-purpose languages such as Ada, C, and Pascal. Each environment and language has its own set of commands.

The result? The sheer volume of terms is too great for anyone, even a specialist, to remember. (Feel better?) And most people involved in database management are relative newcomers, often with only a few years' experience. Yet they are expected to quickly get databases designed, programs working, and information management systems running smoothly and producing useful reports. Under these circumstances, knowing what the terms and jargon mean is vital.

General-purpose dictionaries contain some terms, and computer and other special dictionaries have others. But if you work with databases regularly, you need a dictionary specifically for definitions related to them. In other words, you need **The Database Dictionary.**

WHO IS THE AUDIENCE?

The dictionary is intended for anyone who works with databases on a personal computer (IBM PC or PC-compatible, or Macintosh), workstation, VAX or other minicomputer, IBM or other mainframe, or network. He or she may use a database at work or in hobbies or volunteer activities. The reader may be an experienced database administrator, programmer, developer, or vendor, or a newcomer to the field. Teachers, trainers, students, consultants, analysts, system integrators, accountants, information systems (IS) specialists, technical writers, and sales and customer engineers are other potential audiences.

You do not have to be a computer professional to understand the terms. Definitions in this dictionary are in plain English – no jargon. In fact, the dictionary decodes computer and database jargon. Its definitions are intended specifically for database users, and examples from widely used databases and operating environments are included wherever possible.

WHAT DOES THE BOOK CONTAIN?

The Database Dictionary has two parts. The first is a general dictionary of over 1,300 terms describing databases and related subjects, including accounting, artificial intelligence, communications, data structures, file management, graphics, languages, operating systems, personal computer hardware and software, security, and software engineering. Each entry contains a brief definition of the term and its area of special use, if any; if it has more than one meaning, each is given. The entry may also relate the term to database commands or functions from widely used systems, giving examples.

Each defined term is divided into syllables; for single words, the part of speech is given. All important terms are shown in **boldface** and cross-referenced. Terms to be consulted for additional information are *italicized*.

The listing is strictly alphabetical, ignoring spaces and hyphens. Numbers are handled as if they were spelled out. For example, "2NF" appears under "two NF".

"dBASE" always means Ashton-Tate's dBASE III PLUS and dBASE IV (these are trademarked names), unless otherwise stated.

The second part is a series of Appendixes covering foreign language (French, Italian, and Spanish) equivalents of common terms, British usages, sources of information, standards, common symbols, and major database developments.

HOW DOES THE READER BENEFIT?

Most software manuals are confusing because they assume familiarity with specialized terms and jargon. The same is true of magazine articles and advertisements. This dictionary helps the reader understand such materials.

Anyone who works with databases encounters different types of software and hardware. To use powerful database programs effectively, you may have to program in the built-in language and perhaps in other computer languages as well. If you use these languages, you should become better acquainted with software engineering. You may have to use operating system functions for file and disk management. Graphics is important for displaying data in reports or business presentations. Using remote databases or local area networks requires familiarity with communications. Each of these specialties comes fully equipped with many new terms that you must understand. The dictionary covers all of them.

Furthermore, programmers, consultants, and system designers can use the dictionary to become familiar with the terms their customers use. This means knowing terms from information management and applications (accounting or personnel management, for instance). Database users or information managers, who know the applications terms, can use the dictionary to find the meaning of computer terminology. In addition, the growing linkages between mainframes and personal computers means that many people will need to understand terms associated with both types of machine.

In short, with this dictionary to consult, you can avoid that uneasy feeling when you open a database manual for the first time, deal with a database consultant or customer, or begin creating a new database. Keep it handy.

The dictionary is also available in disk form, organized with all its cross-references in an easily accessible structure. Ordering information is at the rear of the book.

A

*-prop•er•ty

See *star property*.

ab•stract da•ta type

See *data type*.

ab•strac•tion

n. An item, object, or concept separated from specifics; in skeletal form.

(Programming languages)

The hiding of programming details from the user, often by dividing the program into modules. The process is called **lay•er•ing**, with each layer implemented at a lower level of abstraction.

Also see *layer; modularity; module*.

ab•stract syn•tax

See *data type*.

ac•cess

v. To gain entry into a place or the use of something.

(Computer operations)

To acquire and use information. For example, to gain entry into a computer system or to use data from within an application.

Also to read or write memory or an I/O device, as in "to access the memory" or "to access the disk."

n. The ability to make such entry or use.

Also used adjectivally, as in "access mode" or "memory access time."

(Security)

n. A user may be granted entry to only certain kinds or levels of data or programs, and to make only certain uses of them, such as **read access, write access,** or **ex•e•cute access** (the permission to run a program).

Also see *grant; permission.*

ac•cess, con•cur•rent

(Security)

Simultaneous entry into a database by several users.

Multiuser databases should contain locks and other features to protect the data and also assure that each user is working with the latest update.

Also see *lock.*

ac•cess con•trol

(Security)

Determination of which users and subjects should have access to a system and what type of access they should have, and the granting of such access.

Also see *access; authorization; grant.*

ac•cess con•trol, dis•cre•tion•ary

(Security)

A level or degree of system or file access that can be changed. Contrast with *access control, mandatory.*

Also see *access.*

ac•cess con•trol list

(Security)

Abbreviated ACL (pronounced "akkle"). List of a file's authorized users and each one's degree of access, contained within the file. The user's identifier must be in the list for the file to be opened. The process of determining whether access should be granted involves searching the list.

The user's access level may be changed, referred to as discretionary access control.

Controls access well, but searching the list takes time. An access control list does not require any distribution of capabilities. Contrast with *capability list*, which is faster, but less secure.

Also see *access; access control, discretionary.*

ac•cess con•trol, man•da•to•ry
(Security)

Restriction of system or file access that cannot be overridden. Contrast with *access control, discretionary.* Also restricts duplication or changes in data.

Also see *access.*

ac•cess mode
(Security)

Privilege granted a user for entry to a database. A user may be permitted to view data, change specified data, add or delete data, or have unlimited ability to use all data. Also called **access right.**

Also see *grant.*

ac•cess per•mis•sion
(Security)

The degree of access a database user is granted by the administrator. May be limited according to the sensitivity or type of data or by the degree of interaction permitted, such as reading or writing.

Also see *grant; privilege.*

ac•cess right

See *access mode.*

ac•cess, syn•chron•ous
(Data management)

Provision for a database user to access current data, that is, the latest version of the database, at any time. Contrast with *snapshot*, the provision of periodic updates.

Whether the latest information is necessary depends on the user's requirements and also how closely the update corresponds to the actual situation the data represents. For instance, if there is a backlog of data to be added, even the latest update may not accurately reflect current conditions.

ac•counts pay•a•ble

(Accounting)

Debit account listing the status of suppliers from whom one has bought products or services, but to whom full payment has not yet been made. Also records payments that have been made. Requires cross-referencing to checks, cash outlays, and scheduled periodic payments.

Computerized version usually provides routines that automatically perform the cross-referencing and link accounts payable to a general ledger and often to inventory as well.

ac•counts re•ceiv•a•ble

(Accounting)

Credit account containing the status of clients or customers to whom products or services have been provided, but for which payment has not been received in full. May require payment in full by a certain date, after which interest or surcharges will be added, or time or revolving payments, with interest charged on the unpaid balance. The process of grouping accounts based on length of time in the system is called **ag•ing**. Also records payments that have been received.

Computerized versions often provide routines for automatic calculation of these options. Complete accounting software usually links accounts receivable to the general ledger, to inventory, and to programs that prepare sales invoices and periodic billings or statements.

ACK

(Data communications)

See *acknowledge*.

ac•knowl•edge

(Data communications)

n. A positive reply by a system that it has received data or another signal from a sender. For computers that use ASCII, a typical reply often consists of the control character ACK. See table under ASCII. Also called an **acknowledgment**.

Also see *ASCII; negative acknowledge* (NAK).

ACL

See *access control list*.

ac•ro•nym

n. A pronounceable word composed of the first one or two letters of each word in a phrase.

A popular construction in the computer world. Examples are BASIC (Beginner's All-purpose Symbolic Instruction Code), WYSIWYG (What You See Is What You Get), LAN (Local Area Network), and BIOS (Basic Input/Output System).

ac•tion di•a•gram
(Software development tools)

Type of diagram giving a system's or program's overview and also its logical detail. Depicts a hierarchical structure and indicates process flow, repetitions, conditions, and modules with left brackets or rectangles.

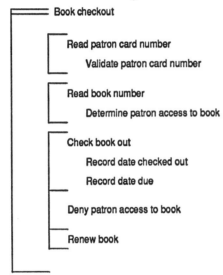

ac•tive da•ta dic•tion•ar•y

See *data dictionary*

ac•tive win•dow

See *window*

Ada
(Computer languages)

n. Structured high-level programming language developed in the late 1970s for the U.S. Department of Defense by a team headed by Jean Ichbiah. Its original purpose was for use in computerized weapons, communications, and guidance and control systems (so-called embedded systems), but it was developed for general programming. Ada has many characteristics of Pascal, but also supports modular compilation (of units called packages), abstract data types, tasking, process synchronization, and encapsulation (within packages). It was heavily influenced by the simulation-oriented Simula 67 language.

The programming environment is composed of hardware; a kernel called the Kernel Ada Program Support Environment (KAPSE); a set of tools for developing Ada programs, called the Minimal Ada Program Support Environment (MAPSE); and specialized Ada Program Support Environments (APSE's).

Defined in MIL-STD-1815A-1983.

Named for Augusta Ada, Countess of Lovelace, 19th century English mathematician, who worked with Charles Babbage (conceptualizer of the Analytical Engine) and developed the idea of a computer program. She is often regarded as the first programmer.

Also see *kernel*.

Ada Pro•gram Sup•port En•vi•ron•ment
(Computer languages)

An extension of a minimal set of Ada tools for a specialized purpose or application. Abbreviated APSE.

Also see *Ada*.

ADC

See *analog-to-digital converter*.

add
(Mathematics)

v. To combine numbers. To sum; to give an arithmetic sum. For example, in binary notation,

$1 + 1 = 0$ (plus a carry to the next bit position).

(Logic)

Synonym: OR. As with two binary digits, if either is one, the result is one. This is sometimes called logical addition.

$1 + 0 = 1$

$1 + 1 = 1$

If both operands are zero, the result is zero.

$0 + 0 = 0$

Also see *Boolean operator; logical addition*.

(Data management)

The process of adding records or rows to databases is generally called *appending*.

add•i•tive col•ors

See *primary colors*.

add-on

n. A supplement. Something that enhances the value or usefulness of the item or system to which it is added.

(Hardware)

A device added to a computer or system. Examples include printers, memory cards, modems, database processors, and data-gathering devices, such as bar-code readers.

(Software)

A program that enhances an application, but has no stand-alone function. Typical examples used with databases are report writers, statistical programs, graphics programs, application generators, 4th generation (nonprocedural) languages, and print utilities.

ad•dress

n. An identifier used to select one of a set of items, such as memory locations, I/O ports, or devices.

(Data communications)

The name of a device on a computer network. Synonym: *node name*.

v. To select a location according to its address, as in "to address memory." Roughly synonymous with *access* in this usage.

ad•dress space

The total range of addresses to which a particular computer may refer.

ad hoc que•ry

See *query, ad hoc*.

ad•min•is•tra•tor, da•ta•base

See *database administrator*.

ADP

See *automatic data processing*.

ADP se•cu•ri•ty

See *security*.

ad•vanced pro•gram-to-pro•gram com•mu•ni•ca•tions

(Data communications)

Abbreviated **APPC**. IBM's SNA session layer protocol, implemented by LU 6.2. A version for the IBM PC is called APPC/PC.

Also see *LU 6.2; systems network architecture.*

af•fer•ent branch

(Data management; Programming languages)

Input to a data flow diagram including the processes that change data from physical to logical form. Contrast with *efferent branch.*

Also see *transform analysis.*

af•ter im•age

(Data management)

Copy of a database or record after modification. Contrast with *before image.*

ag•gre•ga•tion

n. Formation of a mass or whole from a group or collection of individual items, parts, or life forms.

(Data management)

A method of data abstraction, as with a Cartesian product. Contrast with *generalization.*

Also see *abstraction; Cartesian product.*

AI

See *artificial intelligence.*

ALGOL

(Computer languages)

Stands for ALGOrithmic Language. A general purpose high-level language for implementing algorithms, developed in the 1960s by Working Group 2.1 of the International Federation of Information Processing (IFIP). A later version is known as ALGOL 68.

The language features five primitive value modes (types): bool (Boolean), char (character), int (integer), real, and format. It also has five rules for creating new modes from those already defined.

Values, called references, point to other values. Routines or procedures also return values.

Now largely superseded by Pascal and Modula-2. Often used as a standard form for describing algorithms.

al•go•rithm
(Programming)

A set of rules for solving a problem in a given number of steps. A formal method, often based on mathematical or logical techniques. For a contrasting approach, see *heuristic*.

alias

n. Alternative, false, or substitute name; pseudonym.

(Data management; Programming languages)

An alternative name used as shorthand or a convenience in programming or querying. Provides flexibility by allowing easy changes in definition, for example, between files or between printers or other devices or tables. Aliases also provide abbreviations for long names, better documentation, greater portability among systems and applications, and more generality in programs. An alias is simply an alternative name, not a memory variable.

(UNIX)

Command built into the C and Korn shells that permits creation and display of aliases.

alias•ing
(Graphics)

The broken appearance on a screen of a diagonal line produced by raster graphics, caused by the rectangular shape of pixels. A term originating in signal processing.

Some displays provide anti-aliasing, which improves the appearance, but not the resolution.

al•pha•bet•ic
(Data management; Programming)

adj. Consisting of letters and a few symbols such as hyphens, commas, periods, and ampersands. For example, an alphabetic field can contain a city name or a job title.

Also see *alphanumeric; numeric*.

al•pha•nu•mer•ic

(Data management; Programming)

adj. Consisting of letters, digits, or a combination. Some punctuation marks and other typed characters, such as periods and underscores, may also be acceptable.

For example, an alphanumeric field, such as a street address, can contain letters, numbers, and other characters (commas, periods, hyphens, #, and perhaps colons).

Also see *alphabetic; numeric.*

Amer•i•can Stan•dard Code for In•for•ma•tion In•ter•change

See *ASCII.*

am•or•ti•za•tion

(Accounting)

n. Regular payment of principal over the life of a loan. The payments are accumulated in a sinking fund, so that the entire amount is available for repayment on the due date. The periodic principal payment may be the same over the life of the loan, or the total of principal and interest may remain constant, but the amount of principal increases over time as the interest payments decrease.

Spreadsheet programs, such as Lotus 1-2-3, have functions for computing amortization schedules automatically.

ana•log

adj. Containing, generating, or relating to continuously variable data. Contrast with *digital.*

Analog da•ta takes on a continuous range of values, which may be transmitted by a modulated signal. Also see *modulate.*

An analog de•vice is one that generates or records such a range of values, for example, an oscilloscope or a video camera.

An analog com•put•er (now largely obsolete) consists of analog rather than digital circuits. Mainly used in engineering applications (particularly flight simulators and power plant simulators), analog computers were a significant alternative to digital computers in the 1950s. They declined in popularity due to programming difficulties and limited precision.

ana•log com•put•er

See *analog.*

ana•log da•ta

See *analog*.

ana•log de•vice

See *analog*.

ana•log I/O board

See *digital-to-analog covnerter*.

ana•log-to-dig•i•tal con•vert•er
(Hardware)

Device that converts analog signals to digital ones, for instance, into a form that can be entered into a computer. Examples are data from sensors and optical character recognition scanners. Abbreviated **ADC**.

Often available in chip form or combined with other parts in an **analog I/O board** or **da•ta ac•qui•si•tion sys•tem**.

Also see *analog; digital*.

Ana•lyt•i•cal En•gine
(Hardware)

The name Charles Babbage, 19th century English mathematician, gave to his innovative design of a forerunner of modern computers. Babbage's mechanical Analytical Engine used the metaphor of a cotton mill. He designed it in two parts, the **Mill**, wheels on an axis for each number column, where the operations were performed, and the **Store**, where the original numbers were placed and where the computed numbers were returned. Data was entered on punched cards. The full design was never built.

ANSI/X3/SPARC da•ta•base frame•work
(Data management)

Generalized framework developed in the 1970s for data management, using three **sche•mas: con•cep•tual**, describing the objects and relationships needed by users; **in•ter•nal**, the design for data storage; and **ex•ter•nal**, the ways the data is presented and made available to users. Provides data description, data mapping, and data manipulation languages, as required for the schemas. Often called the "ANSI three-schema standard."

The framework greatly influenced the development of database management systems in the 1970s and 1980s, including relational models.

Defined in D. Tsichritzis and A. Klug, eds. *The ANSI/X3/SPARC DBMS Framework - Report of the Study Group on Database Management Systems* (Montvale, NJ: AFIPS Press, 1977). Also published in *Information Systems 3* (1978).

API

See *Applications Programming Interface.*

APP

See *Applications Portability Profile.*

APPC

See *advanced program-to-program communications.*

ap•pend

(Database management)

v. To add a record after the latest one previously added to a database or after the highest record number.

(dBASE)

To add a record to the file ADDRESSES, enter

> .USE addresses
> .APPEND

A blank record will be displayed, in which the user can enter data.

(R:BASE)

To add a row using a data form, the command is ENTER. For a data form ADDRESS-FORM, at the R prompt, type

> ENTER addressform

The user can also specify the number of rows to be added. To add four rows, type

> ENTER addressform FOR 4 ROWS

R:BASE uses the command APPEND to copy rows from one table or view and add them to the end of another table. This works only if source and destination have the same column headings. For example, suppose you have the names and addresses of new customers in a table NEWCUST and want to add those in Ohio to the table OHIOCUST. Use

> R> APPEND newcust TO ohiocust WHERE state EQ "OH"

ap•pli•ca•tion

(Software)

n. A program that allows a user to perform work on a computer (in contrast to a program that performs overhead functions, such as an operating system). Examples are database managers, spreadsheets, and accounting programs.

Also describes a program that performs a specialized database task. For example, an accounting package might be called a "database application" or a package for drug stores might be called a "vertical application."

An **application gen•er•a•tor** is a routine or program that allows a user to create an application without writing code, for example, with menus or graphical screens (as in R:BASE).

Ap•pli•ca•tions Por•ta•bil•i•ty Pro•file

(Software)

A set of standards developed or endorsed by the U.S. National Institute for Science and Technology (NIST) to make it easier for Federal employees to use applications on a variety of computer systems. Abbreviated **APP.** Standards cover operating systems, database management, data interchange (documents, graphics, and product data), programming languages, and user interfaces.

Ap•pli•ca•tions Pro•gram•ming In•ter•face

(Software development tools)

Development tool for creating user interfaces to operating systems and applications on distributed computer systems. Abbreviated **API.** An example is an interface for using IBM's OS/2 operating system over a local area network.

ap•plic•a•tive language

See *language, functional*.

APSE

See *Ada Program Support Environment*.

arc

(Graphics; Mathematics)

n. A smooth curve representing a section taken through a solid or a path of data points that is not a straight line. An arc may have multiple vertices. A form drawn by a tool in some graphics programs.

Also see *vertex*.

(Data management)

Line connecting parent-child files in a data tree.

Also see *tree*.

ar•chi•tec•ture

(Computer architecture)

The physical structure of a computer, including the organization, capacity, and intercon-nections of its CPU, memory, and I/O sections. Often refers specifically to the organiza-tion of the CPU, including its registers, flags, buses, arithmetic/logic unit, instruction decoding and execution facilities, and timing and control unit.

Also see *closed architecture; open architecture.*

ar•chi•val

(File management)

adj. Referring to long-term storage of data, usually separate from what is in current use.

ar•chive

(File management)

n. Place for permanent or long-term storage of data, from which retrieval is infrequent. A computer archive, for instance, may be on magnetic tape.

v. To store data permanently. For example, to transfer it from a hard disk to tape or floppy disk, allowing it to be erased from the original medium.

area

(Data management)

n. In network databases, a designed part of secondary storage to which access may be granted. Synonym: **realm.**

(dBASE)

An independent workspace in which the user can open databases, indexes, and format files. Several may exist simultaneously. Most commands affect only databases in the active area. Also called a **work area.**

ar•gu•ment

(Mathematics)

n. An independent variable that determines the value of a function.

(Programming languages)

A variable for which a command or function is performed, or one that sets the conditions for performance. In many languages and operating systems, each command is followed by one or more arguments (sometimes called **com•mand line arguments** to differentiate them from ones passed through the stack or by other methods).

Also see *parameter*.

(dBASE)

In the command line

APPEND FROM addressfile TO masterfile

the arguments are ADDRESSFILE and MASTERFILE.

Also see *syntax*.

ar•ith•met•ic mean

See *mean*.

arith•me•tic pro•ces•sor

See *floating point processor*.

ar•ray

n. A set of elements usually, but not necessarily, of the same type. An array may be unordered, such as a data table. Or it may be ordered, for example, alphabetically or numerically. May be multidimensional.

ar•ray pro•ces•sor

(Hardware)

A high-speed parallel mathematical attachment used to do array operations in applications such as signal processing, simulation, and computer aided design.

ar•ti•fi•cial in•tel•li•gence (AI)

The performance by computers of processes ordinarily identified with the human brain. These include learning, decision making, creation of intellectual products, and the ability to adapt to changing conditions.

An AI system may incorporate vision (pattern recognition) and speech. A self-contained AI unit that can move or manipulate tools or other objects, for example, in manufacturing, is called a **ro•bot**. An AI system that recreates the decision making process of a knowledgeable human in a particular field or on a single topic is called an **ex•pert sys•tem**.

ASCII CHARACTER TABLE (HEXADECIMAL AND DECIMAL)

Hex	Dec	Character
0	0	NUL (null or blank)
1	1	SOH (start of header)
2	2	STX (start of text)
3	3	ETX (end of text)
4	4	EOT (end of transmission)
5	5	ENQ (enquiry)
6	6	ACK (acknowledge)
7	7	BEL (bell)
8	8	BS (backspace)
9	9	HT (horizontal tabulation)
A	10	LF (line feed)
B	11	VT (vertical tabulation)
C	12	FF (form feed)
D	13	CR (carriage return or enter)
E	14	SO (shift out)
F	15	SI (shift in)
10	16	DLE (data link escape)
11	17	DC1 (device control 1)
12	18	DC2 (device control 2)
13	19	DC3 (device control 3)
14	20	DC4 (device control 4)
15	21	NAK (negative acknowledge)
16	22	SYN (synchronization)
17	23	ETB (end of text block)
18	24	CAN (cancel)
19	25	EM (end of medium)
1A	26	SUB (substitute)
1B	27	ESC (escape)
1C	28	FS (file separator)
1D	29	GS (group separator)
1E	30	RS (record separator)
1F	31	US (unit separator)

Hex	Dec	Character
20	32	SP (space)
21	33	! (exclamation point)
22	34	" (quotation mark)
23	35	# (pound sign)
24	36	$ (dollar sign)
25	37	% (percent sign)
26	38	& (ampersand)
27	39	' (apostrophe or closing single quote)
28	40	((left parenthesis)
29	41	) (right parenthesis)
2A	42	* (asterisk)
2B	43	+ (plus sign)
2C	44	, (comma)
2D	45	- (hyphen)
2E	46	. (period)
2F	47	/ (slash)
30	48	0
31	49	1
32	50	2
33	51	3
34	52	4
35	53	5
36	54	6
37	55	7
38	56	8
39	57	9
3A	58	: (colon)
3B	59	; (semicolon)
3C	60	< (less than)
3D	61	= (equal sign)
3E	62	> (greater than)
3F	63	? (question mark)

Hex	Dec	Character
40	64	@ (at sign)
41	65	A
42	66	B
43	67	C
44	68	D
45	69	E
46	70	F
47	71	G
48	72	H
49	73	I
4A	74	J
4B	75	K
4C	76	L
4D	77	M
4E	78	N
4F	79	O
50	80	P
51	81	Q
52	82	R
53	83	S
54	84	T
55	85	U
56	86	V
57	87	W
58	88	X
59	89	Y
5A	90	Z
5B	91	[(left bracket)
5C	92	\ (backslash)
5D	93	] (right bracket)
5E	94	^ (circumflex or caret)
5F	95	_ (underscore)

Hex	Dec	Character
60	96	' (opening single quote)
61	97	a
62	98	b
63	99	c
64	100	d
65	101	e
66	102	f
67	103	g
68	104	h
69	105	i
6A	106	j
6B	107	k
6C	108	l
6D	109	m
6E	110	n
6F	111	o
70	112	p
71	113	q
72	114	r
73	115	s
74	116	t
75	117	u
76	118	v
77	119	w
78	120	x
79	121	y
7A	122	z
7B	123	{ (left brace)
7C	124		(vertical line)
7D	125	} (right brace)
7E	126	~ (tilde mark)
7F	127	DEL (delete)

AS•CII

(Data communications)

n. Acronym for American Standard Code for Information Exchange. It is commonly used as a word, often in the redundant "ASCII code." (Pronounced ass' key.)

The code (see Table) consists of 128 letters, numbers, punctuation marks, and control characters, each composed of 7 bits. It is used in most small computers and their peripherals and networks. Extended sets with even parity or graphics characters (IBM PC) are also used.

Note: On most computers and terminals, one can enter non-printing ASCII characters by pressing the Control (Ctrl) key and the key for the character 40 hex (64 decimal) higher. For example, one can enter 03 by pressing Ctrl-C, as C is 43 hex.

The code is specified by American National Standard X3.4-1986 with additions specified by ANSI X3.64-1979 and extensions by ANSI X4.31-1974.

Also see *bits; control characters; hexadecimal.*

AS•CII file

(File management)

Also called a text file. A file composed only of ASCII letters, numbers, and symbols, without non-printing characters or specialized commands for formatting or other applications purposes. It may contain carriage returns, line feeds, or both between entries.

Almost any word processor or text processor can read an ASCII file, as it contains no special codes. This makes it a simple portable format, but with no provisions for error detection, error correction, or length restrictions. Sometimes called a **straight ASCII file.**

as•sem•bler

(Programming)

n. Translator of a program written in assembly language line by line into one that can be executed directly by the computer with no further conversions other than numerical ones. Unlike a compiler, an assembler is dependent on the particular CPU in use.

as•sem•bly lan•guage

See *language, assembly.* Sometimes improperly called assembler (language).

as•set

See *object.*

---

asyn•chro•nous trans•mis•sion

(Data communications)

A mode of data transmission that transfers data at irregular intervals rather than regularly. Often used in computer systems to handle devices that produce data irregularly, such as keyboards. Asynchronous transmission requires starting and ending markers, as well as the actual data. A common method is to precede each character with a start bit and follow it with one or more stop bits. Synonym: **start-stop transmission**. Contrast with *synchronous*.

(MS-DOS)

To send or receive data with the Asynchronous Communications Adapter for the IBM PC via communications port COM1 (AUX) or COM2. The user must specify transmission rate, from 110 to 9600 baud; odd, even, or no parity; number of data bits, either 7 or 8; and number of stop bits, either 1 or 2.

atom•ic

adj. Indivisible.

(Data management)

Refers to the integral nature of a data transaction, which must be completed in its entirety before it can be committed; otherwise, the database is rolled back to the last completed transaction.

Also a single value, as in a table that is in first normal form.

at•tri•bute

n. Distinguishing characteristic or quality commonly applied to, inherent in, or symbolic of a person or thing.

(Data management)

The type (such as alphanumeric or numeric) or name of a field or column in a flat file. dBASE IV, for example, has six types: character, date, floating point, logical, memo (long text), and numeric.

In relational databases, the logical form of a table column.

Also, a quality of a file, for instance, system or read-only.

(Hardware)

Quality of part of a screen display, such as its color, brightness, or font (**vid•e•o attribute**).

au•dit trail

(Data management)

Documentation of a data processing operation to clearly show its original sources, derived or associated data, and reports. The trail should be continuous, and for some databases may be constructed automatically. Its uses include accounting, workload analysis, capacity and facility planning, security management, and permanent records. For example, in an accounting system, an audit trail should trace a paid voucher to the service or operation performed, its location, the people who authorized the activity and the payment, the check number, and the bank reconciliation.

(Security)

An audit trail can also be an important component in maintaining a database's integrity against unauthorized use and changes. Government security standards (such as DoD S200.28-STD, the so-called "Orange Book") often require the keeping of an audit trail both as a historical record and to check for unusual behavior, changes in behavior, attempts to violate security, or repeated efforts to guess at passwords or keys.

au•then•ti•cate

v. To determine the genuineness of an object, identity, or claim.

(Security)

To validate or verify the identity of a subject (a user or process) seeking entry into a computer system, especially regarding access rights. Also, to identify the creator of an object. Authentication may involve passwords, key codes, answers to questions, fingerprint matching, or other techniques.

au•then•ti•ca•tion

n. Verification of the genuineness of an object, identity, or claim.

Also see *authenticate*.

au•thor•i•za•tion

n. Permission by an authority to take specified action.

(Security)

Determination that a user or subject will be granted access rights to certain objects within a computer system. This may be done by defining subject and object attributes or by listing capabilities.

Also see *access; capability; grant.*

au•tho•rize

See *authorization.*

AU•TO•EX•EC.BAT

(MS-DOS)

Startup batch (procedure) file in MS-DOS.

au•to•in•dex•ing

(Programming)

n. Automatic updating of an index (a number used to modify an address) during each use.

Also see *index*.

au•to•mat•ic da•ta pro•cess•ing (ADP)

(Data management)

The use of a computer system for entry, storage, organization, and processing of data and its retrieval in a desired format.

Also see *data processing*.

au•to•mat•ic in•gest

(Data management)

A function of an expert DBMS that, upon receipt of data, automatically places it in a database for immediate querying or use.

av•er•age

See *mean*.

av•er•age, mov•ing

(Mathematics)

A series of averages centered around each item in an ordered list. For example, a list of total sales for the years 1975-1990 might be averaged over 5 year periods, such as 1975-1979, 1976-1980, 1977-1981, and so on. The result is to reduce the impact of an unusual year, perhaps caused by a model changeover, plant closure or opening, adverse publicity, natural disaster, labor dispute, political upheaval, or other one-time event.

Where values fluctuate, a graph of moving averages may provide more useful information about trends than the periodic totals themselves. For example, a moving average of monthly sales tends to smooth out variations caused by different numbers of weekends in a month, seasonal factors, different placement of floating or movable holidays (such as Easter), weather, and special events.

B

B tree

(Data management)

A tree with several keys per node, designed for large databases in which searches require repeated access to data on disk, rather than in the computer's memory. Allows for rapid access to the data according to a key value.

Also see *B+ tree; key; tree.*

B+ tree

(Data management)

A tree with many keys in each intermediate node and the values for comparison only in leaf nodes. During a search, all leaf nodes can be searched in sequence, skipping the branching. The search method used in dBASE queries.

Also see *B tree; node; tree.*

Bach•man diagram

(Software development tools)

Diagram for data modeling, particularly for network databases. Uses a line for one-to-one relations, an arrow for one-to-many relations, and boxes for records or sets. Does not indicate functional dependencies.

Defined by C.W. Bachman, who introduced data diagrams, in "Data Structure Diagrams," *Data Base*, 1 (2), Summer 1969.

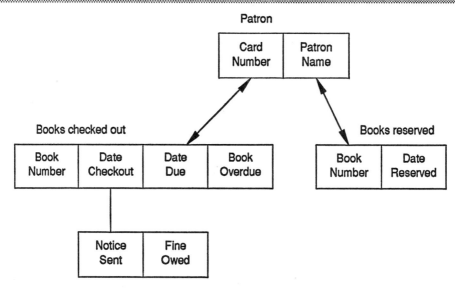

Bachman diagram

back•bone

n. A supporting structure, such as the spine.

(Data communications)

A network that connects other networks or communications systems so each station can send and receive data as if connected to a single network.

Also see *Internet*, a primary example.

back end

See *database server*.

back•ground

(HyperCard)

n. Underlying structure of a HyperCard card. Similar to the structure of a table, except that a HyperCard stack may contain cards with different backgrounds.

Also see *card; HyperCard; stack*.

(Computer operations)

Referring to off-screen data processing (such as printing, sorting, spell checking, or compiling) while a user is performing other tasks on a computer that are visible on the screen (in the foreground). As in **background pro•cess•ing** or **background pro•gram**.

In some cases, background processing may also use the screen through special windows.

MS-DOS supports only limited background processing through a simple print queue, whereas OS/2 and UNIX allow multiple background tasks (processes). UNIX also uses the term de•tached pro•cess.

backing store
(British usage)
See *store*.

back•up
(File management)
A copy of a saved file for archival purposes. For instance, a file on a non-removable hard disk could be backed up on a floppy disk or a tape.

Also see *restore*.

(Hardware)
A duplicate or redundant piece of equipment, used if the main piece fails or requires servicing.

back•up store
(British usage)
See *store*.

Backus-Naur form
(Programming)
Abbreviated BNF. A standard format for syntactic description of a programming language, named after John W. Backus and Peter Naur. Also called a meta•lan•guage.

The following symbolic notation is used:

a variable is enclosed in < >

equivalence is ::=

a required choice is indicated by |

Symbols and words used by the language stand alone.

For example, in dBASE

SET CLOCK ON|OFF

means the user must set the clock either on or off.

GO ::= GOTO <database position>

means GO is the equivalent of GO TO a given position.

<scope> ::= ALL | NEXT <digit> | RECORD <digit>

means the scope of a specified command must be either all records, the next given number of records, or a specified record number.

Synonym: **Backus normal form.**

Back•us nor•mal form

See *Backus-Naur form.*

back•ward chain•ing
(Artificial intelligence)

Processing method used in some expert systems and other AI applications that constructs a hypothesis, then works backward through the rules, testing the hypothesis against them. Contrast with *forward chaining*, noting that some applications use both.

Also see *expert system.*

back•ward re•cov•ery

See *rollback.*

band•width
(Computer operations; Data communications)

n. Range of frequencies within which acceptable transmission will be accomplished. For data communications, the bandwidth of a cable or network is usually delimited by the frequencies at which the response is three decibels less than (or down about one-half from) the reference value.

By extension, also refers to the maximum rate at which operations can be performed, as in mem•o•ry bandwidth or trans•ac•tion bandwidth.

bar code
(Applications)

Symbolic system or **sym•bol•o•gy** of machine-readable light and dark (or black) spaces representing data. The encoded space intervals are converted to time intervals for computer entry by use of a **bar code reader**, such as a light pen, laser beam scanner, or other analog detector. Used in management information and production control systems, including point-of-sale, manufacturing, and inventory.

Many bar codes exist. Some are **dis•crete**, meaning that the dark bars have meaning, but the light spaces (in•ter•char•ac•ter gaps) do not. In con•tin•u•ous bar codes, both the dark bars and the spaces or light bars have meaning. In some codes, the bars are of equal thickness. In others, they consist of modules, with widths ranging from one to four modules. Codes that use bars of various widths are called interleaved codes.

In some codes, a dark bar is a binary 1 and a light bar a 0. In others, a wide light or dark bar represents 1 and a narrow bar represents 0.

The narrowest bar in any code is its conceptual element, and the encoded width bars are its components. Encoding is done according to an algorithm unique to each code. Besides the coded data, each complete example contains beginning and ending characters (guard bars) and usually a check digit, such as a parity check.

Also see *checksum*; *parity*.

In many codes, such as the familiar one on grocery items, the symbolic number is also shown in numeric (human readable) form, called the echo line. Most codes represent only numeric data; others use alphanumeric data and certain symbols.

Some frequently used bar codes are:

• **Uni•ver•sal Pro•duct Code** or **UPC** (also called the **Uni•form Pro•duct Code**), for groceries and other consumer products in North America. Administered by the Uniform Code Council, Inc. A continuous code using a combination of thick and thin bars that are from 1 to 4 modules wide. Five versions exist.

• **EAN** or **Eu•ro•pe•an Ar•ti•cle Num•ber**, the international equivalent of UPC, which is partially compatible. Similar codes include **IAN** (**In•ter•na•tion•al Ar•ti•cle Num•ber**), **WPC** (**World Pro•duct Code**), and **JAN** (**Jap•an•ese Ar•ti•cle Num•ber**).

• **Co•da•bar** (Welch Allyn, Inc), used by North American blood banks and many libraries.

• **Code 39** (Intermec, Inc.), also called **3-of-9 Code**. Discrete code used by the U.S. Department of Defense.

• **In•ter•leaved 2-of-5 Code**, a discrete code used in the U.S. automobile industry, and for containers and warehousing.

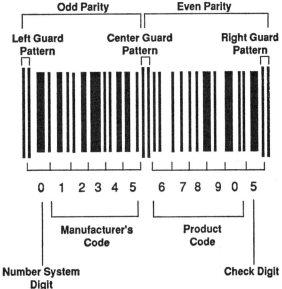

bar code read•er

(Hardware)

Analog scanner used to "read" or convert bar coded data into digital data for computer entry. Types include light pens, laserbeam scanners, laser guns, and laser wands.

Also see *bar code*.

base•band trans•mis•sion

(Data communications)

Low-frequency transmission of data in digital form. Usually used over distances of no more than a few miles on twisted-pair wire or coaxial cable. The data is carried as voltage changes or sequences representing digital zeros and ones. May transmit a single signal or use time division multiplexing.

Contrast with *broadband transmission*.

Also see *Ethernet; multiplexing*.

base ta•ble

(Data management)

In a relational database management system, a table containing the data.

Also see *database; table*.

BA•SIC

(Computer languages)

n. Acronym for Beginner's All-purpose Symbolic Instruction Code. A procedure-oriented, high-level programming language developed in the 1960s by John Kemeny and Thomas Kurtz (Dartmouth College). Designed for ease of use and interactive operation in solving small-scale scientific and engineering problems. Widely used by beginning programmers on personal computers. Supports user-defined functions, subroutines, string variables, and matrix operations.

Unlike Ada, C, FORTRAN, and Pascal, BASIC is usually implemented as an interpreter, although compilers do exist. A particularly popular version is Microsoft BASIC or GW-BASIC for IBM PCs or compatibles (Microsoft Corp.).

Also see *interpreter; language, procedure-oriented*.

Defined in American National Standard X3.113-1987.

batch com•put•ing

See *batch processing*.

batch file

(MS-DOS)

MS-DOS's version of a procedure file. Used to submit a sequence of commands to the operating system automatically.

Also see *procedure file*.

batch mode

See *batch processing*.

batch pro•cess•ing

(Data management)

Data processing that is performed non-interactively, with the results returned to the user at a later time. Often used for long production jobs such as payroll preparation, other financial and accounting functions, and scientific or engineering programs. Database uses include report generation, updating of permanent records from a transaction file, and archiving. Also called **batch com•put•ing** or **batch mode.** Contrast with *interactive processing; on-line transaction processing*.

baud

(Data communications)

n. The common unit for computer data transmission speed, usually defined as 1 bit per second, but including bits used for signaling, synchronization, error checking, and other purposes, as well as actual data bits. Used as a synonym for bit rate, but the two differ, as bit rate includes only data bits. Plural: baud.

Baud was originally defined by telegraphy, and actually refers to the number of signal modulations per second. The equivalent of the reciprocal of the duration in seconds of the shortest code element. The most common speeds for modems are 300, 1200, 2400, 4800, and 9600 baud.

Since a character consists of 8 data bits plus 2 or 3 bits used for other purposes, the character transmission rate is approximately the baud rate divided by 10 (300 baud or higher) or 11 (110 baud). Thus 300 baud, for example, generally corresponds to 30 characters per seconds (cps), assuming one start bit and one stop bit with each character. 110 baud corresponds to 10 characters per second.

On a network, the nominal data transmission speed may be unrealistic, because the speed of the slowest device determines actual speed. Named for J.M.E. Baudot, 19th century French inventor.

BCNF

See *Boyce/Codd normal form*.

be•fore im•age
(Data management)

Copy of a database page or record before modification. Contrast with *after image*.

Bell-LaPadula mod•el
(Security)

A formal computer security model widely used by the U.S. Department of Defense. It is a state machine model based on system states, rules, and security properties. It defines the ability of subjects to access objects in terms of access modes (view and alter). Pronounced "bell' - la pad' ula."

The model permits a user at a particular security level to read only at that or lower levels (called a **sim•ple se•cu•ri•ty con•di•tion**) and to write only at that or higher levels (called a **star, *-,** or **con•fine•ment prop•er•ty**). It provides for trusted subjects and processes.

Also see *access; object; reference monitor; state machine model; subject; trusted.*

bench•mark
n. A reference point.

(Computer operations)

A standard program or problem for comparing the performance of computers, other hardware, or software according to speed, ease of use, features, or other criteria. For example, two database programs might be evaluated from their speed in sorting, using index files, appending records, or searching for records.

Popular benchmark programs for general computer applications include the Sieve of Eratosthenes, the Whetstone problem (and its Dhrystone derivative), and the Linpack package.

Also see *Dhrystone program; Linpack benchmark; Stanford (Hennessy) benchmark; Whetstone program.*

Berke•ley Soft•ware Dis•tri•bu•tion

See *Berkeley UNIX* or *BSD*.

Berke•ley UNIX
(Computer environment)

Versions of UNIX supported by the Computer Science Department of the University of California, Berkeley. Version 2, in several revisions, is used on 16-bit computers. Version 4, including revisions, is for 32-bit computers. Often identified by the tag BSD, for example, as in UNIX 4.3 BSD.

best fit

See *fit, best*.

Biba in•teg•ri•ty mod•el

(Security)

Mathematical model of access limitation to maintain data integrity. Prevents writing from a process to a file with higher integrity and reading a file with lower integrity than the user or subject file.

Also see *access; integrity*.

big end•i•an

In *Gulliver's Travels* by Jonathan Swift (18th century English cleric and satirist), a political party whose basis was the members' belief in opening soft-boiled eggs at the big end. The opposition was composed of people who believed in opening eggs at the little end – little endians.

(Hardware)

Referring to computers that assign the lowest memory address occupied by a number to the most significant bits – that is, to the largest value. Examples are IBM mainframes and the Motorola series of microprocessors (68000, 68020, 68030, and 68040), used in Apple Macintosh computers and in computers from Apollo, Atari, Commodore, and Sun Microsystems.

Contrast with *little endian*.

bill•ing

(Accounting)

n. Sending of statements to customers giving the amount owed, the payment due, and the due date.

bill of ma•te•ri•als

(Manufacturing)

Statement of the materials, parts, and amounts needed to construct a facility or manufacture a product. In CAD/CAM systems, this information is usually kept in a master database and compiled automatically for the task after being specified in the design.

Also see *CAD/CAM*.

bi•na•ry

(Mathematics)

n. Number system with base 2. Numbers are composed of zeros and ones. For example, one is expressed as 01, two as 10, and 39 as 100111. Because of their length, binary numbers are difficult to handle and interpret. For this reason, binary digits are often grouped in threes or fours and handled as octal or hexadecimal numbers, respectively.

Also see *hexadecimal; octal.*

bi•na•ry code

(Computer operations)

Programs in the form suitable for direct execution by a computer. Usually the output of a translator such as a compiler or assembler. Also called object code. Not in a form suitable for examination by a person. On the IBM PC, binary code is usually in the form of COM, EXE, or OBJ files.

Also see *COM file; EXE file; OBJ file.*

bi•na•ry tree

See *tree.*

bi•na•ry vari•able

See *Boolean variable.*

bind

v. To join; to commit to an action.

(Programming)

To translate an expression in a program into a form that can be immediately interpreted by the machine that will run the program. The goal of binding is to translate expressions into machine representations involving physical addresses, but there may be several immediate steps. Binding may be done by a compiler, a linker, or even at run time. The trend is toward binding as close to run time as possible to allow more flexibility.

(DB2)

For example, a command that converts the results of precompiling to an application, creating access paths and checking authorization.

BIOS

(Computer operations)

n. Acronym for Basic Input/Output System (pronounced buy′-ohss). Set of operating system routines or utilities that directs signal flow among devices, such as keyboard, monitor, printer, and disk. Usually applies specifically to the low-level, machine-specific routines (generally in ROM) required to make an IBM PC (or compatible) functional. The IBM BIOS is copyrighted, so manufacturers of PC-compatibles must write their own or obtain one from an independent source. Such independent BIOSes often differ from IBM's in minor details.

bit

(Computer operations)

n. Abbreviation for binary digit, referring to a basic unit of information with just two possible states. The two states are often called true and false, 0 and 1, or "on" and "off."

bit block

(Graphics)

Bits representing a rectangular array of graphical data at a particular screen location, for example, a font character, an image, or a pop-up menu.

A **bit block trans•fer** is the moving of a bit block between memory locations, such as from storage to display or from one place on the screen to another. This allows motion simulation as well as the transfer of objects between windows and their movement between containers in a graphical interface.

Abbreviation is **bitblt**, pronounced "bit-blit." Graphics hardware often provides special support for bit block transfers.

bit block trans•fer

See *bit block.*

bitblt

See *bit block.*

bit map

See *map.*

bit-map•ped graph•ics

See *raster graphics.*

bit rate

(Data communications)

Synonym: *bits per second.* Measurement of the speed at which bits are transmitted.

Also see *baud.*

bits per sec•ond

(Data communications)

Synonym: *bit rate.* Measurement of the speed at which bits are transmitted. Abbreviation: **bps.**

Also see *baud; bps; characters per second.*

block

(Computer operations)

n. Units of information storage for a device such as a disk or tape. Often the capacity of one disk sector or tape segment. Synonym: *physical record.*

For example, in dBASE III PLUS, a block for memo fields and multiple index files is 512 bytes. In dBASE IV, the user can select block size in multiples of 512 bytes, from 1 to 32, by using the command SET BLOCK SIZE.

Also refers to an area of memory. **Block move** transfers data from one area to another. **Block I/O** transfers data between an area of memory and an input or output device. Other common operations are block compare, block fill, and block search.

(Data communications)

The amount of data, usually variable in length, transmitted as a unit. The methods for ensuring its proper transfer are a protocol.

(Data management)

A data unit composed of files, words, or characters. May also be called a string, although that term is often restricted to units composed of characters.

(Programming)

A complete syntactic unit in a block-structured language, such as Ada, C, Modula-2, or Pascal. It has its own starting and ending markers and can have its own declarations, statements, and other features. A block can generally replace a simple statement at any point in a program. There may be limitations, such as C's refusal to allow functions within functions.

block I/O

See *block.*

block move

See *block*.

BNF

See *Backus-Naur form*.

Bool•ean op•er•a•tor

(Data management)

A symbol in **Boolean al•ge•bra** for a logical (rather than mathematical) operation. Examples are AND, OR, NOT, and EXCLUSIVE-OR. Such **log•i•cal op•er•a•tors** are used in database queries to define or limit the information sought. Because logical operators lend themselves to true-false statements, they are suited to creating conditions for queries, searches, and program branches.

(dBASE)

dBASE provides the Boolean operators .AND., .OR., .NOT., != (not equal), and ( ) (grouping). For example, the user can give the following command to search a file ADDRESSES, with fields for name, address, city, state, Zip Code, area code, telephone number, and occupation:

LOCATE FOR Occupation='plumber'.AND. State='NY'.AND. Area code='212'.

The result will be records for plumbers in New York state in area code 212 (the heart of New York City).

Also see *binary; character operator; numeric operator; relational operator*.

Bool•ean vari•able

(Programming)

A variable that can have only the values true (on or 1) and false (off or 0). Also called a **yes/no vari•able, true-false vari•able, log•i•cal variable,** or **flag.** Supported explicitly in such languages as Ada, Modula-2, and Pascal, but not in C.

boot

See *bootstrap loader*.

boot•ing

See *bootstrap loader*.

boot load•er

See *bootstrap loader*.

boot•strap load•er

A small program, often in read-only memory, that gets a computer started, often by reading in part of the operating system from secondary storage. Also called a **boot load•er**; its activation is called **boot•ing** the computer or a **sys•tem boot**.

bot•tom-up design

(Data management; Programming languages)

Method of system or program design characterized by concatenation. Produces a hierarchical, modular structure, in which design begins with the lowest levels or functions and then combines them, finally producing an overall design. Ideally, each level or module is designed, written, and tested before the next one is begun.

Also see *concatenation*.

Contrast with *top-down*, noting that most designs and analyses use both.

Bourne shell

See *shell*.

Boyce/Codd nor•mal form

(Data management)

More rigorous version of third normal form to resolve anomalies for data whose relation involves a composite, multiple, or overlapping unique identifier (**can•di•date key**). Requires every attribute on which another attribute is functionally dependent (called a **de•ter•mi•nant**) to be a candidate key. Abbreviated **BCNF**.

Devised by E.F. Codd in the 1970s.

Also see *fifth normal form; first normal form; fourth normal form; normalize; second normal form; third normal form.*

bps

(Data communications)

Abbreviation for *bits per second*. Sometimes erroneously used for bytes per second, but the two differ by a factor of 8.

branch

(Data management)

n. In a data tree, a path between nodes. **Branching** refers to paths leading from parent to child node. Some data structures have one parent node for several child nodes. Others have **mul•ti•ple in•her•i•tance** – many parent nodes for many child nodes.

Also see *child; node; parent; tree.*

(Programming)

A path, junction, or transfer of control in a program.

branch•ing

See *branch.*

bridge

(Data communications)

n. A hardware connection between two networks of the same type, such as local area networks employing Ethernet. Contrast with *gateway.*

broad•band trans•mis•sion

(Data communications)

High-frequency transmission of modulated analog or digital data, or both. Used over long distances on coaxial or fiber optic cable. May carry a single signal. Multiplexing divides the frequency into several lower frequencies, each carrying a data signal, such as voice or video. However, multiplexing is slower than single signal transmission.

Contrast with *baseband transmission.*

Also see *Ethernet; modem; modulate; multiplexing.*

browse

(Data management)

n. A mode or command that lets a database user examine or query some or all of the data without being able to make additions or changes. This may be done by presetting the level of access or by requiring passwords.

Also an alternative to querying to obtain information, especially from text data. Searching for a general pattern, then looking in its vicinity, similar to going to a shelf of books on a topic, then leafing through several of them to find a particular subtopic or reference.

v. To examine or query a database, or to search for a data pattern.

Sometimes also used to refer to an unauthorized database entry.

Also see *navigate.*

BSD
(Computer environment)

Abbreviation for Berkeley Software Distribution. An identifier for versions of UNIX supported by the Computer Science Department of the University of California, Berkeley. Referred to in various ways, for example, as UNIX 4.3 BSD.

Also see *Berkeley UNIX*.

buf•fer
(Computer operations)

n. A memory area used for temporary storage of data.

v. To store data in such an area before transferring it on to its final destination.

buf•fer/driv•er

See *driver*.

buf•fer•ed in•put

See *canonical*.

buff•er pool
(Data management)

In DB2, the main storage buffers for tablespaces and indexes.

Also see *tablespace*.

bug
(Computer operations)

n. An error in a computer system or application. Computer lore says that the term originated when an insect was found to be disrupting the operation of an early computer.

Also see *debug*.

bul•let proof
(Software)

(Slang) Resistant to user mistakes. Refers primarily to user interfaces.

but•ton

n. An object that connects two things, such as the two sides of a jacket.

(Data management)

A hypertext link.

Also see *hypertext; link.*

Also an alternative to a dialog box in graphical interfaces, usually allowing only a simple yes or no choice or confirmation.

bus driv•er

See *driver*.

byte

(Computer operations)

n. A basic grouping of bits, almost always 8, although historically it could have other lengths. By extension, a basic unit of storage capable of holding one character in a standard code, such as ASCII.

C

(Computer languages)

n. A procedure-oriented high-level language intended for systems applications, such as operating systems, compilers, text processors, and communications packages. It is block-structured and contains the logical forms required for structured programming. Regarded as close to assembly language, it provides direct access to basic machine facilities. Developed by Dennis Ritchie at Bell Laboratories in the early 1970s, it is now defined in American National Standard X3.159.

Also see *C++*, which is an object-oriented extension.

In database work, C programs are often used to implement low-level functions, such as screen or file control, write I/O drivers, and speed up sorts, searches, and other critical algorithms.

CA

See *collision.*

C++

(Computer languages)

n. Object-oriented extension of C, developed by Bjarne Stroustrup of Bell Laboratories in the middle 1980s. Described in his *The C++ Programming Language* (Reading, MA: Addison-Wesley, 1986). Combines C with class concepts from Simula 67.

cache

(Computer operations)

n. A memory area used to hold frequently accessed data and instructions. Pronounced "cash." Usually consists of a small amount of high-speed memory.

A cache can significantly improve the performance of computers at a fraction of the cost of upgrading the entire memory.

v. To put something into such a memory.

adj. Un•cache••able means that something cannot be put into a cache, for example, objects residing in shared memory or I/O devices addressed as memory.

CAD

See *computer aided design.*

CAD/CAM

See *computer aided design; computer aided manufacturing.*

CAE

See *computer aided engineering.*

cal•cu•lat•ed field

See *field, calculated.*

call

(Programming)

n. An instruction that causes the execution of a subroutine, while retaining the information required to resume the calling routine at a later time.

v. To effect such an execution.

(dBASE)

A binary file can be placed in memory with the LOAD command. CALL executes it from within a dBASE program.

In dBASE IV, the function CALL( ) permits use of a loaded binary file during data entry or when generating a report.

call-back mo•dem

See *modem, call-back.*

CAM

See *computer aided manufacturing*.

can•di•date key

(Data management)

In establishing a relational data table, a unique identifier that may be selected as a primary key.

Also see *database; key*.

ca•non•i•cal

adj. The property of acting in agreement with a rule or canon.

(Mathematics)

In a set of equivalent objects, an object in a subset and an object in the set are also equivalent. The object in the subset is the **canonical form** for the object in the set.

(Data management)

The property of procedures and queries being standardized so they are interpreted identically within a system, that is, so they all fulfill the rules of the data model.

In structured systems, a **canonical struc•ture** is a unique model for a group of data, in which redundancies have been eliminated. This permits structuring of the data apart from applications.

(UNIX)

Canonical or **cooked** mode input processing refers to terminal processing in units of lines, with an end-of-line, end-of-file, or newline character added. Distinguished from the **raw** mode, in which bytes are not assembled into lines, but are handled one-by-one. Canonical mode is also called **buff•ered in•put**.

ca•non•i•cal form

See *canonical*.

ca•non•i•cal struc•ture

See *canonical*.

ca•pa•bil•i•ty

(Security)

n. A user's or subject's right to access an object, for example, data or a device, within a computer system. A capability defines a subject's right to an object, whereas an access right defines an object's availability to a subject.

A capability is sometimes called a ticket, as it identifies a subject that is allowed entry. Synonym: *ticket*.

Also see *access mode; access right.*

ca•pa•bil•i•ty list

(Security)

Tabulation within a computer system of the capabilities of each user or subject. Grants or denies access quickly, as no list has to be searched. Contrast with *access control list*, which is slower, but provides greater security, as there is no problem with the transfer or distribution of capabilities.

card

(Data management)

n. The equivalent of a record in HyperCard, displayed on the screen in the form of an index or telephone file card, with user-defined fields. Cards are grouped in stacks.

Also see *HyperCard.*

car•di•nal•i•ty

(Mathematics)

n. The number of elements a set contains.

(Data management)

Characteristic of a relation. The number of tuples or rows a relation contains. Unlike a relation's degree, its cardinality can change as rows are added, or a relational operation is performed.

Also see *degree.*

car•ri•er sense mul•ti•ple ac•cess

(Data communications)

Abbreviated CSMA. Protocol for a network system that allows a station to transmit at any time the line or cable is not in use. It may be combined with collision detection (CD) or collision avoidance (CA) to handle the situation where multiple stations try to transmit simultaneously.

Also see *carrier sense multiple access/collision avoidance* (CSMA/CA); *carrier sense multiple access/collison detection* (CSMA/CD).

car•ri•er sense mul•ti•ple ac•cess/col•li•sion avoid•ance

(Data communications)

Abbreviated CSMA/CA. Combination of the transmission protocol CSMA and a method of collision avoidance, in which the station checks whether the line or cable is in use before transmitting.

Contrast with the more common *carrier sense multiple access/collision detection* (CSMA/CD). Also see *carrier sense multiple access.*

car•ri•er sense mul•ti•ple ac•cess/col•li•sion de•tec•tion

(Data communications)

Abbreviated CSMA/CD. Combination of the transmission protocol CSMA and a method of collision detection, in which the station retransmits in case the data collides with other data on the line.

Defined in the Ethernet-like IEEE Standard 802.3. It is also the physical layer (cabling and signaling) for Technical and Office Protocol (TOP).

Contrast with *carrier sense multiple access/collision detection* (CSMA/CA).

Also see *carrier sense multiple access; Ethernet; Technical and Office Protocol* (TOP).

Car•te•sian pro•duct

(Mathematics)

A set containing pairs of designated elements, each member of which comes from one of two other sets.

(Data management)

A set containing all possible pairings of elements from two given sets. For example, given the sets (A_1, B_1) and (A_2, B_2), the Cartesian product would be the set $(A_1A_2, A_1B_2, B_1A_2, B_1B_2)$.

In relational databases, a set containing all possible rows from two given tables. The same as an unconditional join if the tables have no common attributes.

Supports the data abstraction method called aggregation.

Also see *aggregation; join.*

CAS

See *communication application specification.*

CASE

See *computer aided software engineering.*

cat•a•log

See *data dictionary*

cat•e•na•tion

See *concatenation.*

CCEP

See *Commercial COMSEC Endorsement Program.*

CD

See *collision.*

CD-ROM
(Data management)

n. Compact disk read-only memory, a laser-written optical disk used for mass storage instead of a magnetic disk. The first CD systems were actually read-only; they did not allow the user to change or add material. However, the term is no longer precise, since later CD systems allow the computer user to save files to the disk once (WORM, or Write Once, Read Many times). One CD can hold much more material than magnetic floppy or hard disks, making them suitable for large databases, including those with large blocks of text and many illustrations, such as encyclopedias.

Defined in ISO Standard 9660.

cen•tral pro•cess•ing unit
(Computer architecture)

The section of a computer that fetches, decodes, and executes instructions; performs arithmetic and logical operations; and generates or responds to timing and control signals. Abbreviated CPU. Also called a processor or (master) control unit.

cen•tral trans•form
(Data management; Programming languages)

In transform analysis, the logical processing furthest removed from the physical layer.

Also see *transform analysis.*

CGA

See *color/graphics adapter*.

chain•ing

See *piping*.

chan•nel
(Data communications)

n. A hardware path or a frequency for data transmission.

Also see *I/O channel*.

chan•nel, co•vert
(Security)

A surreptitious communications path for unauthorized data transfer, violating a computer system's security. For example, a covert channel might transfer information by using particular file names in a particular order.

A co•vert stor•age chan•nel is one in which data stored legitimately is read clandestinely, for example, by intercepting it by file name.

A co•vert tim•ing chan•nel transmits data by manipulating processor timing.

Contrast with *channel, overt*.

Also see *confinement*.

chan•nel, overt
(Security)

A communications path for authorized data transfer.

Contrast with *channel, covert*.

Chap•in chart

See *Nassi-Shneiderman chart*.

char•ac•ter•is•tic

See *floating point*.

char•ac•ter op•er•a•tor
(Data management)

An operator that performs a character-based manipulation, such as placing one string after another (concatenation). dBASE, for example, uses + and - for concatenation.

Also see *Boolean operator; concatenation; numeric operator; relational operator.*

char•ac•ters per sec•ond
(Data communications)

Unit for measuring computer data transmission speed. Abbreviated cps. Usually each character requires 10 or 11 bits, 8 bits for the character plus a start bit and 1 or 2 stop bits. A rule of thumb is that each 10 characters per second approximates 100 baud.

Also see *baud.*

chart

See *graph.*

check•point

See *synchronization point.*

check•sum
(Data communications)

n. A computational result used to verify the accuracy of data transmission. It is obtained by summing the values of a transmitted packet of data (sometimes without carries between digits). In communications, a receiver will compare the computed value to the one sent with the packet. If the two are identical, the data was transmitted correctly. A simple checksum can detect errors, but cannot locate or correct them.

check sum•ma•tion

See *checksum.*

child
(Data management)

n. In a tree data structure, a node connected by a branch to a node above it. Also, in an alternative to indexing, a database file for which a query is organized around another (parent) file through the use of pointers.

Also a process created by another (parent) process.

Also see *branch; node; parent; tree.*

chunk•ing
(Data management)

n. In hypertext, searching for or specifying a single alphanumeric character or an arbitrary series of characters within a field or file.

Also see *hypertext.*

(HyperCard)

For example, assume that a stack Addresses has the state and Zip Code in the same field, named State, as

IL 60515

Chunking permits the field entry to be considered as two words:

word 1 - the state abbreviation

word 2 - the Zip Code

To make the state and Zip Code into separate fields, create a new field called ZIP, then write the Hypertalk instruction

put word 2 of field "State" into ZIP

CICS
(Data communications)

Abbreviation for customer information control system, IBM communications program for mainframes that permits both on-line and batch data processing. Uses its own commands, which can be embedded in assembly language, COBOL, and other programming languages. Permits user-designed screens for access.

CIM

See *computer integrated manufacturing.*

CISC

See *RISC.*

class

See *object oriented.*

clas•si•fi•ca•tion, se•cu•ri•ty

See *security classification.*

clear•ance, se•cu•ri•ty

See *security clearance.*

click

n. A brief, sharp monotone or noise.

(Hardware)

The sounds made by pressing and releasing the key on a mouse. If performed quickly, the two motions make what seems to be a single sound.

v. To make such a noise, as in "click the left mouse button."

(Data management)

To issue a command by pressing a mouse key, such as highlighting text or data, opening or closing an application or file, or selecting an item from a menu.

In some instances, the user moves the pointer to a box or button, then depresses and releases the key. In others, as in a Macintosh pulldown menu, the user points to the displayed menu name, then depresses the key, opening the menu. The user holds the key down while moving the pointer to highlight menu items. Releasing the key selects the highlighted item.

Similarly, on the Macintosh desktop, pointing to an icon and depressing the key allows the user to drag (move) the icon to a new location or to the trash (deleting it from the directory). Releasing the key completes the action.

The HyperCard language Hypertext uses the terms mouseDown and mouseUp to program the depression and release of the key to initiate and complete actions.

Also see *double click; mouse.*

cli•ent

(Data communications; Data management)

n. A network node that requests services from other nodes. Examples are a personal computer requesting printing or access to a database residing in a mainframe or minicomputer. Contrast with *server.*

Also part of an operating system that requests services from other parts (in a cli•ent-serv•er ar•chi•tec•ture).

cli•ent-serv•er ar•chi•tec•ture

(Data management)

Architecture in which specific functions, such as file management, are handled by specific hardware and software, rather than being distributed over many units.

For a distributed database, the splitting of management functions so that some reside in the file server and others on client computers. Sometimes called **re•quest•or-server architecture**.

Also see *client; server.*

clip•board

(Data management)

n. Temporary memory storage for cut or copied material (data, text, or graphics) under the Macintosh operating system and Microsoft Windows. Material on the clipboard may be pasted into other applications and also may be saved on disk.

Clip•per

(Data management)

Widely used compiler for the dBASE procedural language. A product of Nantucket Corp.

Also see *dBASE.*

CLOS

See *Common Lisp Object System.*

closed ar•chi•tec•ture

(Computer architecture)

A computer architecture that does not provide for the easy attachment of add-ons or expansion facilities.

Also see *architecture.*

closed se•cu•ri•ty en•vi•ron•ment

See *security environment.*

CM

See *configuration management.*

CO•BOL

(Computer languages)

n. Acronym for COmmon Business Oriented Language. Procedure-oriented, high-level programming language developed in 1950s by a military and civilian team headed by Grace Hopper (U.S. Navy). The most widely used computer language, primarily in business applications. Each program consists of identification, environment, data, and procedure divisions. It is heavily oriented toward data processing applications (such as accounting, billing, inventory, order entry, and personnel management) that involve large amounts of formatted input and output, but only relatively simple calculations.

Also see *language, procedure-oriented.*

Defined in American National Standard X3.23-1985.

Co•da•bar

See *bar code.*

CODASYL

(Data management)

n. Acronym for Conference On DAta SYstems Languages. Organization in 1970s whose Data Base Task Group (DBTG) developed the data model for network databases. In its final 1978 form, the model rests on a data description language (DDL) and three schemas: logical organization, storage structure (using a data storage description language, or DSDL), and a series of subschemas for views and other user applications (using a data manipulation language, DML). In addition, there are defined database facilities for COBOL and FORTRAN.

Defined in the *CODASYL Data Description Language Committee Journal of Development 1978* (Material Data Management Branch, Department of Supply and Services, 11 Laurier St., Hull, Quebec, Canada K1A 0S5).

Also see *database.*

code

(Programming)

n. Synonym for program, especially executable machine language instructions. Also rules for data representation. Also used as a synonym for encrypt, as in coded data.

Also see *encrypt; language, machine.*

v. To write a program or to encrypt.

Cod•ing is the stage of software development in which the actual program is written. **Cod•er** is an obsolete synonym for programmer, usually referring to a person with a relatively low skill level.

code con•ver•sion

See *conversion, code.*

cod•er

See *code.*

Code 39

See *bar code.*

cod•ing

See *code.*

co•her•en•cy

n. Logical consistency.

(Data management)

In a distributed system, assurance that only one valid updated version of data exists, that is, that data copies are not updated instead of the main data.

co•he•sion

n. The state of being unified or sticking together.

(Data management; Programming languages)

In structured design, the degree to which the elements in a module are related.

As identified by J. Martin, the weakest degree of cohesion is coincidental, followed by logical, temporal, procedural, communicational, sequential, and functional.

A feature of systems analysis, in which good design is believed to feature loose coupling and strong cohesion.

Also see *coupling.*

col•li•sion

n. A forceful encounter between particles, people, or other entities, often when they are trying to occupy the same place at the same time.

(Data communications)

The attempt by more than one station to transmit on the same path simultaneously. Two popular methods for handling collisions are **col•li•sion avoid•ance** (CA), in which a station checks that the path is clear before transmitting, and **col•li•sion detec•tion** (CD), in which a station retransmits if a collision occurs.

Also see *carrier sense multiple access/collison avoidance; carrier sense multiple access/collison detection.*

col•li•sion avoid•ance

See *collision.*

col•li•sion detec•tion

See *collision.*

col•or/graph•ics adapt•er
(Hardware)

Abbreviated **CGA**. The original color/graphics video display standard for IBM PCs. Provides 320 x 200 resolution with four colors or 640 x 200 with two colors. Supports only 8 x 8 dot-matrix characters in text mode. For current standard, see *video graphics array* (VGA). For other IBM PC display standards, also see *enhanced graphics adapter* (EGA); *monochrome display adapter* (MDA).

col•umn
(Data management)

n. In a flat file, a vertical listing of a single category of data, such as all addresses in a file. The logical form is called an **at•tri•bute.**

(Hardware)

A horizontal position on the screen.

col•umns for•mat
(Data management)

A database report format presenting data in columns, for example:

Name	Order No.	Date of Death
Jefferson	3	1826
Madison	4	1836

Also see *labels format; rows format.*

COM file

(MS-DOS)

A file containing loadable object code in the exact form it will appear in memory. MS-DOS needs to do almost nothing to execute a COM file, so it loads faster (and is more compact) than an EXE file. Designated by the COM extension. Contrast with *EXE file*.

com•mand

(Programming)

n. An instruction to a computer.

com•mand, ex•ter•nal

(Programming)

Abbreviation **XCMD**. A command for the Macintosh database manager HyperCard written in a general programming language, such as C, FORTRAN, or Pascal, rather than in its own language HyperTalk. Can also be written in assembly language. An XFCN is a routine not provided in HyperTalk, such as handling non-HyperCard files.

An XCMD is incorporated ("glued") into a HyperCard stack by means of two special files that contain the driver and glue routines for the particular language.

Also see *function, external.*

com•mand file

See *procedure file*.

com•mand verb

See *operation code*.

Com•mer•cial COM•SEC En•dorse•ment Pro•gram

(Security)

Method of data encryption developed by the U.S. National Security Agency (NSA) and adopted by it in 1988, superseding the data encryption standard DES. Abbreviated **CCEP**.

com•mit

See *transaction.*

Com•mon LISP

See *LISP*.

Com•mon LISP Ob•ject Sys•tem
(Artificial intelligence; Programming languages)

Object oriented programming adaptation of Common LISP, featuring class objects, other objects that are instances of classes, generic function objects, and objects containing method functions (methods).

Defined in ANSI X3J13 Document 88-002R.

Also see *LISP*.

Com•mu•ni•ca•tion Ap•pli•ca•tion Spec•i•fi•ca•tion
(Data communications)

Application program interface that lets a program send and receive files, independent of the underlying hardware. Abbreviated CAS. Intended primarily for background file and image transfers. Uses a device-independent resident manager. Developed by Intel and Digital Communications Associates (DCA).

com•mu•ni•ca•tions front end

See *front end*.

com•mu•ni•ca•tions se•cu•ri•ty

See *security*.

com•pac•tion
(Data management)

Combining separated areas of free memory or disk space into a single unit. Sometimes called "garbage collection," although that term is more general and often refers to the collection of free areas into a queue or linked list.

com•par•i•son op•er•a•tor

See *relational operator*.

com•part•men•tal•iza•tion

See *isolation*.

com•pat•i•bil•i•ty

n. Similarity; commonality; harmonious interaction.

(Computer operations)

Similarity in operating systems, protocols, interfaces, or programming methods that allows computer hardware and software to work together. May refer to a computer and peripheral devices, such as printers and modems; different brands of computers, such as IBM PCs and others that use MS-DOS; or software packages, such as database programs that can import each other's data or can replace each other on various brands of computers.

com•pil•er

(Computer languages)

n. A translator of a high-level language program into a form a computer can execute, either directly or with the aid of a run-time package. The compiler translates the entire program, without executing any of it. Contrast with *interpreter*.

The compiler is advantageous for completed programs that will be run repeatedly, as they have to be translated only once.

(dBASE)

In dBASE IV, the command COMPILE translates a source program into executable form. Clipper (Nantucket Corp.) is a compiler that handles most dBASE code.

com•plete•ness

n. Having all necessary elements. Also a measure of how many or what part of the necessary elements something has, as in a job that is 50 percent complete (or half done).

(Statistics)

A component of uncertainty, the limits on what is known about a problem being analyzed.

An element in risk assessment. For example, the success of a computer security system depends in part on the degree to which all possible methods of breaching security have been considered.

Also see *risk assessment; uncertainty*.

com•pres•sion, data

(Data communications; Data management)

n. Reduction of the size of a data block in storage or during transmission. There are many methods for doing it. When compressed data is retrieved or received, it must be expanded before use.

Compression is particularly important in data transmission, since it can reduce the time required and the cost significantly. It is most often applied to the transmission of screen images, pictures, and other graphics due to their large size. Also applied to disk storage.

Dif•fer•en•tial compression involves replacing predictable data, such as the first or last letters of items in an alphabetical index, with an indicator of the difference between the item and the one preceding it. The indicator might be the number of similar characters removed.

Hi•er•ar•chic compression eliminates redundant fields or other data and combines the remaining fields in a hierarchy. For instance, a database of names and addresses has several records whose state field contains SD. Compression will store as a unit one field containing SD and the remainder of the records.

com•put•er aid•ed de•sign
(Applications)

An integration of database, drawing, and simulation applications to produce a design and specifications for manufacturing or construction. Common application areas include electrical, mechanical, and architectural design.

For instance, the designer of a piece of equipment must specify the materials for simulation and manufacturing. Each material's physical properties, cost, and source of supply are contained in databases, which the designer uses in the course of the design process.

Sometimes known as Computer Aided Design and Drafting, or CADD.

Also see *computer aided manufacturing*.

com•put•er aided engineering
(Applications)

Abbreviated CAE. The use of computers to provide general engineering tools for both design and non-design tasks.

com•put•er aid•ed man•u•fac•tur•ing
(Applications)

Narrowly, the use of computers to control manufacturing equipment. More broadly, a computer-oriented system of manufacturing, inventory control, and accounting, depending heavily on databases. Often used with CAD, in the expression CAD/CAM. May involve robotics, decision support systems (DSS), manufacturing resource or materials requirements planning (MRP), and expert systems.

Also see *computer aided design*.

com•put•er aid•ed soft•ware en•gi•neer•ing
(Software development tools)

n. Acronym: **CASE.** The use of a computer-based set of tools to aid in software development.

Planning tools include configuration and project managers.

Design tools draw flowcharts and other graphics, generate code for screens, compile data dictionaries, track data elements, and model data paths.

Implementation tools generate code, provide libraries of subroutines, edit code and detect errors, validate test data, test data modules, and debug on-line code.

Other tools aid in maintenance, documentation, and project management.

com•put•er in•te•grat•ed man•u•fac•tur•ing
(Data management)

Abbreviated **CIM** (pronounced "sim"). The linking of computerized design, process planning, and manufacturing and their related computerized office and support functions, such as communications, data management, inventory control, and accounting. An extension of CAD/CAM.

Also see *computer aided design; computer aided manufacturing; MAP/TOP*.

com•put•er se•cu•ri•ty

See *security, computer*.

com•put•er's store

See *store*.

com•put•er sys•tem

See *system*. Often just a longer name for a computer, but may also include peripherals and software.

con•cat•e•na•tion
(Data management)

n. Combining strings by placing one after another.

Also see *string*.

(dBASE)

dBASE uses + and - for concatenation. For example, to place 60515 after ILLINOIS, with a space in between, enter

"Illinois " + "60515"

A character field will be filled with spaces, called trailing blanks, if the string is shorter than the field length. For example, the field CITY contains CHGO - - - - and the field FACILITY contains 7531 - - - -. It may be desirable to create a new field ID by concatenating the two strings and transferring the trailing blanks from the end of CITY to the end of FACILITY. This is done with

STORE City - Facility TO Id.

The result is

CHGO7531 - - - - - - - -.

con•cep•tu•al model

See *model, conceptual.*

con•cur•ren•cy

n. Property of several processes or operations being carried out at once, that is, in parallel. Shared.

For example, **con•cur•rent ac•cess** to data means that several people may have access to it at the same time.

Also see *access.*

Concurrent processes are ones that are active simultaneously. Concurrent languages (such as Ada, Modula-2, and Concurrent Pascal) have facilities for specifying concurrent processes and allowing them to communicate. Often called **concurrency con•trol** or **trans•ac•tion pro•cess•ing** mechanisms.

con•cur•ren•cy con•trol

See *concurrency; locking.*

con•cur•rent ac•cess

See *access, concurrent.*

Con•fer•ence on Da•ta Sys•tems Lan•guages

See *CODASYL.*

CONFIG.SYS
(MS-DOS)

MS-DOS's system configuration file. Provides commands by which the user can specify whether breaks in operations are allowed, number of buffers, time and date style, devices to be used, number of open files allowed, number of drives, and shell name.

con•fig•u•ra•tion man•age•ment (CM)
(Data management; Programming)

The specification, design, task allocation, and maintenance of a process or system, such as a computer system or network, so that it is effective and efficient for present uses and can be altered or expanded in the future. May include the design, control, and documentation of data management systems, process planning, and product development and operation.

CASE (computer-aided software engineering) tools are available to aid in its implementation.

con•fine•ment

n. Keeping within bounds.

(Security)

The prevention of leakage or release of data by a computer program that has access to it. Methods include elimination of surreptitious data copying and restrictions on storage and timing channels.

The ability of a program to thwart unauthorized access to its data. Or its ability to detect covert channels, allowing their elimination.

Also see *channel, covert.*

con•fine•ment prop•er•ty

See *star property.*

con•junc•tion

n. A combination.

(Data management; Mathematics)

A series of propositions joined by Boolean and's. Contrast with *disjunction.*

con•nec•tion
(Data communications)

n. A path in a network, allowing nodes to send and receive data.

(Programming)

A functional path for transferring information. Also a reference in a program to something elsewhere in the same program.

con•nec•tiv•i•ty

(Data communications)

n. The ability of a computer or other device to be connected to a network, especially one that accepts different operating systems. Generally requires both software and hardware.

con•sis•ten•cy

(Data management)

Assurance by a database management system that data integrity is maintained despite system crashes and other unusual circumstances. This is done through locks, techniques for data recovery, and interfaces that isolate the database from users, nodes, and communications hardware.

Increasing the availability of the database generally decreases the probability of data consistency.

con•sole

(Hardware)

n. A computer terminal, particularly the main one used by a manager to control the system. Also called a **con•trol pan•el.**

Con•stan•tine Your•don struc•ture

See *Yourdon-Constantine structure.*

con•straint

n. A boundary, limitation, or restriction on action.

(Data management)

In relational database managers, a **ref•er•en•tial constraint** is a rule that defines automatic updating across all tables, preventing it unless certain conditions are met. A method of assuring referential integrity. For example, it forbids an update that would change or delete data that must not be changed and a data addition that is not provided for in related tables.

Also see *integrity, data; integrity, referential.*

con•text sen•si•tive help
(Applications)

Help routine that provides on-screen assistance specific to the part of the application currently being used, rather than more general assistance.

con•tin•u•ous bar code

See *bar code*.

con•tin•u•ous sim•u•la•tion

See *simulation*.

con•trol char•ac•ter
(Computer operations)

A non-printing character often used to start, stop, or change a computer or communications operation. Typical ASCII control characters, for example, include ACK (acknowledge), LF (line feed), CR (carriage return), ESC (escape), and NUL (null). In ASCII, all characters below 20 hex (32 decimal) are control. On many keyboards, one enters control characters by using the Ctrl or Control key. See table under *ASCII*.

con•trol pan•el

See *console*.

con•trol pro•gram

See *operating system*.

con•trol store

See *store*.

con•ver•sa•tion•al mode

See *interactive processing*.

con•ver•sion, code
(Data management)

The changing of data representation from one code to another, such as ASCII to EBCDIC or decimal to binary.

con•ver•sion, da•ta

(Data management)

Transferring of data from one operating system, file, or application format to another. For example, when two application formats are incompatible, changing data from the original format to ASCII format, in which it can be loaded into the second application.

Also transferring from one storage medium to another, as from disk to tape.

cooked

(Data management)

adj. Input processing mode that refers to the usual way of handling terminal input in units of lines, with an end-of-line, end-of-file, or newline character added. Distinguished from the raw mode, in which bytes are not assembled into lines, but are handled one-by-one.

Also see *raw.*

(UNIX)

Synonym: *buffered I/O.*

co•op•er•a•tive pro•cess•ing

(Data management)

Application execution that occurs simultaneously on two or more processors in a distributed system. An example is a database management system that permits some data storage and manipulation on a personal computer and some on a host.

co•pro•ces•sor

(Hardware)

Secondary processor that performs specialized operations in parallel with the main CPU. The most common application is floating point arithmetic; other proposed or implemented functions include graphics, communications, signal processing, memory management, and security.

Also see *floating point processor.*

copy

v. To duplicate an original.

(Data management)

To duplicate a file or block of text for placement elsewhere without destroying the original. A file may be copied from one disk or storage device to another, for example, as a backup. In a database, the contents of a field, record, row, or table may be copied to another. A spreadsheet cell, group of cells, row, column, or other block may be copied for placement elsewhere in the same spreadsheet or in a different one. Text, ASCII, or graphics files may be copied from many applications for inclusion in report, word processing, presentation graphics, or page layout files.

n. A duplicate of an original.

(Data management)

A duplicate file or block of text created for placement elsewhere without destroying the original.

core dump

(Computer operations)

(Obsolete) Listing of complete contents of memory, often used as a last resort to pinpoint errors that cannot be identified by standard means.

Synonyms: **dump, mem•o•ry dump**

cou•pling

n. Joining or bringing together.

(Data management; Programming languages)

In structured design, the degree to which modules are independent. A high degree of independence is called **loose coupling**. A high degree of dependence is **tight coupling**.

As identified by J. Martin, the loosest degree is data coupling, followed by stamp (communication through a record or other data composite), control (data from one directing the action of the other), common (sharing global data), and content (affecting each other's content).

A feature of systems analysis, in which good design is believed to feature loose coupling and strong cohesion.

Also see *cohesion.*

co•vert chan•nel

See *channel, covert.*

co•vert stor•age chan•nel

See *channel, covert*

co•vert tim•ing chan•nel

See *channel, covert.*

cps

See *characters per second*.

CPU

See *central processing unit*.

crash

(Computer operations)

v. (Slang) Sudden and unexpected action of a computer to shut down or cease operations because of a malfunction in the hardware, operating system, application, or data file.

n. (Slang) Such a computer shutdown, as in "system crash."

CRC

(Data communications)

Abbreviation of cyclic redundancy check. Method of error checking during transmission. Also called polynomial code, because it treats bit strings as representations of polynomials with coefficients of zeros and ones only. All arithmetic is done modulo 2, with no carries or borrows.

Also see *checksum*.

C shell

See *shell*.

CSMA/CA

See *carrier sense multiple access/collision avoidance*.

CSMA/CD

See *carrier sense multiple access/collision detection*.

cur•ren•cy in•di•ca•tor

(Data management)

A position within a network database. For example, in IDMS, the value of an indicator is either null or a key (a record ID). Synonym: *pointer*.

(dBASE)

A string used to mark money values (such as $, ¥, or £). Also called a **currency sym•bol.**

cur•ren•cy sym•bol

See *currency indicator*.

cur•rent win•dow

See *window*.

cur•sor

n. Indicator that moves across a surface to allow something to be read or entered accurately. May be a line for an instrument or an underscore or highlighted area for a computer screen.

(SQL)

Named area in a program in which query results are held. Functionally similar to a buffer. The user must first issue the command

DECLARE cursorname CURSOR FOR specificquery

OPEN cursorname

When all data is found, the user issues the command

CLOSE cursorname

curve

(Graphics; Mathematics)

n. A line representing a point moving in accordance with the value of an equation variable.

v. To bend at other than a sharp angle.

cyc•lic re•dun•dan•cy check

See *CRC*.

D

DA

See *database administrator; desk accessory.*

DAC

See *digital-to-analog converter.*

Da•plex
(Artificial intelligence; Data management)

Query language based on predicate calculus for use with functional databases. Defined in K.G. Atkinson and K.G. Kulkarni. "Experimenting with the Functional Data Model." in P.M. Stocker, ed. *Databases: Role and Structure* (Cambridge, U.K.: Cambridge University Press, 1984).

da•ta
(Data management)

n. Facts without context in a form – words, numbers, images, sounds – that can be entered into a computer. Human organization and interpretation give data context and meaning, producing information.

Also see *information.*

Note: Although the term is plural, it is often used today as a singular noun. For example, one might say, "Data moves from one node to another." The Latin singular, datum, has become rare.

data ab•strac•tion

See *abstraction.*

da•ta ac•cess map

See *data navigation diagram.*

da•ta•base
(Data management)

n. An organized set of data. It consists of subunits called records, which in turn are composed of fields. There are many different types, including flat files, relational databases, and network databases. Often synonymous with database management system (DBMS), the software that allows users to manipulate databases.

Also see *field; record.*

By extension, fields in some databases can contain entire bodies of information, such as maps, music, pictures, videos, sounds, and text.

Sometimes appears in the original form as two separate words, as in "data base design."

Database types include:

• **flat file** Also known as a **file.** A two-dimensional matrix of rows and columns. For instance, each horizontal row may contain a name and its associated address, area code, and telephone number. This is known as a record. Each entry is called a field. Each field is also in a vertical column, so that all names or all telephone numbers can be considered together, as for sorting.

• **re•la•tion•al** One or more tables, each of which is a flat file, associated through linking. This organization permits more efficient entry, use of more types of data, and querying by establishing relationships among data categories. Examples include dBASE (Ashton-Tate) and DB2 (IBM).

Also see *relational database.*

• **net•work** A database governed by data description and data manipulation languages (but not Structured Query Language). Records have multiple links and are identified with pointers. Example are DBMS-11 (DEC), IDMS/R (Cullinet), and KnowledgeMan/2 (Micro Data Base Systems).

Also see *network database.*

• **hi•er•ar•chi•cal** A database organized in a tree structure. An example is IMS (IBM).

Also see *tree.*

• **in•verted file** Database in which the entire file is indexed by key word, with all data associated with each key word stored with it. Examples include ADABAS (Software AG of North America, Inc.), DATACOM/DB (Applied Data Research, Inc.), and Model 204 (Computer Corporation of America).

Also see *column; database management system; field; file; index; link; record; pointer; query; row; spreadsheet; table; tree;* also specific database programs: *dBASE, DB2, FoxBASE, HyperCard, Ingres, Oracle, Paradox, R:BASE.*

data base

(Data management)

Original spelling of database (popularized by Cullinet), which has now largely replaced it.

da•ta•base ad•min•is•tra•tor

(Data management)

The person responsible for determining and maintaining a database's structure and use. Abbreviated **DA**. Responsibilities include maintaining data integrity and security, providing for backup and error or damage recovery, helping users with queries, enforcing rules for use, assigning priorities and passwords, determining access, and maintaining the underlying software.

da•ta•base, dis•trib•ut•ed

(Data management)

A database that resides on several computers, for example, partly on a personal computer and partly on a VAX minicomputer or IBM mainframe.

da•ta•base, expert

See *database, logic*.

da•ta in•de•pen•dence

See *independence, data*.

da•ta•base, log•ic

(Data management)

A database management system that incorporates an expert system in its querying abilities. Also called an **ex•pert da•ta•base**.

Also see *expert system*.

da•ta•base ma•chine

(Hardware)

Peripheral that performs database management tasks. It is composed of a specialized processor (**database pro•cess•or**) and operating system and database management software. The primary manufactures are Britton-Lee (Intelligent Database Machine, IDM, for mainframes and minicomputers, and Relational Server, RS, for minicomputers and workstations) and Teradata.

da•ta•base man•age•ment sys•tem

(Data management)

Abbreviated **DBMS**. Application program (sometimes a series of programs) that defines a database, stores and retrieves data, and, in a distributed system, manages communications. Usually contains a data description language (DDL) and a data manipulation language (DML). Also called a **database man•ag•er**. Examples are dBASE (Ashton-Tate), DB2 (IBM), Ingres (Relational Technology), and Oracle (Oracle Corp.).

The phrase sometimes refers to a combination of hardware and software, such as a distributed database available to users over a network.

Also see *database server*.

The terms database manager, DBMS, and database are often all used with the same meaning. However, database more properly refers to just the data, not the management software.

da•ta•base man•ag•er

See *database management system*.

da•ta•base, ob•ject or•i•ent•ed

(Data management)

Database whose structure uses the principles of object oriented programming, including modules (objects) containing data and methods (procedures) and the inheritance of methods by new classes. An example is GemStone (Servio Logic Development Corp.)

Also see *object oriented*.

da•ta•base own•er

See *database administrator*.

da•ta•base pro•ces•sor

See *database machine*.

da•ta•base pub•lish•ing

(Output formatting)

Page layout and publishing software for database reports and catalogs. Permits importing of database, graphics, spreadsheet, and word processing files.

Also see *desktop publishing*.

da•ta•base serv•er

(Data management)

In multiuser and distributed database management, software that contains the command structure for entering data into a database, querying, and making changes or deletions. The user interacts with the server through a "friendly" front end or interface. Generally the server and database reside on a network server, minicomputer, or mainframe. Synonym: **engine.**

Also see *server*.

(MS-DOS)

An example is the database server SQLBase (Gupta Technologies), which provides the user with information by means of SQLWindows, a 4GL front end. Another is SQL Server (Ashton-Tate, Microsoft, and Sybase).

da•ta com•pres•sion

See *compression, data*.

da•ta con•trol lan•guage

See *Structured Query Language*.

da•ta con•ver•sion

See *conversion, data*.

da•ta def•i•ni•tion lan•guage

A language used to define a conceptual model (schema) of a database, including size of records, data types, formats, tables, columns, and relationships. Used in the relational model.

Also see *Structured Query Language*.

da•ta de•pen•den•cy di•a•gram

See *dependency diagram*.

da•ta de•scrip•tion lan•guage

(Data management)

A language used to define a conceptual model (schema) of a database, including size of records, data storage capacity, data types, formats, tables, columns, relationships, views, and privileges. Used in the CODASYL model.

Also see *ANSI/X3/SPARC database framework; CODASYL; Network Database Language; schema.*

da•ta dic•tion•ar•y

(Data management)

A system database that contains information about a user database, such as location of data, lists of fields and tables, and data types and lengths. Also called a **catalog**.

May be part of a database management system (**de•pen•dent**), for example, Integrated Data Dictionary (Cullinet) or DB/DC Data Dictionary (IBM). Or it may be independent (**free•stand•ing**) for data files, such as Datamanager (MSP).

An **act•ive data dictionary** contains all the system's data descriptions and must be accessed for each operation. In a **pass•ive data dictionary**, such access is either optional or not required, since the information also exists elsewhere in the system.

An **in•ter•ac•tive data dictionary** is one that can be queried and updated from within the open database.

da•ta driv•en ap•pli•ca•tion

(Data management)

An application, such as a database, that uses the data input design of another database. The design is in the form of an algorithm from which a secondary database containing the data structure is designed. This database becomes the driver for the one that will contain the actual data.

Da•ta En•cryp•tion Stan•dard

(Security)

Abbreviated **DES**. Data encryption/decryption algorithm widely used commercially and by the U.S. government for unclassified, but sensitive data. Developed in early 1970s at IBM, and supported by the U.S. National Bureau of Standards (now the National Institute of Science and Technology, NIST).

Defined in FIPS 46 and FIPS 46-1 and American National Standards X3.92-1981 and X3.106-1983.

Enciphers 64-bit blocks of data with a 56-bit key. Special circuits (chips) are widely available to implement the method.

Formerly endorsed by the U.S. National Security Agency (NSA) for unclassified uses, but superseded in 1988 by its Commercial COMSEC Endorsement Program (CCEP). There have been public arguments over the efficiency of DES and how much security it provides.

Also see *decryption; encryption.*

da•ta flow di•a•gram (DFD)
(Software development tools)

Type of diagram used in structured analysis, showing the flow of physical and logical data through a system's or program's processes. Abbreviated DFD. Data flow is represented by arrows, processes by circles or rounded boxes (depending on notation), data store by double lines, and external data or processes by boxes. Synonym: **flow•chart.**

Also see *flowchart; Gane and Sarson analysis; structured analysis; Yourdon-DeMarco diagram.*

da•ta flow sys•tem
(Data management)

Computer built from modules connected by message-passing links. Each module performs part of a computation and communicates a result.

da•ta in•de•pen•dence

See *independence, data.*

da•ta in•teg•ri•ty

See *integrity, data.*

da•ta in•ter•change for•mat

See *DIF.*

da•ta-link con•trol

See *protocol.*

da•ta ma•nip•u•la•tion lan•guage
(Data management)

Language that defines queries, views, addition, changing, and deletion of data, and other types of user access to a database. Abbreviated **DML.** Several database models employ such a language, including network and relational.

For network databases, also see *ANSI/X3/SPARC database framework; CODASYL; Network Database Language.*

For relational databases, also see *Structured Query Language.*

da•ta map•ping lan•guage

See *ANSI/X3/SPARC database framework.*

da•ta nav•i•ga•tion di•a•gram

(Graphics; Software development tools)

In relational systems, a diagram showing the path through a normalized data model. Appropriate either for users or for developing applications procedures. Synonyms: *data access map; logical access map.*

da•ta pro•cess•ing

The organization of data into easily used forms, its processing, and reorganization into usable information. Commonly associated with modern business, data organization and use is recorded as far back as the Stone Age. Modern data processing probably has its origins in the 17th century.

Auto•mat•ic da•ta pro•cess•ing is the use of a computer system for data entry, storage, organization, and processing and its retrieval in a desired format. This method became popular beginning with the punched card system devised by Herman Hollerith for the U.S. Census of 1890.

da•ta re•cov•ery

See *recovery, data.*

da•ta set

See *file.*

da•ta stor•age de•scrip•tion lan•guage

See *CODASYL.*

da•ta stream•ing

See *streaming.*

da•ta struc•ture

(Data management)

A form for storing data in an organized manner. Typical examples are lists, arrays, queues, sets, stacks, trees, and graphs. The structure may include pointers or links.

da•ta type

(Data management)

A classification of data according to characteristics such as bit length, range, format, structure, accuracy, associated or applicable functions, or specific values. Typical types (sometimes called **prim•i•tives**) are Boolean (binary or yes/no variables), integer (whole numbers), character, decimal, floating point, string, and record or structure. Some languages have extended types and type definition facilities. **Ab•stract** data types are defined by a declaration of a set of primitive types. Different computer languages and applications support different data types.

Enu•mer•at•ed types have a specific range of values. For example, a type SEASON could have possible values SPRING, SUMMER, FALL, and WINTER. Other types might be DAYOFWEEK or MONTH.

(dBASE)

dBASE III PLUS supports the following types:

• ASCII characters, which can be manipulated by linking or concatenating strings, dividing a string into substrings, or comparing strings

• decimal numbers, permitting addition, subtraction, multiplication, division, and exponentiation; also mathematical functions for absolute value, exponential value, integer value, natural logarithm, maximum value, minimum value, modulus, rounding, and square roots

• logical expressions – true and false, as well as the relational operators equal to, not equal to, less than, greater than, less than or equal to, and greater than or equal to

Also see *Boolean operator; Boolean variable.*

• calendar dates

• long text, called memo, which is handled like character data, but can only be manipulated in a very limited way

dBASE IV also supports floating point numeric data, as defined in IEEE Standard 754.

Also see *floating point.*

da•ta val•i•da•tion

See *validation.*

DB2

(Data management)

General purpose distributed relational database management system using SQL, designed for mainframes (IBM). Querying and report writing are performed with the Query Management Facility (QMF). Access to the database is by means of associated front end applications. DB2 runs on the IBM MVS/370 and MVS/XA systems.

Interactive version is called DB2I.

dBASE

(Data management)

A widely used series of relational database management programs for personal computers (Ashton-Tate). User may issue screen commands ("dot commands") or write programs in the provided procedural language. Common versions include dBASE IV, dBASE III PLUS, and dBASE III.

Follows the relational model, but uses the terminology of flat file and network databases, such as record instead of tuple.

The original version was dBASE II (also known as Vulcan), developed by Wayne Ratliff. There was no dBASE I, nor has there even been an "Ashton." There are also dBASE "clones" or "lookalikes" such as Clipper (Nantucket), dBXL (WordTech Systems, Inc.), FoxBASE and FoxPro (Fox Software), and Quicksilver (WordTech Systems, Inc.).

DBMS

See *database management system.*

DBTG

See *CODASYL.*

dBXL

(Data management)

A relational database management program (WordTech Systems, Inc.). dBXL is a "lookalike" for dBASE (Ashton-Tate). It is an interpreter, but its commands can be compiled using the related Quicksilver (also WordTech Systems, Inc.).

DDL

Ambiguous abbreviation. See *data definition language* or *data description language.*

dead•lock

n. A standstill; a tie score.

(Data management)

Condition in which multiple users are all waiting for the availability of resources that others among them control. No progress can occur until at least one user is forced to release a requested resource. The resources may, for example, be database files (or pages), I/O devices, or memory areas. May involve many users, and may be **glob•al**, tying up the entire system.

Many picturesque phrases exist to describe this condition, such as **dead•ly em•brace**.

dead•ly em•brace

See *deadlock*.

de•bug

(Programming)

v. To remove errors from computer programs. Computer mythology says that the term originated when an insect was found to be disrupting the operation of an early computer.

de•bug•ger

(Software development tools)

n. A routine that allows a programmer to control the execution of a program and to obtain information to use in correcting errors. Tools may include trace, breakpoint, single-step, and dump.

(dBASE)

To manually debug a program, first SET ECHO ON, which will display the lines as they are executed. Then use SET DEBUG to print the executed lines for comparison with source code.

dBASE IV contains an interactive debugger, which is invoked with the command DEBUG to control a specified program. The command SET TRAP ON automatically activates the debugger during program execution if an error is detected.

(UNIX)

The widely available low-level debugger is adb.

In System V (AT&T) UNIX, sdb is a symbolic debugger for programs written in C, FORTRAN, or Pascal.

In Berkeley UNIX, dbx is a symbolic debugger.

Also see *debugger, symbolic*.

de•bug•ger, sym•bol•ic

(Software development tools)

A debugger that allows the user to analyze program execution at a language (such as C, dBASE, or Pascal) or symbolic level, that is, using names and labels defined within the program rather than absolute addresses. It generally lets the user trace program variables, set breakpoints at program statements, and execute the program one statement or one line at a time. It can be told to locate information in a named variable or field (for example, Accounts Receivable), perform operations, control program execution, and display results.

As opposed to a low-level, machine-level, or absolute debugger that only allows analysis in terms of machine language instructions and absolute addresses.

Typical examples that work with several languages are CodeView (Microsoft) and Turbo Debugger (Borland International).

Also see *debugger*.

(UNIX)

In System V (AT&T), sdb is a symbolic debugger.

The Berkeley UNIX command ln -s creates a symbolic link that permits use of the symbolic debugger dbx.

de•bug•ging

(Programming)

n. The process of removing errors, often included as a stage in the development of a finished program. Sometimes also called **pro•gram ver•i•fi•ca•tion.**

Also see *verification*.

de•ci•pher

v. To decode. Synonym: *decrypt*.

Also see *encryption*.

de•ci•pher•ment

n. The process of decoding. Synonym: *decryption*; decipherment is the preferred word of the International Standards Organization (ISO).

Also see *encryption*.

de•ci•sion sup•port sys•tem

(Data management)

Abbreviated **DSS**. A computer program that provides a tool an organization's executives can use to help make decisions about future actions and operations. Often involves budgeting, analysis, modeling, and other analytical applications that can project current data into the future.

A DSS usually has a specific purpose and provides help with a particular type of decision, as opposed to a more generalized management or executive information system. There are special packages for creating DSS's, such as IFPS (Execucom).

Also see *executive information system.*

de•ci•sion ta•ble

(Software development tools)

Table designed to assist in problem solving. In one dimension, it presents the elements or conditions of the problem under consideration; in the other, the possible actions or outcomes. Each cell can contain either a yes-no or a true-false decision. This may dictate the course of action, or the pattern on which a final decision is based.

May also be used as an alternative to a flowchart in constructing a computer program.

dec•la•ra•tion

See *type declaration.*

de•com•po•si•tion

n. Breaking up or disassembly of an entity into smaller parts.

(Data management; Programming languages; Software development tools)

The dividing or partitioning of data, a system, or a program into small parts that can be easily handled individually. May be represented graphically with a **decomposition di•a•gram.**

Func•tion•al de•com•po•si•tion is a feature of structured programming and systems design and analysis.

There are several types of decomposition – into functions, such as a tree structure organization chart; data types, with inputs and outputs for each function; and rule-defined, in which only certain types of decomposition are permitted and carried out.

Also see *top-down.*

de•com•po•si•tion di•a•gram

See *decomposition.*

de•crypt

v. To decode. Synonym: *decipher*.

   Also see *encryption*.

(dBASE)

In dBASE IV, users of the PROTECT security program can COPY a file in decrypted form after using the command SET ENCRYPTION OFF.

de•cryp•tion

n. The process of decoding. Synonym: *decipherment*, though decryption is the preferred U.S. usage.

   Also see *encryption*.

ded•i•cat•ed

adj. Reserved for a single or special purpose.

(Computer operations)

A computer, device, or system designed or used for a single application or purpose. Examples are a graphics computer and a word processing machine.

(Data communications)

A device or transmission line reserved for data communications, such as a dedicated telephone line.

   A **dedicated serv•er** is one that does not perform any user tasks on its own. It is a separate machine given over entirely to communications (networking) tasks, not a user machine.

   Also see *server*.

ded•i•cat•ed serv•er

See *dedicated; server*.

de•duc•tive da•ta•base

(Artificial intelligence)

A database composed of a set of deductive rules.

de•fer•red up•date

See *snapshot*.

de•gree

n. A rank in an order or classification. A unit of measure on a scale. The extent of a relation.

(Data management)

Characteristic of a relation. The number of attributes or columns a relation contains. If there is one column, the relation is said to be **unary**. If there are two columns, it is **bi•nary**. A three-column relation is **ter•nary**. If there are n columns, the relation is **n-ary**.

Used in relational mathematics to determine the size of a relation produced by an operation.

Unlike a relation's cardinality, its degree is said not to change, because adding an attribute or column, or performing a relational operation, creates a new relation characterized by its own degree.

Also see *cardinality*.

de•lete

(Data management)

v. To erase a file from a floppy or hard disk or other storage medium. Also to erase a record from a database, data from a field, or text from a word processing file.

Many applications have two ways to remove data, one that allows the user to restore it and one that removes it irrevocably.

(dBASE)

The DELETE command marks records for deletion. Deleted records remain in the file, but are marked with an asterisk (*). Many commands will ignore them if the DELETED flag is on. RECALL reinstates deleted records. The PACK command removes them and reindexes open index files.

The ZAP command removes all records from the file and packs them; it is the equivalent of DELETE ALL, followed by PACK. It also removes records from all open index files.

Deleted records are still in the file, unchanged except for the delete status. Even records removed by PACK or DELETE may be temporarily retained on disk in MS-DOS systems and may sometimes be recovered by a standard "un-erase" utility.

To prevent accidental deletion, use SET SAFETY ON. dBASE then asks for a confirmation from the user before deleting anything.

Also see *pack*.

de•lim•it•er

n. A marker or separator.

(Data management)

A character or symbol (such as a comma, period, space, or semicolon) used to separate items. For instance, in many database management systems, when entering a text file into a database, the sequence

        item1, item2, item3, ...

puts item1 in the first field, item2 in the second field, and so on.

(Programming)

A symbol used to separate or mark elements (such as variables, strings, statements, or blocks) within a program. For example, many languages, such as BASIC and C, require a semicolon at the end of each statement.

(Data communications)

Patterns, characters, or sequences of characters that separate words, paragraphs, and lines and mark the end of a transmitted message. For example, a message may end with a null character (ASCII 0). In standard asynchronous protocols, stop bits (logic 1's) serve as delimiters between characters.

De•Mar•co anal•y•sis

See *Yourdon-DeMarco diagram*.

de•pen•den•cy di•a•gram
(Data structures; Software development tools)

Similar to data flow and decomposition diagrams, showing the structure of a system or program.

de•pen•den•cy, func•tion•al

See *functional dependence*.

de•pen•dent da•ta dic•tion•ar•y

See *data dictionary*.

de•ref•er•ence
(Programming)

v. To refer to an object (such as a data item or structure) via a pointer. May be specified by an operator, such as the * in C that serves as a prefix (not to be confused with the * meaning multiplication).

DES

See *data encryption standard.*

de•scrip•tor

n. An identifier, particularly an entry in an index.

(Data management)

In describing a relationship, the object of the association (verb). For example, in "library card No. 4567 expires on November 30," the descriptor is November 30.

In the database management program ADABAS (Software AG of North America, Inc.), the term for an inverted field.

(Security)

Access to a single process. Like a capability, but for a single process.

desk ac•ces•so•ry

(Applications)

An application for the Macintosh that is loaded into the system folder using the Font/DA Mover; always accessible through the Apple menu, even when another program is open. Abbreviated DA. Calculators and notepads are two common DAs. Others include database, graphics, word processing, communications, telephone dialer, and mathematics programs.

Also see *terminate and stay resident.*

desk•top

(Computer environment)

n. The opening screen display of the hierarchy of files on a floppy disk or hard disk under the Macintosh operating system. The files appear as labeled icons, and may be grouped in folders, represented as file folder icons. The idea has been carried over to other user interfaces on other computers.
Synonym: **root di•rec•to•ry.**

Also see *directory; folder; icon; root.*

desk•top pub•lish•ing

(Output formatting)

Use of a personal computer system to produce camera ready copy without involving outside vendors. Originally referred to performing publishing with equipment that fit on a desktop. Increased sophistication of hardware and software is making the term obsolescent.

Basic tools include a personal computer; word processing, graphics, and page layout software; and a laser printer. May include other applications software and a typesetting machine, sometimes available at outside facilities called service bureaus.

Also see *service bureau.*

desk•top com•put•er

(Hardware)

A machine that can be placed comfortably on a desk, rather than requiring a rack, stand, or other mounting.

DES stan•dard

See *data encryption standard.*

de•struc•tive up•dat•ing

(Data management)

The deletion of previous versions of data and data structures as new ones are added.

de•ter•mi•nant

n. Something that identifies another or decides an outcome.

(Data management)

In a data relation, an attribute on which another attribute is functionally dependent. For example, in a table LIBRARY CARDS, the column EXPIRATION DATE is functionally dependent on the primary key CARD NO. Here CARD NO is the determinant.

de•vel•op•er

(Software)

n. A person who designs, writes, and tests computer applications programs. Some programs (such as dBASE IV) have special developers' versions aimed at those who will add features of their own, rather than just use the software.

For example, a developer might write a banking, accounting, manufacturing, or retailing application based on a dBASE package.

Also see *end user.*

de•vice

(Hardware)

n. A keyboard, printer, modem, terminal, or other piece of equipment that can send or receive data when attached to a computer or a network. A device attached to a network is also called a node.

In MS-DOS, UNIX, and other operating systems, also a named, numbered, or otherwise designated port, such as COM1 or standard output. MS-DOS and UNIX treat devices like files, and the two can be used interchangeably in commands.

de•vice driver

See *driver*.

DFD

See *data flow diagram*.

Dhry•stone pro•gram

(Computer operations)

A synthetic integer-only benchmark that tries to simulate the performance of system code. Described in R.P. Weicker, "Dhrystone: A Synthetic Systems Programming Benchmark," *CACM*, 27 (10), Oct. 1984.

di•ag•nos•tic

A program that checks the operation of a hardware unit and reports its findings.

di•a•gram

See *graph*.

di•a•lect

(Computer languages)

n. A variation of a standardized computer language specific to an application or brand of computer. Variations may include additional commands, deactivation of commands, or differences in command meaning or execution. For example, the dialect of dBASE implemented in dBXL adds new commands and functions, and enhances some commands. BASIC has many dialects, some of which include commands for graphics, real-time control, business functions or arithmetic, and structured programming.

di•a•log box

(Data management)

A pop-up screen in an application or operating system that elicits decisions or choices from the computer user before program execution continues. An example is a request to indicate number of copies and other options in response to a user's instruction to print a file. Dialog boxes are a standard feature of the Macintosh operating system and of other graphical interfaces.

DIF

(File formats)

A standard format that allows data files created in one application to be used in another. Acronym for Data Interchange Format, pronounced "diff." Orginally used with the now obsolete VisiCalc program to allow the transfer of data files from a spreadsheet to a graphics program, database, or word processor.

dif•fer•en•tial pro•gram•ming

(Programming languages)

Description of object oriented programming involving polymorphism and inheritance. Also called programming by modification.

Also see *inheritance; object oriented; polymorphism.*

dig•i•tal

adj. Having to do with the fingers, that is, individual or discrete entities. Thus, having only discrete values, rather than continuous ones. **Digital cir•cuits** operate on digital data and produce digital results. The creation of systems from digital circuits is **digital de•sign.**

A **digital com•put•er** is one that operates on discrete data. The term is now largely obsolete (or at least redundant), as the alternative (the analog computer) has fallen out of use.

dif•fer•en•tial com•pres•sion

See *compression, data.*

dig•i•tal cir•cuit

See *digital.*

dig•i•tal com•put•er

See *digital.*

dig•i•tal de•sign

See *digital*.

dig•i•tal-to-ana•log con•vert•er

(Hardware)

Device that converts digital signals to analog ones, for instance, digital voltages into an analog signal for broadband transmission. Also used to activate or control analog devices, such as motors, actuators, valves, or gears. Often available in chip form or combined with other parts in an **analog I/O board**. Abbreviated **DAC** (pronunciation rhymes with "tack").

Also see *analog; digital*.

di•graph

See *graph*.

di•rect ac•cess

(Data management)

Data storage in which each record location has an address, allowing any record to be retrieved directly. Contrast with *indexed sequential access; sequential access*.

di•rect•ed graph

See *graph*.

di•rect mapping

See *mapping*.

di•rec•to•ry

(File management)

n. A file that contains information about other files, such as their names, sizes, dates and times of creation, attributes, positions on a disk or tape, and other characteristics. Used to organize files and to answer queries about them.

May itself be organized in a variety of ways. Popular options are a **flat directory** that contains information about all files and a **tree-structured directory system**, in which directories themselves may contain information about other subordinate directories or **subdirectories**, as well as actual data or program files.

In a tree-structured system, the base is the **root** or primary **directory**. However, the root is considered to be the top of the system, despite the biological awkwardness.

In the Macintosh operating system, the root directory is called the **finder** or **desktop.** Subdirectories are represented as **folders.**

Also see *tree.*

(MS-DOS)

In MS-DOS, subdirectories are indicated by a \. For example, to open the hard disk file ADDRESSES in a subdirectory PERSONNEL, enter

> \PERSONNEL\ADDRESSES

To change from the current directory to one named CUSTOMERS, enter

> CD \CUSTOMERS

(UNIX)

In UNIX, subdirectories are indicated by / (not to be confused with MS-DOS's \). The "change directory" command is cd (lowercase).

(Computer operations)

A list of data addresses that allows the operating system to copy data from backup storage, such as disk, into the computer's memory. When new data is stored, the operating system automatically updates the directory.

dis•am•big•u•ate

v. To remove double or uncertain meanings; to establish a single meaning or interpretation.

(Data management)

To define or establish a meaning for each entity and dependency in a database model.

dis•crete bar code

See *bar code.*

dis•crete-event

See *event.*

dis•crete sim•u•la•tion

See *simulation.*

dis•cre•tion•ary ac•cess con•trol

See *access control, discretionary.*

dis•joint

adj. Something taken apart.

(Mathematics)

Referring to sets having no elements in common.

(Data management)

A **dis•joint union** is one having no elements in common. It supports the data abstraction method called generalization.

Also see *generalization; union.*

dis•joint union

See *disjoint.*

dis•junc•tion

n. A separation.

(Data management; Mathematics)

A series of propositions joined by Boolean or's.

dis•trib•ut•ed com•put•er sys•tem

(Computer architecture)

Referring to a system involving many computers in which operations may occur on more than one. Software and appliations may run on several machines and may even *migrate* from one to another.

Also see *database, distributed.*

dis•trib•ut•ed da•ta•base

See *database, distributed.*

DK/NF

See *domain-key normal form.*

DML

See *data manipulation language.*

do•main

n. Area of activity or control.

(Mathematics)

Set that defines a mathematical or logical variable.

(Data communications)

May refer to a network or series of networks.

(Data management; Security)

Objects that a subject or principal may access.

do•main-key nor•mal form

(Data management)

In relational database management, a theoretical method of data normalization based on the constraints of domain value and candidate key. The value of every attribute or column must fall within a given domain or set of values and must also meet the constraints of the candidate key. Abbreviated **DK/NF**. Such a relation is also in fifth normal form.

Described in R. Fagin. "A Normal Form for Relational Databases That Is Based on Domains and Keys." *ACM Transactions on Database Systems,* 6 (3), Sept. 1981.

Also see *attribute; fifth normal form; key.*

DOS

(Computer environment)

General acronym for Disk Operating System. Now usually refers specifically to the widely used MS-DOS (Microsoft Corp.) for IBM personal computers. However, for users of large computers, refers to an operating system for smaller IBM mainframes, derived from OS/360.

Also see *MS-DOS; operating system.*

DOS com•pat•i•bi•li•ty box

See *OS/2.*

dot prompt

(dBASE)

In dBASE, a dot at the left margin indicating to the user that a command can be entered. The prompt was the original dBASE II user interface, but later versions largely replaced it with interactive or menu-driven shells.

The user can open a file Addresses and prepare to add a record with the dot prompt commands

.USE Addresses

dots per inch
(Desktop publishing)

Measure of printing resolution. Abbreviated dpi. The larger the number, the higher the resolution. Laser printers are capable of approximately 300 dpi and typesetting equipment of 1200 dpi.

dou•ble click
(Data management)

n. Two successive press-release motions on a mouse key.

v. To press and release a mouse key twice in rapid succession. Sometimes used to issue two commands at once, for example, pointing to text and selecting it, or selecting a file and opening it.

dou•ble-pre•ci•sion float•ing point
(Computer operations)

Floating point numbers stored with twice the standard precision. In IEEE Standard 754, defined as a 64-bit number with a 53-bit significand or mantissa, an 11-bit exponent, and an exponent bias of 1023.

Also see *floating point; precision; single-precision floating point.*

dou•ble word

See *word.*

down•load
(Data communications)

v. To receive data on one computer that was sent from another computer or device. Unlike import, download has a strong hierarchical meaning, with the more complex unit (or central unit) at the sending end.

For example, one would download data from a minicomputer or mainframe to a personal computer.

Also see *upload.*

dpi

See *dots per inch.*

draw pro•gram

(Graphics)

An application for producing line drawings, using line-oriented (or vector) graphics, which creates smooth edges. The draw application stores the end points of a straight line rather than the line itself. It also allows drawing of a curve limited by the end points and defined by direction points; a common implementation is called a Bezier curve. In a complex curve, smoothness depends on the user's skill in placing the external points.

Compare to *paint program.*

Also see *vector graphics.*

driv•er

(Software)

n. A program that performs the detailed manipulations required to connect an I/O device to a computer. Also called a **de•vice driver.**

The software required to actually make something run. For example, one might use a driver to run an interactive program before the shell has been written or to test it in isolation.

(Hardware)

An amplifier required to transmit a signal over long distances or to connect the output of one device to the inputs of many devices (often called increasing the **fan-out**). Also called a **bus driver, driver am•pli•fi•er, buff•er/driver,** or **line driver.** This usage means that hardware-oriented literature often refers to I/O driver programs as **soft•ware drivers,** a redundancy in the software or general computer world.

driv•er am•pli•fi•er

See *driver.*

DSS

See *decision support system.*

dump

See *core dump.*

du•plex

See *duplex, full.*

du•plex, full

(Data communications)

Transmission mode in which each end can send and receive data simultaneously. Sometimes called simply **duplex**. Contrast with *duplex, half; simplex.*

du•plex, half

(Data communications)

Transmission mode in which each end can only send or receive data at one time.

Also see *simplex.*

dy•nam•ic

adj. Changing over time.

A **dynamic var•i•able** is one whose values change over time. Also applies to **ar•rays** and **da•ta struc•tures. Dynamic link•ing** means that the program is started before all linking is completed and the linker is invoked as required. **Dynamic mem•o•ry al•lo•ca•tion** refers to allocation at procedure execution; the purpose is to improve space utilization.

Contrast with *static.*

dy•nam•ic link•ing

See *dynamic.*

dy•nam•ic mem•o•ry al•lo•ca•tion

See *dynamic.*

dy•nam•ic var•i•able

See *dynamic.*

E

EAN

See *bar code*.

EBCDIC

(Data communications)

n. Acronym for Extended Binary Coded Decimal Interchange Code (pronounced eb' see dik). A character code often used in larger computers, particularly those made by IBM. Consists of representations of letters, numbers, punctuation marks, and control characters, each composed of 8 bits. Allows 256 combinations, not all of which are assigned.

EDA

See *electronic design automation*.

edge

n. A line representing the intersection of two planes or two plane faces.

(Graphics)

Line or path connecting nodes on a graph.

EDI

See *electronic business data interchange*.

EDIF

See *electronic design interchange format*.

ef•fer•ent branch
(Data management; Programming languages)

Output from a data flow diagram including the process that changes data from logical to physical form. Contrast with *afferent branch*.

Also see *transform analysis*.

EGA

See *enhanced graphics adapter*.

EIS

See *executive information system*.

elec•tron•ic busi•ness da•ta in•ter•change
(Data communications)

Standard format for transferring business documents, such as invoices, purchase orders, and quotations, among applications and devices by modem or electronic mail. Used by large corporations. Abbreviated **EDI** and often called **electronic data interchange**.

Defined in a series of American National Standards X12.1-12.16, 12.20, and 12.22, dated 1986 or 1987.

elec•tron•ic da•ta in•ter•change

See *electronic business data interchange*.

elec•tron•ic de•sign auto•ma•tion
(Applications)

A specialized form of computer aided design, used primarily for designing circuit boards and integrated circuits. Abbreviated **EDA**.

Also see *computer aided design*.

elec•tron•ic de•sign in•ter•change for•mat
(Data communications)

Public domain format for transferring data among computer-aided design, engineering, and manufacturing systems. Abbreviated **EDIF**.

Provides syntax and structure for cell and library organizations, and descriptions for cell interfaces (boundaries, feedthroughs, functional-test patterns, logic symbols, parameters, ports, and port-to-port timing), cell details (gate arrays, geometric layouts, logic models, schematic diagrams, simulation parameters, and symbolic layouts), and processing technology (device-size scaling information, layer definitions, and simulation values).

elec•tron•ic mail

(Data communications)

A system for sending and receiving messages non-interactively. It may be a distributed computer system, such as multiuser VAXes. It may also be a network in which all messages move through a central storage device rather than directly, in other words, an electronic "spoke and hub," in which a sent message is stored for a given period of time or until retrieved. Abbreviated **e-mail**. Also refers specifically to the software required to implement the system.

Unlike a public postal service, an electronic mail network usually can be entered only by qualified users, either from within an organization or by subscription. Each user receives a unique address from which "mail" (a message) is sent and from which it can be retrieved. Typical network services include text editing, message forwarding, copies to multiple users, and extended storage.

el•e•ment

n. A basic part of a group, or a piece of data, such as a number in an array.

e-mail

See *electronic mail.*

em•bed

(Word processing)

v. To place a formatting, printing, or other command within the screen text for later execution.

Also see *WYSIWYG.*

(Dedicated systems)

To place entirely within a single application. For example, an **em•bed•ded com•pu•ter** or **em•bed•ded con•trol•ler** performs specified functions for a single system, such as communications, data analysis, guidance, or adaptive control. It is not shared among multiple users or applications. Embedded computers are common in instruments, test equipment, vehicles, military systems, appliances, communications equipment, computer peripherals, process and industrial controllers, robots, and business equipment. The computer is a system component and is not visible or accessible from outside.

(Programming)

To insert assembly or machine language code into a program written in a high-level language. Also to insert commands from a language within the framework of a package as, for example, to embed SQL within dBASE or Oracle.

em•bed•ded com•put•er

See *embed*.

em•bed•ded con•trol•ler

See *embed*.

em•bed•ded SQL

See *Structured Query Language*.

em•u•la•tion

n. The imitation or duplication of the function of another.

(Hardware)

Property of a computer or device so that it can operate like another. For example, a personal computer may duplicate the operation of a mainframe terminal, or one brand of printer may function like another brand. Emulation is accomplished with hardware, software, or a combination. In some cases, emulation is built into the device, such as a printer that operates like one or more popular brands, making it usable with applications containing drivers for those brands.

When applied to computers, the term emulation is often limited to copies implemented in hardware or at the instruction (firmware) level, whereas those implemented in software are simulations. Emulations run much faster than simulations, but are more difficult to develop. Emulations generally involve microprogramming (that is, changing the extremely low-level code that actually performs the computer instructions).

Also see *simulation*.

en•cap•su•la•tion

n. Enclosing or surrounding.

(Programming languages)

Hiding the details of an implementation within a structure or object.

A feature of object oriented programming in which not all information is visible to the user. A feature of a class or abstract data type in which only the results of its behavior are visible, whereas its structure is concealed. May involve the combination of data structures and procedures within a unit (such as an Ada package) with a defined external interface.

Contrast with *pointer*.

Also see *abstraction; modularity; object oriented*.

(Data communications)

Addition of transmission information to data being sent. Also see *header*.

en•ci•pher

v. To put into code. Synonym: *encrypt*.

Also see *encryption*.

en•ci•pher•ment

n. The process of putting into code. Synonym: *encryption*; encipherment is the preferred word of the International Standards Organization (ISO), because encryption does not translate well into French.

Also see *encryption*.

en•crypt

(Data management)

v. To put data into code, for secrecy or security, or to show that it is authentic. An example is the encryption/decryption (DES) algorithm used by the U.S. government, defined in FIPS 46-1977 and American National Standard X3.106-1983. Synonym: *encipher*.

Also see *decrypt; DES; encryption*.

(dBASE)

In dBASE IV, users of the PROTECT security program can encrypt files created by COPY, JOIN, and TOTAL after using the command SET ENCRYPTION ON.

en•cryp•tion

n. The process of putting into code. Synonym: *encipherment*, though encryption is the preferred U.S. usage.

(Security)

A method of protecting data during storage or transmission. Types of encryption include:

end-to-end – encryption is performed at the sending node and decryption at the destination node.

link – meaning decryption and encryption are performed at each intermediate network node on a data transmission path as well as at the sending and destination nodes.

pub•lic key – which uses different keys to encrypt and decrypt, allowing one of them to be public knowledge.

This still leaves open the problem of managing the remaining private keys.

An example is RSA encryption, available for networks and various sizes of computers (RSA Data Technology, Inc.) Developed at MIT in 1977 by R.L. Rivest, A. Shamir, and L. Adelman. Adopted by Internet in 1989.

Also see *data encryption standard; key; network; node; path.*

end-to-end en•cryp•tion

See *encryption.*

end us•er
(Applications)

n. Individual or organization that employs a computer system and applications software to manage data, solve problems, or produce information or materials. The end user, for instance, interacts with a distributed database management system through its front end.

A distinction is often made between end users and intermediaries, such as consultants, developers, OEMs (original equipment manufacturers), system integrators, and VARs (value added resellers).

Synonym: *user.*

en•gine

See *database server.*

en•hanced graph•ics adapt•er
(Hardware)

Abbreviated EGA. Video display standard for IBM PCs, developed by IBM. Lacks the resolution and variety of colors of VGA. EGA provides text and graphic modes, with graphics resolution of 640 x 350 pixels in 16 colors. For other IBM PC video display standards, see *color/graphics adapter* (CGA); *monochrome display adapter* (MDA); *video graphics array* (VGA).

en•queue

See *queue.*

en•roll

v. To put one's name on a list; to sign up or register for an activity.

(Data management)

Registration of a user or node to become part of a federated database system.

Also see *federated database system*.

en•ter•prise mod•el
(Data management)

Synonym for conceptual model.

Also see *model, conceptual*.

En•ter•prise Sys•tems Ar•chi•tec•ture
(Computer architecture)

Abbreviated ESA. IBM computer architecture for older IBM 4381 and 3090 mainframes to increase the size of their virtual memory and allow them to use a version of the MVS/XA (Multiple Virtual Storage, eXtended Architecture) operating system, called MVS/ESA.

en•ti•ty

n. A distinct thing, object, or concept.

(Data management)

A data object that identifies something.

Also see *relationship*.

en•ti•ty re•la•tion•ship da•ta•base
(Data management)

Database that uses the entity/relationship model. Also called an *extended relational database*. Includes both data and relationships. Examples are Infoexec SIM (Unisys) and Adabas Entire (Software AG).

Also see *entity/relationship (ER) model; relationship*.

en•ti•ty/re•la•tion•ship (ER) mod•el
(Graphics; Software development tools)

A model developed by Peter P.-S. Chen that defines the relationships among data objects (entities); also includes data types, keys, and other information necessary for construction of a database schema.

The model may be depicted by an **ER di•a•gram**. Entities are enclosed by rectangles and relationships by diamonds. Directional lines connect them, indicating whether the relation is 1 (one to one) or M (many to one); line thickness may indicate the strength of the relation.

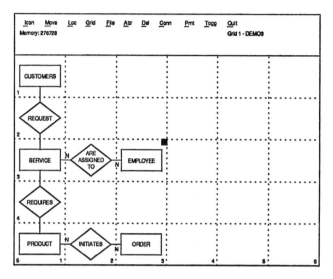

en•tro•py

(Information theory)

n. The amount of information a message contains, compared to the number of equivalent messages that are possible. From the well-known thermodynamic term measuring the amount of disorder in a system.

enu•mer•at•ed da•ta type

See *data type*.

equi•join

See *join*.

ER di•a•gram

See *entity/relationship model*.

ESA

See *Enterprise Systems Architecture*.

Ether•net

(Data communications)

n. A specification for local area network cabling and connectors that can transmit computer data, voice, and video. It transmits at a rate of 10 megabits per second. Stations must be no more than 2.8 km apart.

The specification covers Layer 1, Physical Layer, and Layer 2, Data Link Layer, of the ISO/OSI Reference Model. Ethernet, developed by Xerox Corp., has several variations defined in IEEE Standard 802.3: 10BASE5 or Thick Cable; 10BASE2 or Thin Cable, also known as Cheapernet; 10BASE36, for broadband cable; and 1BASE5 or StarLAN, which uses twisted-pair telephone wire. At least two other variants, for twisted pair and fiber optic cable, are also being defined.

Also see *carrier sense multiple access/collision detection* (CSMA/CD).

Eu•ro•pe•an Ar•ti•cle Num•ber

See *bar code*.

even par•i•ty

See *parity*.

event

n. A change in status.

(Computer operations)

A change in a system's state. On a state diagram, an event is represented by a node.

Also, an action or occurrence that causes a program to execute a response.

(Data management)

An activity that changes data in a file or allows access to a file.

(Computer simulation)

Any change in status. An event-driven, discrete-event, or discrete simulation considers only the times at which events occur, rather than dealing with time as a continuous variable.

event-driv•en

(Computer operations)

System activity or change of state caused by an input signal or event.

ex•cep•tion

n. An unusual or special event, usually internal, but may include external interrupts.

Typical exceptions are division by zero, bounds errors (accesses beyond an array boundary), protection violations, stack overflow or underflow, breakpoints, numerical overflow, invalid or illegal instructions, page faults, and software interrupts. May also include external interrupts such as input or output device ready, timer signals, bus errors, alignment errors, timeouts, power failure, and parity errors.

Some high-level languages, such as Ada, have facilities for handling exceptions.

Synonyms: **fault, soft•ware in•ter•rupt, trap.** Sometimes synonymous with **su•per•vis•or call.**

Exceptions may be divided into classes according to how serious they are. Some are benign and recoverable; others are fatal or nonrecoverable.

A computer is directed to a routine that responds to exceptions via an exception vector or trap vector. The routine is called an exception handler, trap handler, service routine, or fault handler.

ex•clu•sive lock

See *lock.*

ex•ec•u•tive

See *operating system.*

ex•ec•u•tive in•for•ma•tion sys•tem
(Data management)

Abbreviated **EIS.** Software that provides an organization's top executives with the information they need for an overall picture of operations and comparisons with past performance. Often used in strategic planning. Usually provides information in a variety of formats (for example, summaries or graphics) that can be used for planning sessions, board presentations, and other executive functions. Emphasis is on summarizing information in easily understood formats for rapid perusal.

Formerly part of a management information system (MIS), but now a separate entity. Intended specifically for top management, as opposed to the more generalized MIS.

Also see *decision support system.*

EXE file
(MS-DOS)

A file containing loadable object code in an executable form. MS-DOS must perform a few operations to execute an EXE file, so it loads slightly slower (and occupies more disk space) than a COM file. Some, but not all, EXE files can be converted to the COM format with the EXE2BIN program. Designated by the extension EXE. Contrast with *COM file.*

ex•pert da•ta•base

See *database, logic.*

ex•pert sys•tem
(Artificial intelligence)

Information management system composed of data about a particular area and a series of rules that allow the program to make choices and decisions (logical inferences) as a human expert (specialist) in the area would.

The leading practical application of artificial intelligence in general use. The most popular form (called a **rule-based expert system**) consists of a **rule base** or **knowl•edge base,** containing the expert rules, and an **in•fer•ence en•gine,** which makes the decisions. The rules are usually based on analysis of the decision-making processes of several human specialists in the field. The system is most often specific to a particular area of expertise, and contains information that the engine will use in evaluating user-supplied data.

For example, an expert system for credit checking would contain rules for evaluating people's financial histories to determine creditworthiness. These would be applied to credit histories entered into the system. Or a medical expert system would contain data on symptoms and diseases, and the rules to determine probability of disease. In this case, the user would enter a patient's symptoms and medical history, and the inference engine would predict which disease the patient is most likely to have.

The decision process may be performed by forward chaining, backward chaining, or a combination.

Also see *backward chaining; forward chaining; inference engine; knowledge base.*

ex•plod•ing file
(Data management)

Routine that allows a user working within a program to automatically create a file from a defined structure. The structure is usually that of an existing file. Used in database management programs. Prevents having to define a new file when such a definition already exists.

ex•po•nent

See *floating point.*

ex•port
(Data communications; File formats)

v. To transmit data to another computer.

Also to transfer data from one application to another, as from Lotus 1-2-3 to dBASE or from a graphics program to a word processor. The source exports the data and the destination imports it.

(Computer languages)

To send values from one subroutine for use in others. The exported values are all that is visible externally when functions are encapsulated.

Also see *encapsulation*.

ex•tend•a•ble

See *extensible*.

Ex•tend•ed Bi•na•ry Cod•ed De•ci•mal In•ter•change Code

See *EBCDIC*.

ex•tend•ed da•ta type

Data type that can be defined by the user and added to the language with the same facilities for checking and general management as the intrinsic types.

Also see *data type*.

ex•tend•ed mem•o•ry

In IBM PCs and compatibles, the area above the standard 1 MB boundary. Can only be accessed indirectly using special hardware and software. A popular software interface is XMS, the eXtended Memory Specification (from Lotus, Intel, Microsoft, and AST Research). It is hardware independent and is based on an installable device driver or eXtended Memory Manager (XMM). Often necessary for large spreadsheets, databases, desktop publishing packages, and integrated software.

Ex•tend•ed Pas•cal

(Programming languages)

High-level programming language descended from Pascal that incorporates features of Ada and Modula-2. Features include independent modules connected by a few declarations, information hiding, and abstraction (encapsulating related types and objects, as well as instructions).

Defined in ANSI X3J9/JPC Document 88-151.

Also see *Ada; Modula-2; Pascal*.

Ex•tend•ed POS•IX

(Computer operations)

Operating system interface specified in National Institute of Science and Technology (NIST) Applications Portability Profile for U.S. government computer systems. Expanded version of an interface between UNIX systems and applications written in C.

Defined in FIPS 151 (IEEE Standard 1003.1-1988) and proposed IEEE standards P1003.2 (draft 8) and P1003.7.

ex•tend•ed re•la•tion•al da•ta•base

See *entity relationship database*.

ex•ten•si•ble

adj. Ability to be extended. Synonym: **ex•tend•a•ble.**

(Computer languages)

An **extensible lan•guage** is one to which functions can be added or from which routines in another language can be called. For example, a high-level language in which a machine language routine can be called or SQL commands can be embedded. Sometimes refers specifically to languages that allow user-defined or extended data types.

Also see *data type; user-defined function*.

ex•ten•si•ble lan•guage

See *extensible*.

ex•ten•sion

n. In logic, the denotation or specific meaning of a term. Its breadth; the number of subjects contained under a predicate.

(Data management)

The domain or values for each defined attribute and the set of instances allowed for each entity type.

Also see *intension*.

ex•tent

(Computer operations)

n. A group of data pages, stored in adjacent memory locations.

ex•ter•nal com•mand

See *command, external.*

ex•ter•nal func•tion

See *function, external.*

ex•ter•nal security

See *security.*

F

fac•tor•ing

(Mathematics)

Resolution of a product into constituent quantities. For example, 15 may be factored as 3 times 5.

(Data management; Programming languages)

Division of a function into subfunctions. In transform analysis, includes addition of operations such as error handling.

fault

See *exception*.

fea•ture ori•ent•ed GIS

See *geographic information system*.

fed•er•at•ed da•ta•base sys•tem

(Data management)

A database management system design involving a voluntary association of nodes and users, for example, for a CAD team or workgroup operation. Called a **fed•er•a•tion.**

Typically the database is defined by a single user at a single site. Other users and sites may be added or **en•rolled.**

Access to the system is through a virtual user or capability, such as a unique name and password. Usually several levels of access are provided.

fed•er•a•tion

See *federated database system*.

field

(Data management)

n. The fundamental unit of data in a database file, having a unique location within a record. If the database is in the form of a table, for example, a field can be identified by record (row) and column. A field is typically characterized by its type and length. The C language uses the term *member* instead for a constituent of a structure (record).

Also see *column; file; record.*

field, cal•cu•lat•ed

(Data management)

A database, spreadsheet, or form field containing a formula whose variables are defined in other fields. For example, a field COMMISSION could be calculated using values from the fields SALES and COMMISSIONRATE.

field lock

(Security)

Exclusive ownership by one user or process of a field in a multiuser database, for updating or some other operation. A lock prevents other users from performing a simultaneous, conflicting operation or reading obsolete data.

Also see *file lock; lock; record lock; unlock.*

FIFO

See *first-in, first-out.*

fifth nor•mal form

(Data management)

In relational database management, a theoretical method of assuring that a join creates a relation in which all tuples result from a dependency on a candidate key. It assures, for example, that a join does not produce spurious tuples and that the relation is the same as the sum of its projections. Abbreviated **5NF.** Synonym: **pro•jec•tion join nor•mal form (PJ/NF).**

Also see *Boyce/Codd normal form; first normal form; fourth normal form; normalize; second normal form; third normal form.*

5NF

See *fifth normal form.*

file

(Data management)

n. The basic named unit of stored information in a computer system. Also refers to a simple database or flat file. A file may contain continuous text, such as an ASCII file. Or it may be composed of units called records, rows, or tuples, as a database file is. Some operating systems, such as MS-DOS and UNIX, treat I/O devices as files. Called a **da•ta set** in IBM mainframe terminology.

Also see *database; device.*

file head•er

See *header.*

file lock

(Security)

Exclusive ownership by one user or process of a file in a multiuser database, for updating or some other operation. A lock prevents other users from performing a simultaneous, conflicting operation or reading obsolete data.

(dBASE)

dBASE III PLUS has both automatic and explicit locking by which users can claim and relinquish specific files. When a file is locked, associated files are locked automatically.

Files are locked automatically during execution of the commands APPEND, APPEND FROM, AVERAGE, BROWSE, COPY, COPY STRUCTURE, COUNT, DELETE ALL, INDEX, JOIN, RECALL ALL, REPLACE ALL, SORT, SUM, TOTAL, and UPDATE. After execution, the file is unlocked automatically.

Also see *field lock; lock; record lock; unlock.*

file serv•er

(Data communications)

A network node that stores files in shared or private subdirectories. The node may be a dedicated server, or it may function independently.

Also see *server.*

file shar•ing

(Data management)

Ability to use a file on several network stations, or its use by several stations at the same time.

file trans•fer

(Data communications)

Moving of a file from one computer memory, storage device, operating system, or application format to another. Often refers to moving a file from one computer to another via a modem, LAN, or other communications method. A basic function of a file server.

fil•ter

(Data management)

n. A command or routine that transforms data in accordance with specified criteria. A filter passes the main part of the data in analogy with an electrical or material filter. It may, for example, sort the data, remove extraneous delimiters or duplicate elements, convert codes, restrict numerical values, assign values to nulls, or perform other incidental operations.

By extension, it also means transforming data for display on the screen. Also importing by one application from another while, for example, retaining selected formatting commands, as from a spreadsheet to a database or from a word processor to a page layout program.

Also refers to the specification of conditions for selecting records in database operations. A filter may involve a range of values, a logical condition, or an attribute. For example, dBASE IV has a SET FILTER command that restricts the user's view of the database in all operations.

Also see *pipe*.

find•er

(Computer operations)

n. In the Apple Macintosh operating system, a program that locates stored files, loads them into main memory, and opens them.

fin•ger•print

n. Pattern of the lines on the pads of fingers left by ink or other substances on a surface. A unique identifier, since each person's set is different. May also be sensed electronically.

(Security)

By extension, term for a checksum that is unique to a file. Used, for example, in RSA public key encryption. Referred to as a **signed file.**

Also see *access; checksum; encryption; identifier.*

firm•ware

(Software)

n. Program permanently stored in read-only memory (ROM) within a computer rather than in ordinary memory (RAM). Typical examples are the basic input/output system (BIOS) in a personal computer or a word processing application in a laptop computer. Classically refers specifically to low-level programs (so-called **mi•cro•pro•grams**) used to decode instructions, but later extended to any ROM-based software.

first-in, first-out

(Data management)

A waiting line, **queue,** or buffer organized so that items are removed in the same order in which they were entered. Acronym: **FIFO** (pronounced "fie-fo"). Often used to hold data temporarily while in transit without affecting its ordering.

first nor•mal form

(Data management)

A normalized table. Abbreviated **1NF.**

First, second, and third normal forms are sufficient for most data management. However, more advanced and theoretical normalizations are possible.

Also see *Boyce/Codd normal form; fifth normal form; fourth normal form; normalize; second normal form; third normal form.*

fit, best

(Data interpretation)

The best approximation to an actual set of data. Often refers to a curve drawn from points on a graph.

fit, good•ness of

(Data interpretation)

A measure of how close an approximation is to an actual set of *data.* Often refers to how close a curve passes to points on a graph. There are several measures, including average absolute deviation and standard deviation (least squares fit).

flag

n. Marker, indicator, or signal.

(Programming languages)

An indicator of a true-false or other condition or of an occurrence, such as end of file. May be used as a reference later in a program.

(Data communications)

In data transmission, a marker for the end of a data word.

v. To make such an indication.

(UNIX)

An argument that limits or changes the way a command is executed. Usually indicated by a "-" sign and a single letter after a command name, such as ls -l for a "long" (complete) listing of the user's current directory. Synonym: *option.*

flat di•rec•to•ry

See *directory.*

flat file

(Data management)

A two-dimensional matrix of rows and columns. For instance, each horizontal row may contain a name and its associated address, area code, and telephone number. This is known as a record. Each entry is called a field. Each field is also in a vertical column, so that, for example, all names or all telephone numbers can be sorted as a unit.

float•ing point

(Computer operations)

A method of mathematical notation used to represent very large or very small numbers that otherwise would be impossible to represent in a specified number of digits. The form is a number or **man•tis•sa** (also called **sig•nif•i•cand**) raised to an **ex•po•nent** or **char•ac•ter•is•tic**, usually in base 10. For example,

$$93,000,000 = 9.3 \times 10^7$$

$$.93 = 9.3 \times 10^{-1}$$

$$.00093 = 9.3 \times 10^{-4}$$

"Floating" refers to the fact that the base or radix point is not in a fixed position, but floats, depending on the size of the exponent.

With this method, numbers are limited by length in significant digits and the size of the exponent, rather than by the size of the number itself.

Floating point data are often entered using the letter E, for exponent. For example, 9.3×10^6 would be entered as

9.3E6

and 9.3×10^{-2} as

9.3E-2

The number of digits that the language or application can maintain accurately is called its pre•ci•sion. The usual format is called sin•gle precision. Maintenance of twice the usual number of digits is called dou•ble precision.

Specified by IEEE Standard 754. See table and format below, where s is the sign, e is the biased exponent (actual exponent E plus bias), and f is the fraction (normalized mantissa).

Defined as a data type in some database management systems, including dBASE IV.

Also see *data type; double-precision floating point; FLOPS; precision; single-precision floating point.*

SUMMARY OF FLOATING POINT PARAMETERS

Parameter	Format			
	Single	Single Extended	Double	Double Extended
p	24	≥ 32	53	≥ 64
E_{max}	+127	$\geq +1023$	+1023	$\geq +16383$
E_{min}	-126	≤ -1022	-1022	≤ -16382
Exponent bias	+127	unspecified	+1023	unspecified
Exponent width in bits	8	≥ 11	11	≥ 15
Format width in bits	32	≥ 43	64	≥ 79

Single Format Floating Point

1	8	23
s	e	f

Double Format Floating Point

1	11	52
s	e	f

float•ing point pro•ces•sor

(Hardware)

A coprocessor chip or an add-on device or board that performs floating point calculations. It may also do decimal arithmetic and functions such as square root, exponentials, logarithms, and trigonometric functions.

Synonyms: **a•rith•met•ic pro•ces•sor, co•pro•ces•sor, math co•pro•ces•sor, nu•mer•ic pro•ces•sor.** These terms usually refer specifically to single-chip implementations, whereas floating point processor may also refer to multichip or board-level implementations for workstations, minicomputers, or even mainframes.

Also see *floating point.*

FLOPS

(Computer operations)

Acronym for FLoating point Operations Per Second. Pronounced "flops." Always used, as a plural. Measure of a computer's speed in performing floating point operations. Often quoted in hundreds of FLOPS or in millions (megaFLOPS).

Also see *floating point.*

flow•chart

(Graphics; Software development tools)

n. A diagram of the design, logic, and operation of a computer program.

(Computer operations)

Diagram of the design and flow of data in a computer system during an operation or operations. Synonyms: **da•ta flow di•a•gram, pro•gram flow•chart, sys•tem flow•chart.**

Flowcharts employ standard symbols for annotation, decision point, connector, terminal, input/output, and other functions. These are defined in American National Standard X3.5-1970.

Focus

(Computer languages; Data management)

The most widely used 4th generation language (Information Builders, Inc.) for mainframe DBMS's, such as DB2 and IMS. Includes menus for query development and report writing, and a procedural language for applications development. A version for personal computers permits downloading, processing, and uploading of data.

Also see *language, 4th generation.*

Book checkout   STANDARD SYMBOLS

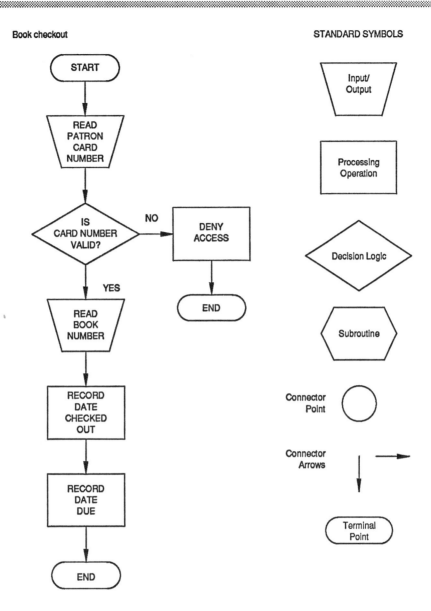

fold•er

(File management)

n. A grouping of files under the Macintosh operating system, displayed on the screen as a file folder. Each folder may contain files, other folders, or a combination. Primary folders on a floppy disk or hard disk are displayed on the opening screen, known as the desktop. Synonyms: *directory, subdirectory*.

Also see *desktop*.

font
(Output formatting)

n. A set of type of a specific face, style, and size, such as Times roman 10 point. Often used imprecisely to mean type face.

There are two kinds of computer fonts: those used on the screen and those used by the printer or typesetting equipment. **Screen fonts** often are only representations of the actual **print•er fonts**, so that what the user sees on the screen is not necessarily exactly what appears on the printed page.

The word refers to a complete group of individual type pieces – letter, numbers, and symbols – used for hand or hot-metal typesetting.

Also see *point; type face*.

Four fonts of the Times typeface
Times roman 10 point

Times roman 12 point

Times italic 10 point

Times italic 12 point

foot•er
(Output formatting)

n. Page number, name, date, or other information that appears at the bottom of all or selected pages of a printed document. Word processing programs and report writers for databases and spreadsheets allow the user to write and often to set the style for a document's footer. The word is clearly derived by analogy from the common word *header* for information appearing at the top of a page.

Also see *header*.

fore•ground
(Computer operations)

adj. Referring to computer processing that is visible on the screen or with which the user can interact. Contrast with *background*. The foreground jobs are the main ones the system is running.

for•eign key
See *key*.

fork

v. To split, such as the division of a road or river or the branching of a tree.

(UNIX)

Command to the UNIX kernel (a **sys•tem call**) to create a new or child process (an image – a program and its associated data and status information – being executed) by duplicating an existing or parent process.

The two processes share the files that were open at the time of forking, but otherwise execute independently. However, they may execute in parallel. The two consist of the same code but have different identification numbers (PIDs) that can be used to produce different behavior. The fork call itself returns the child's process identification number in the parent, but 0 in the child.

form

n. A printed sheet or document with blanks for inserting data. Also a sheet of paper.

(Data management)

A stylized database and text file presented on the computer screen to be filled in by the user. In some applications, certain data is generated automatically, such as a form number or a repetitive entry. As with a database or spreadsheet, a form's field may contain user-entered data, data from a linked table, values calculated from data in other fields, or default values perhaps obtained from previous forms. Data entered on the form can be used to update the linked tables.

Also see *field, calculated.*

(R:BASE)

A feature called Forms EXPRESS allows the user to select a database, name and customize a form, name tables and designate the region of the form where each table's data is displayed, edit text, locate and customize fields, write expressions, and define variables.

Also see *form feed.*

for•mat•ting

(Output formatting)

n. Arranging text for screen or printed display according to a design or style, perhaps including margins, paragraph indentations, type fonts, line spacing (number of lines per inch), and page dimensions. In some programs, the screen display looks the same as the printed copy. In others, the formatting is for the printed version only.

Also see *WYSIWYG.*

Also refers to low-level printing specifications, such as type of print (for example, compressed, italics, or boldface), number of characters per line, and perhaps line spacing.

User defined formatting is most flexible in word processors and page layout programs. Spreadsheets and database report writers usually offer several preset formats and often allow some user-defined modifications. For data items, these may include specifying form (such as decimal, hex, or character), length, justification (left, right, or centered), number of decimal places, and style (with or without dollar signs, commas, and other markings, such as debit or credit indicators).

Also refers to initializing a disk, that is, preparing it to accept files. In MS-DOS, the FORMAT command does this job. It divides the disk into sections (sectors), initializes the directory, and handles other organizational overhead.

form feed

(Computer operations)

A printer command that ejects the current sheet (also called a form) and makes the next one available for printing. Often a printer control (abbreviated FF) for page ejection.

form let•ter

(Word processing)

Multiple copies of a generic text, each one of which is customized with the recipient's name and address and possibly other text or data. Form letters can be generated in many word processors with a database and a routine for directing the fields in each record to the desired locations in the letter. The generator is sometimes called a **mail merge** feature.

forms gen•er•a•tor

(Applications)

Software that allows a user to create forms.

Also see *form.*

FOR•TRAN

(Computer languages)

n. Abbreviation of FORmula TRANslation language. The first widely used high-level, procedure-oriented programming language, developed in 1950s at IBM by John W. Backus and others. Used mainly in engineering, mathematical and scientific problem-solving, particularly involving numerical analysis techniques (so-called "number crunching").

Also see *language, procedure-oriented.*

Defined in American National Standard X3.9-1978.

for•ward chain•ing

(Artificial intelligence)

Processing method used in some expert systems and other AI applications that begins by identifying a chain of appropriate ("true") rules that lead finally to a conclusion. Contrast with *backward chaining*, noting that some applications use both.

Also see *expert system.*

for•ward re•cov•ery

See *roll forward.*

4GL

See *language, 4th generation.*

4NF

See *fourth normal form.*

fourth nor•mal form

(Data management)

In relational database management, a theoretical method for removing redundancies or repeating groups from data in Boyce/Codd normal form. Abbreviated **4NF**. Devised by R. Fagin in the 1970s.

Also see *Boyce/Codd normal form; fifth normal form; first normal form; normalize; second normal form; third normal form.*

Fox•BASE

(Data management)

A series of relational database management programs (Fox Software). FoxBASE is a "look-alike" for dBASE (Ashton-Tate) with added features. That is, it accepts dBASE files and runs most dBASE programs, but has its own enhancements. FoxPro is a later version.

frag•ment

See *fragmentation.*

frag•men•ta•tion

n. The process of being broken into pieces.

(Data management)

The process of restructuring a linear document so it can become hypertext. The division of a document's text or structure into distinct, independent parts (**frag•ments**) that can be defined as nodes and linked in a nonlinear way.

Also refers to the division of a disk file into many separate units that are dispersed around the medium rather than being stored in consecutive areas. Utilities are often available to reduce fragmentation, as it increases file access time.

frame

(Computer operations)

A unit of physical memory capable of holding a page worth's of information. Called a **page frame** as it is the "slot" into which a page of virtual memory can be placed.

Also see *virtual memory*.

(Data communications)

n. A packet of data for transmission on a network such as a token-ring or Ethernet.

Also an entire asynchronous data transmission, including the starting and ending markers and error-checking facilities, as well as the data.

(Programming)

The stack area used by a particular instance of a routine for its parameters, return address, and local storage. Also called a **stack frame** and addressed by means of a **frame point•er.**

frame point•er

See *frame*.

fram•ing er•ror

See *stop bit*.

free•stand•ing da•ta dic•tion•ar•y

See *data dictionary*.

freeware

See *shareware*.

fre••quen•cy-di•vi•sion mul•ti•plex•ing

(Data communications)

Transmission line or channel for high speed digital communication of multiple data streams simultaneously by transmitting each one at a different frequency. Used, for example, in television transmission for simultaneous handling of voice and data.

Contrast with *time-division multiplexing*.

Also see *multiplexing*.

front end

(Computer environment)

A transitional program between the user and the computer. It displays information in an easy-to-use format. For example, a communications program may present a menu of options for sending a message by means of a particular protocol. Or a front end may allow the user to interact with the computer's operating system. DBMS front ends may translate queries and other user entries into instructions for the application to execute. Synonyms: *interface; shell*.

(Hardware)

Piece of equipment that interfaces between a computer and data sources or destinations, such as a **com•mu•ni•ca•tions front end**. It performs overhead tasks (such as code conversion and error-checking), reducing the burden on the computer.

full du•plex

See *duplex, full*.

full screen

(Data management; Programming)

Description of the display of an entire screen of editable text, rather than a line at a time (Teletype style). The use of such a screen is called **full screen ed•it•ing.**

full screen ed•it•ing

See *full screen*.

func•tion

(Programming)

n. A routine that returns a value. The basic unit in some computer languages, particularly C. Other languages have procedures that may perform a task without returning anything to the caller. C has a special type (void) for such functions.

Also see *procedure.*

func•tion•al da•ta•base
(Artificial intelligence; Data management)

Database model using the structure of a network or plex, in which functional relationships are established between entities, resulting in sets. Combines functional (applicative) or mathematics-based programming with network and relational database concepts of abstraction, data definition, and query languages.

Also see *functional language.*

func•tion•al de•com•po•si•tion

See *decomposition.*

func•tion•al de•pen•dence
(Data management; Programming languages)

One-to-one relationship between two data items or between a data item and a concatenated group of data items. For example, a street address may have a one-to-one relationship with the concatenated 5 digit and 4 digit extended Zip Codes. Or a column may be uniquely defined by another column or columns in the same table.

func•tion•al lan•guage
(Artificial intelligence; Data management)

Programming language that describes functional relationships. Also called an ap•plic•a•tive language. An example is LISP.

Also see *LISP.*

func•tion, ex•ter•nal
(Programming)

Abbreviation XFCN. A function or routine for the Macintosh database manager Hyper-Card written in a general programming language, such as C, FORTRAN, or Pascal, rather than in its own language HyperTalk. Can also be written in assembly language. An XFCN is a routine not provided in HyperTalk, such as one for special graphics needs.

An XFCN is incorporated ("glued") into a HyperCard stack by means of two special files that contain the driver and glue routines for the particular language.

Also see *command, external; HyperCard.*

G

Gane and Sar•son anal•y•sis
(Software development tools)

Method of structured analysis involving logical models, database design, physical modeling, and final system design. Involves a data flow diagramming technique that modifies that of Yourdon and DeMarco.

Described in C. Gane and T. Sarson, *Structured Systems Analysis: Tools and Techniques* (Englewood Cliffs, NJ: Prentice-Hall, 1979).

Also see *data flow diagram; Yourdon-DeMarco diagram.*

gate•way
(Data communications)

n. A hardware connection or node between two networks of different types, for example, a local area network and a wide area network, mainframe, or electronic mail service. Contrast with *bridge.*

Software or **vir•tu•al** gateways are also available.

Also see *virtual network.*

gen•er•al•i•za•tion

n. Movement from the specific to the generic.

(Data management)

A fundamental method of data abstraction, as with a disjoint union. Contrast with *aggregation.*

Also see *abstraction; disjoint; union.*

gen•er•al led•ger

(Accounting)

Overall summary of a financial system, including a list of accounting categories (chart of accounts), payments made and received, and comparisons to budget and prior results.

Computerized version usually requires complete definition of the chart of accounts and performs balancing and cross-checking to the individual accounts before transactions can be completed and committed (posted).

Many computerized systems integrate the general ledger with accounts receivable and accounts payable and sometimes even with payroll, inventory, and other applications.

geo•graph•ic in•for•ma•tion sys•tem

(Data management; Graphics)

Application that maintains databases containing alphanumeric and spatial data and digitized maps that a user can manipulate to create specialized maps and data visualizations. Abbreviated **GIS**. Used, for example, by the U.S. Forest Service to track forest growth and diversity. Also used by city and regional planners, landscape architects, demographers, and researchers. Some systems include specialized graphics workstations.

Data may be stored in two ways. In **sheet-ori•ent•ed** GIS's, the data is part of a large drawing or map sheet. An example is ARC/INFO (Environmental Systems Research Institute, ESRI). In **fea•ture oriented** GIS's, data is stored in smaller units or features (such as boundaries, vegetation, or waterways), not as part of a map. An interface language allows users to combine features, maps, and other data as desired, each one forming a graphics layer. An example is Earth One GIS (C.H. Guernsey & Co.).

GIS

See *geographic information system.*

glob•al

(Data management; Programming)

adj. A value or meaning that is applicable throughout a program or file. For example, a global find or find-and-replace would return all instances of the value within a file. A global variable is one that is defined in all parts (modules) of a program. The range in which a value or meaning is known is called its **scope**.

Contrast with *local.*

glob•al opti•miz•er

(Programming)

A compiler optimizer that works on entire procedures rather than on basic blocks.

glob•al var•i•a•ble

See *global*.

good•ness of fit

See *fit, goodness of*.

GOSIP
(Data communications)

Acronym for (U.S.) Government Open Systems Interconnections Profile (pronounced "go-sip"). Collection of communications standards to be used within the U.S. government.

Defined in FIPS 146.

grant
(Security)

v. Permission by the database administrator for an individual to make specified use of a database. The user may have access to the entire database or specific parts, and have unlimited or strictly limited power to change, add, or delete data.

These privileges are often called **access modes** or **access rights.**

Also see *revoke*.

(R:BASE)

The database owner (administrator) may grant five levels of privileges, from most to least restrictive:

SELECT - viewing and printing from a table or view

UPDATE - changing specified columns in a table or view

INSERT - adding rows

DELETE - removing rows

ALL - selecting, updating, inserting, and deleting

gran•u•lar•i•ty

n. Being in small particles; having a grainy or granular texture. Refers to the basic size of units that can be manipulated, such as in allocating computer memory.

(Security)

The size or level of the object that can be locked or protected. The larger the object, the coarser the granularity. It may be as coarse as a device or a file, or as fine as a record or item. The finer the granularity, the larger the number of locks required.

Also see *lock*.

Also the amount of control provided over exactly which users can be included or excluded, such as the fineness of including or excluding a single specific user.

(Graphics)

The coarseness or fineness of a screen grid, determining the degree of control over placement of a graphic.

(Computer operations)

The degree of interaction between parallel processors.

graph

v. To place data on a graph; to chart.

(Data structures)

n. A figure or data representation in which a set of vertexes is connected by edges or arcs. Often used to represent resource allocation and other problems involving multiple entities and connections.

A graph in which the edges are directional (that is, the order of the nodes matters) is a **di•rect•ed graph** or **di•graph**.

(Graphics)

Also called a chart or diagram. May be based on mathematical and statistical manipulation of data. Types of graphs shown on page 129 are: bar chart, Cartesian, high-low-close, line, pie, regression, and scatter.

graph•i•cal user in•ter•face

(Computer environment)

Front-end program that employs images as well as text. An example is the Apple Macintosh desktop. Now being employed in many operating systems and program envioronments. Abbreviated **GUI.**

Also see *desktop*.

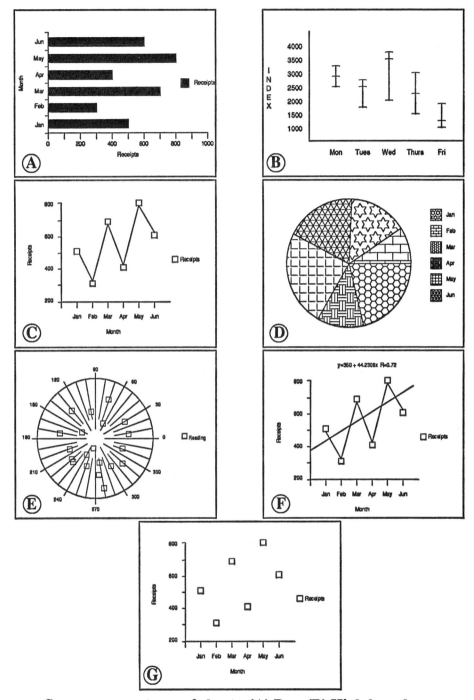

Some common types of charts. (A) Bar. (B) High-low-close.
(C) Line. (D) Pie. (E) Polar. (F) Regression. (G) Scatter.

grep

(Data management)

v. To search for text by entering a combination of specific characters and so-called "wild cards" (or **meta•char•ac•ters**) – characters with a special meaning that stand for any digit, any vowel, a designated number of characters, options, alternatives, or other specified groupings.

For example, ? might be defined as any digit, so that searching for 19?? would return any number between 1900 and 1999.

The term originated in UNIX, but is now in more general use.

(UNIX)

Command to search for text by matching patterns (sets of strings). Derived from the line editor **ed**, whose global request command takes the form **g/re/p**, where **g** is the global request, **re** is the regular expression or pattern, and **p** is the command to print each line containing the pattern.

For example, to search a file CIVILWAR for the string GETTYSBURG, use

    grep gettysburg civilwar

grep may also serve as a filter. In an open file, to print the lines containing the string, use

    ls | grep gettysburg

group

(Graphics)

v. To combine several objects into a more complex entity. Antonym: *ungroup.*

(Data management)

To create a view in which all rows containing similar values for a given column are listed consecutively. Referred to as **par•ti•tion•ing**. For example, the Structured Query Language command GROUP BY.

n. An assemblage of users with something in common, such as geographic location, department, or function. Synonym: *user's group.*

(Mathematics)

n. A closed set.

guard

v. To protect.

n. A protector. Someone or something who prevents unauthorized access to an area and also the unauthorized removal or destruction of life or property, or both, within the area.

(Security)

A processor that filters data being transmitted between security levels or devices, allowing only authorized data to pass through.

Also a process that allows users to receive only the data that is appropriate for their security level, filtering out unauthorized data (called **san•i•tiz•ing**).

guest

(Data communications)

n. A computer or other network device controlled by another during data transmission.

Also see *host.*

GUI

See *graphical user interface.*

han•dle

n. A thing meant to be grasped.

(Graphics; Output formatting)

Square marker on a selected graphic by which it can be moved or changed in shape. In some applications, one or more markers are designated for shape-changing, and others only for moving.

(Computer operations)

In the Apple Macintosh operating system, a number designating a pointer. The use of handles allows more flexibility in memory management at the cost of introducing an extra level of indirection.

Also see *pointer*.

han•dler

n. A thing or person in charge of another person or thing or of an event.

(Programming)

Program or routine that performs or controls one task, such as error detection, or device activity, such as an interrupt signal.

(Ada)

An **ex•cep•tion handler** is a routine that responds to an error (or exception). Executing the response is called **han•dling** the exception.

(Data management)

In the HyperTalk language, similar to a method in object oriented programming.

Also see *HyperTalk; object oriented*.

han•dling

See *handler*.

hard•en
(Security)

v. To protect against or make invulnerable to attack or unauthorized use. Applied to a wide range of security situations, from nuclear missile silos to data communications lines.

hard•en•ing
(Security)

n. The property of being protected against or made invulnerable to attack or unauthorized use.

hard limit
(Computer operations)

An operating limit, such as memory size, set by hardware, rather than software. It can thus be changed only by modifying the physical hardware configuration (for example, by adding memory). Contrast with *soft limit*.

hard•ware

Physical equipment such as CPUs, memory, I/O devices, and connections that forms a computer system.

hash ad•dress

See *hashing*.

hash cod•ing

See *hashing*.

hash field

See *hashing*.

hash•ing
(Data management)

n. A search method that uses a function of a key to locate a starting point. The function may be tabular (a **hash ta•ble**). In a database, the record's location, called the **hash ad•dress**, is calculated as a function of one of the fields (the **hash field**). Given the value of the hash field, the database manager can perform the calculation again to locate the record, then go to it directly. Hashing is generally irreversible and need not produce unique values. The name apparently comes from the arbitrariness of the functions (that is, it makes "hash" out of the key).

Hashing (or **hash cod•ing**) is a general way to transform a key field into a more compact arrangement.

Also see *key*.

hash ta•ble

See *hashing*.

half du•plex

See *duplex, half*.

HDLC

See *high-level data link control*.

head•er

(Output formatting)

n. Information such as page number, document name, or date that appears at the top of all or selected pages of a printed document. Word processors and report writers for databases and spreadsheets allow the user to create a header and often to set its style and placement. The term **running head** is also used.

The equivalent at the bottom of a page is called a **foot•er**, by extension.

(Data communications)

Transmitted information that precedes the actual data being sent; for example, it may specify the sender's name, time of transmission, length of the data, and subject.

Also see *encapsulation*.

(Data management)

A file header contains information about the rest of the contents, usually including its size, number of fields, type and length of fields, and number of records. May include date and time of creation and indexing information. May repeat what is in the directory and contain other information unique to the database.

heap

n. A pile of things.

A memory area organized in an arbitrary manner; it can be subdivided on demand into small blocks. In many computers, the unallocated memory between the program and data areas in the low addresses and the stack area in the high addresses.

(Data management)

Synonym: bi•nary tree.

Also see *tree.*

A heap sort is one that proceeds from the root node systematically through the tree hierarchy.

Also see *sort.*

het•er•o•ge•neous

adj. Of many kinds.

(Data communications)

Describing a communications system that includes a variety of hardware and protocols.

(Data management)

Ambiguous description of a distributed database management system. May refer to one that communicates among many kinds and brands of hardware, data models, or software. Or may refer to one whose server communicates between it and external terminals and workstations. Often only the context indicates which meaning is intended.

heu•ris•tic

(Programming)

n., adj. A method of inductive problem solving that uses rules derived from experience or common sense, rather than from an underlying theory or model. No proof is available of the method's correctness or range of applicability. Applied in artificial intelligence.

For contrasting approaches, see *algorithm; model.*

hex

See *hexadecimal.*

hexa•dec•i•mal

(Mathematics)

adj. A number system with base 16, commonly called **hex.** Used in computer programming as an alternative to writing binary numbers; each hex digit represents a group of four binary digits. The basic set of hexadecimal digits is 0, 1, 2, 3, 4, 5, 6, 7, 8, 9, A, B, C, D, E, F. (The letters A through F may be capitals or lowercase.)

Binary	Decimal	Hex
00000	0	0
00001	1	1
00010	2	2
00011	3	3
00100	4	4
00101	5	5
00110	6	6
00111	7	7
01000	8	8
01001	9	9
01010	10	A
01011	11	B
01100	12	C
01101	13	D
01110	14	E
01111	15	F
10000	16	10

Hexadecimal (or programmers') calculators are widely available, both as stand-alone devices and as programs (often desk accessories).

hi•er•ar•chi•cal com•pres•sion

See *compression, data.*

hi•er•ar•chi•cal database

See *database; tree.*

hi•er•ar•chy plus in•put-pro•cess-out•put di•a•gram

See *HIPO diagram.*

hi•er•ar•chy

(Data management)

n. A graded series or ranked ordering of data, either by size or subsets. For example, files are grouped into subdirectories, and subdirectories into a root directory. Or files are composed of records; records are composed of fields, which are groups of bytes. A data tree structure is composed of a root node, from which are descended parent nodes and child nodes.

Also see *node; tree.*

high-lev•el da•ta link con•trol

(Data communications)

Abbreviated **HDLC**. Protocol for synchronous data transmission that moves bits serially. Performs the functions of ISO/OSI Layer 2, data link, and is used in CCITT Standard X.25. Defined in ISO Standards DIS 3309.5 and 4335.

high lev•el lan•guage

See *language, high level.*

HIPO diagram

(Graphics; Software development tools)

Hierarchy plus input-process-output diagram, a diagram that shows a structured program's or system's inputs, processes, and outputs in three boxes, left to right. May present an overview, or the details of a single component.

Described in *IBM HIPO: A Design Aid and Documentation Technique* (GC20-185D), (White Plains, NY: IBM Corp., 1974).

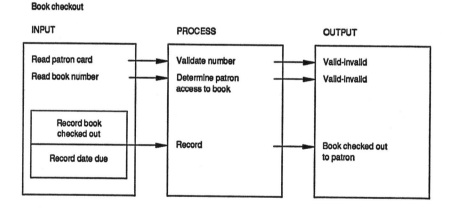

his•to•ry

(Programming)

n. A feature of some user interfaces, such as dBASE and the UNIX C shell, that keeps a record of past commands. This allows for repetition of commands, editing of them, audit, collection into macro or procedure files, and playback.

his•to•ry da•ta•base

(Data management)

A database that preserves past data and data structures, providing a historical record, rather than discarding them (de•struc•tive up•dat•ing) for current versions. Useful in maintaining data integrity and for auditing purposes, as well as for user queries.

ho•mo•ge•neous

adj. Of the same kind.

(Data management)

Ambiguous description of a distributed database management system. May refer to one that communicates only between equivalent types of stations, such as server to server. Or it may mean one that was designed as a system and uses integrated hardware and software and a single data model.

(Data communications)

Describing a communications system consisting of an integrated line of hardware and software.

hor•i•zon•tal par•i•ty

See *parity*.

host

(Computer operations)

n. A computer or central processing unit that runs a program for another computer, terminal, or other device on a network. Contrast with *guest*.

Also see *server*.

(Data communications)

A computer that controls both the sending and reception of a data transmission.

v. To provide the environment required to run a program, such as a DOS application on a UNIX machine. Usually refers to a program that would not normally run on the base machine.

hot key

(Hardware)

(Jargon) Key that interrupts the current routine and transfers control to a special handler. May be used to obtain help, execute functions, bring up special menus or dialog boxes, control execution, or override automatic behavior. Sometimes used simply to mean any key that activates a function directly, rather than requiring the user to select it from a menu.

Hy•per•Card

(Applications)

Database management program and programming environment (Apple Computer, Inc.). It is based on the concept of hypertext, which permits extensive linkage between fields and strings.

Databases, called stacks, are composed of records, called cards. Cards in a stack may have similar or multiple structures, called **back•grounds**. Permits storage of still and moving graphics and sound (including voice and music), as well as text. Uses its own programming language, HyperTalk, which contains many elements of object oriented programming.

Also see *card; HyperTalk; hypertext; object oriented; stack.*

hy•per•cube

n. Geometric shape of more than three dimensions, in which a cube is erected on each node of a three-dimensional cube.

(Hardware)

An architecture for connecting parallel processors or nodes, in which each node is connected to a number n of neighboring nodes. The result is a multidimensional shape with 2^n nodes. Also called an **n-cube**. Theoretically, the more connections there are, the faster the communication of data and results during processing and the faster its completion. On the other hand, more time may be spent coordinating activities and communicating data and results than actually processing.

For instance, in an ordinary or 3-dimensional cube, each node has three connections, or 2^3, giving the cube 8 nodes. If each node has 4 connections, the shape will have 16 nodes, an arrangement only possible in more than three dimensions, or hyperspace.

hy•per•me•dia

See *hypertext.*

Hy•per•Talk

(Computer languages)

n. Programming language for the Macintosh database program *HyperCard*, written in the 1980s by Dan Winkler. Employs features of object oriented programming, and can work with external commands written in C, FORTRAN, and Pascal.

Also see *HyperCard; object oriented.*

hy•per•text
(Data management)

n. A free-form data structure permitting extensive linking among fields, tables, blocks of text or other data, characters, graphics, and sound. For example, each instance of a key word in a text file could be linked to a further explanation, references, supplementary material, maps, videos, sounds, or other parts of the main text. Invoking the link would automatically display or produce the material on the computer. Examples include HyperCard (a partial implementation, by Apple Computer) and Hyperties (Cognetics, Inc.).

In some usage, hypertext refers strictly to alphanumeric data; multimedia applications are called **hy•per•me•dia.**

I

IAN

See *bar code*.

icon

n. A picture that serves as an emblem or a symbol.

(Computer operations)

In some operating systems, part of the graphical interface with the user. In the Macintosh operating system, for example, screen icons represent files, subdirectories, applications, commands such as copy and delete, printers, floppy disks, and hard disk drives.

ID

See *identification*.

iden•ti•fi•er

n. A symbolic name for an element, such as a variable, user, or station.

(Security)

The unique name or set of characters assigned to a computer or network user before access to an application or data is granted. Synonyms: **user ID, user name.**

Also see *authentication*.

Also the name of a network node to which a transmission is addressed. Synonym: *address*.

iden•ti•fi•ca•tion

See *identifier*.

IDMS

See *Integrated Database Management System.*

IDMS/R

See *Integrated Database Management System.*

IGES

See *initial graphics exchange specification.*

im•age

n. A reproduction or replication of an original.

A picture or the contents of a screen, as in **image pro•cess•ing** or **screen image.**

(Programming)

A program and its associated data and status information. Called a **mem•o•ry image** when loaded into the computer's memory.

image pro•cess•ing

Transforming an image to meet some requirement such as improved quality, enhancement of certain features, reduced storage space, noise reduction, or display on a specific output device.

im•port

(Data communications; File formats)

v. To receive data from another computer or application. For example, to import dBASE files into Lotus 1-2-3 or Crosstalk. Contrast with *download.*

Also see *export.*

IMS

(Data management)

Hierarchical database (IBM) for mainframes designed to handle large numbers of transactions, such as in account management for insurance companies and banks.

in•clu•sion de•pen•den•cy
(Data management)

The equivalence of data in two or more tables if the primary key in one table matches a nonkey column in the others. For example, if the primary key column LIBRARYCARD in a table matches a nonkey column LIBRARYCARD in another table, the data in the two columns must be identical (unless the nonkey column contains null values).

in•de•pen•dence, da•ta
(Data management)

Isolation of the database from the user, so that its logical design may be modified or reorganized without requiring changes in applications or user access methods. For example, only those changes, such as addition of new columns, that do not alter the existing logical structure might be permitted. Permitted physical changes might include restructuring the storage method, as long as data integrity is maintained.

Also promotes data integrity and security.

Synonym: *orthogonal.*

in•dex
(Data management)

n. A cross-reference of all fields in a database or other file (similar to an index in a book) giving each item's location in the computer's memory. The index provides direct access to the data requested in a query, and for large databases is more efficient than a sequential search. In some programs, indexes are compiled automatically. In others, the user can create them.

A **unique in•dex** is one that guarantees a table's unique key values.

The preferred plural is indexes, rather than the traditional Latin-derived **in•di•ces.**

Also see *index; key.*

v. To create such a cross-reference.

(Programming)

n. A number used to modify an address, often through addition. Here index approximates "subscript." The terms **in•dex•ing, index•ed ad•dress•ing,** and **au•to•in•dex•ing** (automatic updating of the index before or after each use) are also used.

(dBASE)

A user-created file for a field, fields, or expression, giving the memory location of each occurrence. In a database ADDRSSES, for example, the user can create an alphabetical index NAMELIST of the field NAMES with these commands:

.USE Addrsses

        .INDEX ON Names TO Namelist

To display the indexed data, use

        .LIST Namelist

Indexing a database is much faster than physically sorting it. Furthermore, a database may have many indexes. However, some commands apply only to a **main** or **primary index,** which is the index on the primary key field. They do not apply to **lesser** or **secondary indexes** – those on other fields. Some databases, such as dBASE IV, have **multiple indexes,** that is, indexing on any field, string of several fields, or key expression.

in•dexed ad•dress•ing

See *index.*

in•dexed se•quen•tial ac•cess meth•od
(Data management)

Commonly used method of storing files on disk, using a B tree structure and containing an index of key fields. Abbreviated **ISAM.**

Also see *B tree; index.*

in•dex•ing

See *index.*

in•dex•space
(Data management)

n. In DB2, a pageset (physical structure, object, or tablespace) containing one index.

Also see *pageset; tablespace.*

in•di•ces

See *index*

in•di•vid•u•al li•cense

See *license*

in•dus•tri•al se•cu•ri•ty

See *security.*

in•fer•ence en•gine
(Artificial intelligence)

A system for making logical inferences or decisions. The part of an expert system that uses the rule or knowledge base embodying the "expert's" decision-making process.

Also see *expert system.*

in•for•ma•tion

n. The meaning people derive from data through analysis and the context in which they are working. A collected body of knowledge transferred among people.

Also see *data.*

(Data management)

Data organized for purposeful use, such as the result of a database query.

in•for•ma•tion en•gi•neer•ing
(Data management)

Process of creating an information system (IS), including selection of hardware components, design of software and databases, and integration of user applications.

Also see *information system.*

In•for•ma•tion Re•source Dic•tion•ary Sys•tem
(Data management)

Software tool for recording, storing, and processing information about data and data processing resources. Abbreviated **IRDS**.

Being defined by the U.S. National Institute of Standards and Technology (NIST) and ANSI Committee X3H4.

in•for•ma•tion sys•tems
(Data management)

Comprehensive term encompassing data processing and management applications of computing. Aimed at making computerized data resources more comprehensible and readily available to users than they have been in the past. Abbreviated **IS**.

The term thus includes the routine generation of invoices, ledgers, checks, purchase orders, receipts, stock slips, bills, and other paperwork as well as management aids, such as decision support systems, corporate models, databases, and management or executive information systems.

Creation of such systems is called **in•for•ma•tion en•gi•neer•ing.**

In•gres
(Data management)

A distributed database management program developed at the University of California, Berkeley, but now a commercial product (Ingres Corp., formerly Relational Technology). Intended chiefly for minicomputers, such as the DEC VAX. Uses SQL, as well as its own query language QUEL and the more graphic Query-By-Forms. Available under several operating systems, including VMS (DEC), UNIX, MVS and MVS/XA (IBM), and MS-DOS. Provides a language for creating applications. The user interface features menus.

in•her•i•tance

See *object oriented.*

ini•tial graph•ics ex•change spe•ci•fi•ca•tion
(File formats; Graphics)

Abbreviated **IGES.** File format for transferring graphic two- and three-dimensional data from one CAD/CAM system to another or between applications or operating systems.

Developed by the U.S. Air Force, American National Standards Institute (ANSI), and the U.S. National Bureau of Standards (now National Institute of Standards and Technology) in the early 1980s.

Defined in American National Standard Y14.26M-1987.

in•line
(Programming languages)

v. During preprocessing, to replace a procedure call with the procedure code.

Usage probably an outgrowth of the phrase **in-line cod•ing,** meaning code that is in the main body of a program or routine.

An **inline func•tion** is one that is expanded within the body of a routine, rather than being called. It provides higher execution speed (due to elimination of the overhead involved in transferring control to and from the function), but requires more memory (due to multiple copies of the function existing, rather than a single one).

in•line cod•ing

See *inline.*

in•line func•tion

See *inline.*

in•put

(Data communications)

n. Data received.

v. (Jargon)   To read data, as in "to input data from the keyboard."

adj. Referring to data received, as in "input port" or "input procedure."

in•stall•a•ble de•vice driv•er

(Software)

A driver the user can add to a system, thus customizing it for special peripherals, new or improved peripherals with extra features, or other purposes, such as networks or extended memory.

Also see *driver*.

in•stance

n. An animate, inanimate, or abstract example of a group or category; one that exhibits the group's characteristics.

(Programming languages)

In object oriented programming, a member of a class.

Also see *instantiation*.

in•stan•ti•ate

See *instantiation*.

in•stan•ti•a•tion

n. The concrete embodiment of a concept. Also used as a verb, **in•stan•ti•ate**.

(Data management)

Creation of a data structure embodying a conceptual definition, declaration, or template. For example, one may define or declare the form of an object such as a queue, then instantiate a particular queue for saving commands or tasks.

In object oriented programming, creation of a new class from an existing one or creation of a new member or instance of a class.

Also see *declaration; instance; object oriented; template*.

in•struc•tion

(Programming)

n. A statement in a computer program or a command that results in the performance of an operation. The statement usually states or defines the operation and specifies values or locations of the operands.

(Data management)

Synonym: *query.*

in•struc•tion code

See *operation code.*

in•struc•tions per sec•ond

(Computer operations)

A measure of the maximum speed at which a computer can process data, often given in millions (MIPS). Not always a realistic measurement, since actual processing speed depends on the type of data, how it is entered, how much each instruction accomplishes, and the speed of other devices in the system.

Also see *FLOPS.*

in•te•grate

v. To unify; to create something out of several equals.

(Software)

To join several applications into a larger or coordinated system. Examples are a database manager, spreadsheet, and word processor, and a group of CASE tools. Another example is a database and a rule-based system (expert system). Integration may be provided by the software publisher, or performed by the user with a software tool.

In•te•grat•ed Da•ta•base Man•age•ment Sys•tem

(Data management)

Database management system for mainframes (Cullinet) implementing the CODASYL networking data model. Abbreviated **IDMS**. The related **Integrated Database Management System/Re•la•tion•al** (**IDMS/R**) supports the relational model.

Also see *CODASYL.*

In•te•grat•ed Da•ta•base Man•age•ment Sys•tem/Re•la•tion•al

See *Integrated Database Management System.*

In•te•grat•ed Ser•vices Dig•i•tal Net•work

(Data communications)

Communications network designed to transmit data, video, and voice simultaneously over digital telephone lines. Abbreviated **ISDN.**

in•te•grated soft•ware

(Applications)

Generically refers to any combination of software applications. Specifically refers to combinations of word processing, spreadsheet, database, graphics, and communications functions in such IBM PC (MS-DOS) packages as Symphony (Lotus Development) and Framework (Ashton-Tate).

in•teg•ri•ty, da•ta

(Security)

Assurance that data will not be modified or erased by unauthorized users or accidentally. Also refers to internal consistency of redundant data. Also called **ref•er•en•tial integrity.** A referential integrity check is also called a **con•straint.**

Integrity differs from security in that it refers to the changing or erasing of data, rather than to unauthorized reading of it.

Also see *security.*

in•teg•ri•ty, ref•er•en•tial

(Data management)

Automatic updating of all related data when specific data is updated. A feature usually built into flat file database managers.

In relational DBMSs, integrity among all tables in the database usually must be programmed. In SQL, for example, this is done through the Data Definition Language. Such programmed **ref•er•en•tial con•straints** (restrictions) prevent updating that cannot automatically update related data. Examples are an update that would change or delete data that must not be changed, such as an invoice or account number or the amount of payment received, and a data addition that is not provided for in related tables.

Also see *integrity.*

in•tel•li•gent da•ta•base

(Artificial intelligence)

Database used in artificial intelligence applications, such as expert systems and natural language systems. It may be a knowledge base or incorporate logic rules for data manipulation.

Also see *expert system; intelligent front end; knowledge base; language, natural.*

in•tel•li•gent front end

(Artificial intelligence)

A shell or front end program that uses artificial intelligence techniques, for instance, a natural language interface. Examples include Clout for R:BASE 5000 (Microrim) and Intellect (Artificial Intelligence Corp.).

Also see *language, natural.*

in•ten•sion

n. In logic, the connotation or content of a term; its property or properties. Its depth; the number of predicates a subject contains.

(Data management)

Property names or entity types defined for a database, including attributes, attribute sets, and relationships. Synonym: *schema.*

Contrast with *extension.*

in•ter•ac•tion

n. Two way or reciprocal action; mutual influence. Implies immediacy.

In the computer field, may be between two people, for instance, over a communications network, or between a person and a computer.

in•ter•ac•tive com•put•ing

See *interactive processing*

in•ter•ac•tive da•ta dic•tion•ary

See *data dictionary.*

in•ter•ac•tive mode

See *interactive processing.*

in•ter•ac•tive pro•cess•ing

(Data management)

Ability of a user to obtain immediate results from a computer, for example, after a database query. Also called **con•ver•sa•tion•al mode, in•ter•ac•tive com•put•ing,** or **in•ter•ac•tive mode.** Contrast with *batch processing*.

Also see *on-line transaction processing*.

in•ter•char•ac•ter gap

See *bar code*.

in•ter•face

n. A place for meeting or interaction.

(Computer environment)

A transitional program between the user and the computer. It displays information in an easy-to-use format. It also translates queries and other user entries into instructions for the application or the operating system to execute. For example, Microsoft Windows allows the use of several applications at the same time. HyperCard permits someone to use Oracle without having to learn its commands.

Also see *shell*.

(Data communications)

A connection between two devices, such as a computer or central processing unit and a peripheral device. It may include both hardware (such as electrical and mechanical components) and software. Communications standards include RS-232 (Electronic Industries Association), CCITT (international), and MIL STD 188B (U.S. Department of Defense).

(Hardware)

A connection between components or devices, usually including both electrical and mechanical components. Interfaces are necessary, for example, to connect computers to input, output, or storage devices such as keyboards, printers, or disks. Often supplied as a circuit board or as part of a computer or peripheral. Common types include serial interfaces that handle one bit of data at a time and parallel interfaces that handle many bits.

(Software)

A program that allows a user to interact easily with an application, data, operating system, or devices connected to the computer. For example, an easy-to-understand menu for using a database.

v. To meet or interact. An overused verb (transitive and intransitive) in the computer world, where it refers to human-human interactions, as well as human-computer, hardware-hardware, and hardware-software interactions.

To connect devices, as in "to interface the printer to the computer." (Substandard usage.)

in•ter•laced dis•play

(Hardware)

Video display in which each pass of the electron beam across the screen excites ("refreshes") only every other line of pixels. Two complete passes are required to refresh all lines. Each pass takes less time, but allows more flicker than a pass that refreshes every line. Contrast with *non-interlaced display*.

in•ter•nal mod•el

See *model, physical*.

in•ter•nal security

See *security*.

In•ter•na•tion•al Ar•ti•cle Num•ber

See *bar code*.

In•ter•net

(Data communications)

A large network to which other local and wide area networks are attached. Used primarily by research institutions, including the National Science Foundation (through NSFNET, itself a network of networks) and many universities and laboratories. Internet permits attachment of many makes and brands of computers and devices. Follows the communications protocols TCP/IP and provides a transmission bandwidth of 45 megabits per second. Internet is operated by the Defense Advanced Research Projects Agency (DARPA), U.S. Department of Defense, and is administered by the Internet Activities Board.

in•ter•op•er•a•bil•i•ty

(Computer operations; Data management)

n. Degree of operating compatibility among devices or systems; their ability to exchange data or information. For example, the ability of modems or facsimile (fax) machines to send and receive data at a given speed.

On networks, this may require communications protocols, such as TCP/IP, X.400, or ISO/OSI; multiplex cabling; and common display protocols such as X Window.

Contrast with *connectivity*.

Also see *open system*.

in•ter•pret•er
(Computer languages)

n. A translator of a high-level language program into machine language. The interpreter translates each statement and executes it immediately before translating the next one. This provides immediate feedback that is especially useful during software development and when writing short programs. An interpreter is at a significant disadvantage when applied to long or production programs, as it involves translation overhead during each run.

Contrast with *compiler*.

in•ter•sec•tion
(Data interpretation)

n. In relational databases, an operation that creates a new table composed of all records that appear in both of two specified tables.

(R:BASE)

The command INTERSECT combines two tables with at least one common column containing matching values. An organization-wide table HOMEINFO, with columns NAME, STREET, CITY, STATE, and ZIP could be combined with the departmental table DEPTLIST, with columns NAME and MAILSTOP, to form CARDLIST by

R>INTERSECT homeinfo WITH deptlist FORMING cardlist

CARDLIST contains all rows whose NAME fields are identical, with the columns NAME, STREET, CITY, STATE, ZIP, and MAILSTOP. That is, it contains all rows with names from DEPTLIST, but with fields from both tables.

Contrast with *join; union*.

in•ven•to•ry con•trol
(Accounting)

Management of inventory receipts and shipments by controlling and cross-checking records such as reports of stock levels, purchase orders, back orders, acknowledgments, and shipping tickets.

Computerized packages usually require consecutive numbering of transaction records and other constraints to prevent duplication, lost shipments and receipts, and other errors. Each stage generally involves automatic cross-referencing before it can be completed.

in•vert•ed file

See *database*.

in•voice

(Accounting)

n. A statement of items sold, delivered, or shipped, including amount, price, and terms of sale. May be the same as a bill or shipping ticket.

Some computer accounting packages allow the user to prepare invoices, and may include security provisions, such as preventing duplicate invoice numbers. Such preparation may also include inventory controls, cross-checking with sales orders, and shipping confirmation.

v. To prepare and send such a statement.

in•voke

Synonym: *call*.

I/O

See *input/output*.

I/O chan•nel

(Data communications)

Input/output channel. A hardware path or frequency for data transmission.

IP

See *TCP/IP*.

IRDS

See *information resource dictionary system*.

IS

See *information systems*.

ISAM

See *indexed sequential access method*.

ISDN

See *integrated services digital network.*

iso•la•tion

n. Being separated from others; compartmentalized.

(Data management)

The degree of separation of a database transaction from concurrent transactions that could interfere with it. The greater the isolation, the less the concurrency permitted within the database. DB2, for example, has two isolation levels — one that releases locks upon a rollback and one that requires setting of another synchronization point before releasing the locks. The second level provides more isolation, because it prevents a change by another user, although the original user may not be finished. The first level may give more concurrency, but not necessarily.

Also see *access, concurrent; lock; synchronization point.*

(Security)

A principle of secure systems that restricts access to the system, devices, or data, allowing use only by those who have been granted specific access rights to specific parts.

Also see *access; privilege.*

ISO/OSI Ref•er•ence Mod•el

(Data communications)

International Standards Organization-approved model protocol connecting many different kinds of devices to a computer network, in what is called an open system. The model consists of seven layers:

Layer 7, Application Layer, serves as an interface between the network and an application.

Layer 6, Presentation Layer, translates messages between the network software's format and an international standard format used in transmission.

Layer 5, Session Layer, determines communications paths for transmission.

Layer 4, Transport Layer, assures reliability of the data being transmitted (also see *TCP/IP*).

Layer 3, Network Layer, moves packets of data between the network and Layer 4 (also see *TCP/IP*).

Layer 2, Data Link Layer (hardware), formats outgoing packets of data for transmission and checks that they are received correctly, and checks incoming packets to determine if they are intended for the local node.

Layer 1, Physical Layer, carries the incoming and outgoing unformatted data.

Defined in ISO 7498. In addition, each layer is defined by one or more standards (see Appendix C).

IST/RAMP

See *Risk Analysis and Management Program.*

Jack•son da•ta struc•ture

(Software development tools)

Type of top-down design featuring diagrams and evaluation methods. Diagram uses boxes to represent objects and lines to show data movement. Used in decomposition and code writing.

Described in M.A. Jackson, *System Development* (Englewood Cliffs, NJ: Prentice-Hall, 1983).

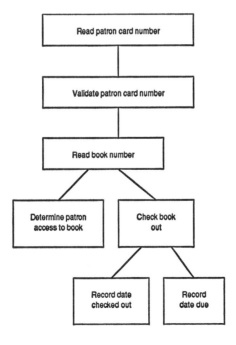

JAN

See *bar code*.

Jap•an•ese Ar•ti•cle Num•ber

See *bar code*.

"Jell-O Books"

(Security)

Refers to the cover colors of two books defining U.S. Department of Defense and National Security Agency security policies, the so-called Orange Book (for individual systems) and the Red Book (for networks).

Also see *Trusted Computer System Evaluation Criteria*.

join

(Data management)

n. In relational databases, the combination of data selected according to specified criteria from several databases to form a new database. For example, two complete tables may be joined, or only selected fields from them. A join is often a time-consuming operation that may create a very large database. For example, an unconditional join of two 100-element databases would create a 10,000-element database including all possible combinations.

An **equi•join** is a join in which the new table contains two identical columns. If one of them is removed, the result is a **nat•u•ral join.**

(dBASE)

An example is a database with two tables: ADDRESSES (fields for name, address, telephone number, and occupation) and CUSTOMERS (fields for name, item purchased, and amount spent). With CUSTOMERS as the active table, a user may create a new table ELITELIST containing name, occupation, and items purchased for amounts over $500, by entering the commands:

> JOIN WITH Addresses TO Elitelist FOR item_purchased >500 FIELDS name, Addresses->occupation, Addresses->item_purchased

v. To connect.

(Graphics)

To connect primitives into an object.

join de•pen•den•cy

(Data management)

The state of a relational database management system in which, after decomposition, it is a join of its subsystems.

K

KAPSE

See *Ada; Ada Program Support Environment*.

KEE

See *knowledge engineering*.

ker•nel

n. A subset or grouping of a set, usually the innermost or most important part.

(Computer operations)

The core of an operating system that provides basic functions, such as assigning memory to applications and data and controlling input and output.

Also see *operating system*.

By extension, used to indicate the core of any large program, excluding the user interface and add-on or supplementary functions. For instance, one might refer to the dBASE kernel or the Lotus 1-2-3 kernel.

Also a central, low-level program dedicated to a particular function, such as a graphics, I/O, or security kernel.

(Security)

A **se•cu•ri•ty kernel** contains all security-controlling software within an operating system. A way of implementing a reference monitor. Also called a **trust•ed kernel**. An example is GEMSOS (Gemini Computers), which runs on an 80286 microprocessor-based computer.

Also see *reference monitor; trusted*.

Ker•nel Ada Pro•gram Sup•port En•vi•ron•ment (KAPSE)

See *Ada*.

key

A means of control, explanation, or identification.

(Data management)

n. A data element whose unique value can be used to locate a record. In a tree search, comparing the key to node values reveals whether the search has succeeded. If not, it indicates which branch to follow or which node to search for the next comparison. For example, in a dBASE B+ tree, intermediate nodes contain the keys and leaf nodes contain the values. A key match leads to a leaf node. An unsuccessful search causes a skip to the next leaf node.

> Also see *B+ tree; node; tree.*

A **pri•ma•ry** key is a unique identifier of a table, having a different value in each field, for example, a column of customer numbers. A **can•di•date key** is a unique identifier that could be designated as the primary key. A **for•eign key** is an attribute or a column in a relation that is identical to a primary key in another relation.

v. To enter data from a keyboard; analogous with type, as on a typewriter. Sometimes used (redundantly) with "in," as in "to key in some changes."

key•board mac•ro

See *macro*.

ki•lo•byte

n. Literally, 1,000 bytes. Actually 2^{10} bytes or 1,024 bytes.
> Abbreviated KB or just K, although the latter also stands for "kilobit" (1024 bits).

knowl•edge base

(Artificial intelligence)

Expert system database containing the rules by which the inference engine makes its logical inferences, or choices. Synonym: **rule base.**

> Also see *expert system.*

knowl•edge en•gi•neer•ing
(Artificial intelligence)

Development of expert system knowledge bases, often by interviewing or observing experts (specialists) and extracting rules from their statements or behavior. There are many computer tools to aid in the process, such as Knowledge Engineering Environment or KEE (IntelliCorp), Knowledge Tool (IBM), and GURU (Micro Data Base Systems, Inc.).

Also see *expert system.*

Knowl•edge En•gi•neer•ing En•vi•ron•ment (KEE)

See *knowledge engineering.*

Korn shell

See *shell.*

la•bel

(Data management)

n. Identifier of a set of data, such as a column, record, or file.

Also a report format, listing fields vertically, as names and addresses appear on mailing labels. dBASE III allows users to create a label format file with the command CREATE LABEL and change one with MODIFY LABEL. LABEL FORM prints a label file.

(Programming)

An identifier associated with a particular memory address or program location. References such as transfers of control can then be done symbolically rather than on an absolute basis (for example, GO TO LABEL or CALL STRCAT instead of GO TO 10756).

la•bels for•mat

(Data management)

The arranging of records' data fields in vertical order, as in mailing labels. This is often a preset option in database programs. An example is dBASE III's LBL file, which can be created with the command

    CREATE LABEL

The R:BASE application called 3Labels enables creation of labels formats.

    Also see *columns format; rows format.*

LAN

See *local area network.*

lan•guage
(Computer languages)

n. A mode of structured, intelligent communication that is spoken, written, or passed on by signals. Natural languages, such as English, are used between people. Computer languages (such as C, COBOL, dBASE, and FORTRAN) are used by people to operate computers; at present, the action is not reciprocal. Computer languages typically have a very restricted vocabulary (often less than 100 words) and precise syntax and format requirements.

Also see *language, natural.*

lan•guage, ap•plic•a•tive
See *functional language.*

lan•guage, as•sem•bly
(Programming)

A low-level language closely related to what the computer executes. Characterized by instruction mnemonics and symbolic names for addresses and data. A mac•ro•as•sem•bler allows macros (named sequences of instructions).

Also see *language, low-level; language, machine; macro.*

lan•guage, da•ta def•i•ni•tion
See *data definition language.*

lan•guage, da•ta de•scrip•tion
See *data description language.*

lan•guage, da•ta ma•nip•u•la•tion
See *data manipulation language.*

lan•guage, ex•ten•si•ble
See *extensible.*

lan•guage, 4th gen•er•a•tion
(Computer languages)

Abbreviated 4GL. A non-procedural, English-like language or set of tools that lets the user specify the desired results, rather than the steps required to obtain them. The largest data object is a database composed of related data files and index files. Fourth generation languages are usually specific to an application. An example is Oracle's SQL*PLUS, which provides a command line and data transfer and reporting options for an SQL database, so that the user need not issue SQL commands.

lan•guage, func•tion•al

See *functional language*.

lan•guage, high-lev•el

(Programming)

A group of strictly defined words with which a user issues instructions to a computer in a structured format, for example, FORTRAN, BASIC, or dBASE. Programs written in them must be translated into machine language before the computer can execute them.

Also see *BASIC; compiler; dBASE; FORTRAN; interpreter; language, low-level; language, 3rd generation; language, 4th generation; language, procedure-oriented.*

lan•guage, low-lev•el

(Programming)

Language written in a form closely related to what a computer can execute directly. Usually specific to a particular model or family of computers. Machine and assembly language are both low-level languages. Sometimes used to refer to a high-level language such as C that allows direct access to machine facilities.

Also see *language, high-level.*

lan•guage, ma•chine

(Programming)

Low-level language written in a form that a computer can execute without further translation. High-level languages must be translated into machine language before execution.

Also see *language, low-level.*

lan•guage, mod•ule

See *Network Database Language.*

lan•guage, nat•u•ral

n. A human language, such as English or American Sign Language.

(Computer languages)

A human language used to communicate with a computer.

A **natural language in•ter•face** permits this use by translating natural language commands or queries into code the computer can understand. Presently in a rudimentary stage of development. The idea is to allow variations and syntax like a human language, although with a restricted vocabulary, often including just 10 or 20 words. Examples are Intellect (Artifical Intelligence Corp.) for DB2 and IDMS and Clout for R:BASE 5000 (Microrim).

lan•guage, non-pro•ce•dur•al

See *language, 4th generation.*

lan•guage, pro•ce•dure ori•ent•ed
(Computer languages)

High level language used to implement procedures or algorithms. Unlike assembly or machine language, a procedure oriented language is independent of the architecture of a particular computer. However, does not include symbolic languages, such as LISP.

Also see specific examples, including *Ada, BASIC, C, COBOL, FORTRAN, Pascal, and PL/I.*

lan•guage, strong•ly typed
(Programming)

Language designed to insure that all operations are consistent with the declared types at compile time. Examples are Ada, Modula-2, and Pascal.

lan•guage, sub•sche•ma def•i•ni•i•tion

See *subschema definition language.*

lan•guage, sche•ma def•i•ni•i•tion

See *schema definition language.*

lan•guage, 3rd gen•er•a•tion
(Programming)

A high-level, procedure-oriented language that is machine-independent and is composed of a series of closely-defined, often English-like statements. The largest data object is a record. Examples are Ada, BASIC, C, COBOL, FORTRAN, Modula-2, Pascal, and PL/I.

Also see *Ada; BASIC; C; COBOL; dBASE; FORTRAN; language, high-level; language, procedure-oriented; Pascal; PL/I.* Contrast with *language, 4th generation* and *language, natural.*

las•er•beam scan•ner

See *bar code reader*.

las•er gun

See *bar code reader*.

las•er wand

See *bar code reader*.

last-in, first-out

See *stack*.

lay•er

n. A thickness, several of which may be placed one on top of another or before another, either physically or conceptually.

Programs, such as operating systems, are said to consist of layers if each level implements its procedures by means of calls to the level immediately below it. The central layer, or kernel, is, of course, an exception that is self-contained and implements the lowest level functions.

Also see *kernel*.

(Graphics)

A figure that can be superimposed on another or placed behind another, for example, a screen over a drawing or a box around text.

(Programming languages)

In object oriented programming, a module whose procedures are implemented by a module at a lower level, that is, closer to the computer's operating system, or one that implements procedures of a higher-level module, that is, one closer to the user.

Also see *modularity; module*.

leaf node

(Data structures)

The final node of a data tree.

Also see *tree*.

leaf rou•tine

(Programming)

A routine that does not call any other routines. That is, when the entire program structure is viewed as a tree, a leaf has no nodes below it.

least priv•i•lege

See *privilege*.

lev•el•ing

(Data management; Programming languages)

n. The process of dividing a system or program hierarchically, that is, into layers or modules of increasing or decreasing detail or levels of abstraction.

Also see *abstraction*.

li•brary

n. Collection of books (from the Latin), and by extension other kinds of reference materials.

(Data management; Programming)

File containing a collection of routines or modules of code or functions, especially those that are often used, known to be error free, and in executable form.

For example, one might have a library of mathematical, statistical, or utility functions. A popular collection of utilities for dBASE III PLUS is Tom Rettig's Library.

MS-DOS library files are produced by compiling or by the user, and have the extension LIB. In UNIX, the command ar is used to create or alter library files; such files have the extension a.

li•cense

n. Permission to act in a defined or specified way.

(Software)

Permission to use software under specified conditions. For instance, purchasing a software package is actually buying the right to use it under specific conditions or restrictions. The user agrees to them by the act of unwrapping the package.

An in•di•vid•u•al license permits use only by the purchaser. It usually allows a backup copy and copying onto one hard disk, as long as the original floppy disk remains unused.

A **run-time license** allows use of the software as part of an application. For example, a developer might sell a manufacturing control package based on dBASE IV, Clipper, or R:BASE. The developer would buy a run-time license for the base software, often with charges depending on the number of copies sold. An **un•lim•it•ed run-time license** involves a one-time charge only.

A **site license** allows multiple users within a single company or installation. The number may be limited or unlimited. A site license is usually more expensive than an individual license, but less than multiple individual licenses. Software publishers offer site licenses as a way of discouraging illegal copying of programs, while still reducing the cost and policing required of large institutional users.

LIFO
See *stack*.

light pen
(Hardware)
Analog scanner shaped and held like a writing pen. Emits a light beam used to read bar codes into a computer. The type of device used at many library checkout desks.

Also see *bar code*.

line driv•er
See *driver*

line-ori•ent•ed graph•ics
See *vector graphics*.

link
(Data structures)
n. A pointer from one part or instance of a data structure to another. For example, one can have links between elements in a queue, stack, or tree.

An automatic transfer of data from one database to another. Linking permits insertions, deletions, or changes made in one list, file, or table, to be reflected automatically in linked lists, files, or tables. For example, if a new customer places an order for a product, when the name is entered in the purchases database, it will automatically be added to a linked mailing list. Such procedures are possible, for example, with programs written in dBASE and Pascal.

(dBASE)
In dBASE II, SET LINKAGE enables or disables the automatic change in a linked field when a change is made in the field on the screen.

In dBASE III, III PLUS, and IV, SET RELATION establishes a linkage.

(MS-DOS)

LINK is a utility that creates an EXE (executable) file to link external object modules.

(Programming)

v. To combine modules for execution. The program that does the job is a **link•er, link ed•i•tor,** or **link•age ed•i•tor.**

link•age ed•i•tor

See *link.*

link ed•i•tor

See *link.*

linked list

See *list.*

link en•cryp•tion

See *encryption.*

link•er

See *link.*

Lin•pack bench•mark

(Computer operations)

A FORTRAN program that solves linear equations. Described in J.J. Dongarra, "Performance of Various Computers Using Standard Linear Equations Software in a FORTRAN Environment," Technical Memorandum 23, Argonne National Laboratory, Argonne, IL, 17 Feb. 1986.

lint

(UNIX)

n. A command that detects errors and inconsistencies in C program files. **lint** options include: assigning long values to its variables and reporting unreachable break statements, bugs, undefined and inconsistent variables and functions, and unaccessed variables.

lint compensates for the very limited error checking provided by most C compilers. Programmers run **lint** before a first compilation.

v. (Jargon) To analyze a program with **lint.**

LISP
(Computer languages)

Acronym for LISt Processing language. Applicative or functional language in several dialects developed by John McCarthy and others at MIT in the 1950s and 1960s. Used in artificial intelligence. Designed to process (or solve problems concerning) lists of non-numeric data, including English sentences and logical and mathematical constructions. A **list** consists of **ele•ments,** each of which may be either a basic atom (such as a character string) or another list. An element may also be called an entity, head, item, node, or record.

Has a reputation as a language that is difficult to use and slow-running, because of the frequent need for memory compaction ("garbage collection").

A widely used version is Common LISP, as defined by Guy L. Steele, Jr. *Common LISP Reference Manual*, 2nd ed. (Bedford, MA: Digital Press, 1990). The actual standard is a product of ANSI Committee X3J13.

list
(Data structures)

n. An ordered set of elements, perhaps including pointers to other elements (a **linked list**).

(MS-DOS)

v. The command DIR lists files.

In the line editor, the command LIST LINES lists 23 lines in a DOS program. The lines to be listed can be entered in a prefix, such as

      10,15L

to list lines 10 through 15.

(dBASE)

v. A command that displays or prints a database's records and fields and can be limited by a scope or with FOR or WHILE. Also used when debugging a dBASE program.

LIST HISTORY shows the commands executed and stored in HISTORY.

LIST MEMORY shows the name, type, size, and number of the memory variables, as well as other memory information.

LIST STATUS gives information about the current session, such as database name, relations, open index file names, search path, and print destination.

LIST STRUCTURE gives information about the active database, including last date changed, size of a record, and number of fields and their lengths and types.

The command DISPLAY is similar, except that scrolling pauses after every 20 lines and resumes when the user presses a key.

lit•tle end•i•an

In Gulliver's Travels by Jonathan Swift (18th century English cleric and satirist), a political party whose basis was the members' belief in opening soft-boiled eggs at the little end. The opposition was composed of people who believed in opening eggs at the big end – big endians.

(Hardware)

Referring to computers that assign the lowest memory address occupied by a number to the least significant bits – that is, to the smallest value. Examples are the Intel series of microprocessors used in IBM PCs and compatible computers (the 8088, 80286, 80386, and 80486).

Contrast with *big endian.*

load

(Computer operations)

v. To copy data from secondary storage or an input device into the computer's memory. Also to copy data from memory into the central processing unit (CPU). Synonym: *read.*

Also see *save; store; write.*

loc•al

(Data management; Programming)

adj. A one-time value or meaning within a program or application, or having a value or meaning only within a single module. For example, a local find or find-and-replace would return only the first instance of the value or text. A local variable is defined only within a single module.

Contrast with *global.*

loc•al area net•work (LAN)

(Data communications)

A computer network limited geographically to one building or site. Although the definition is flexible, maximum distances are usually 2,000-7,000 feet (600-2,100 meters). Devices are generally connected by cables, not telephone lines.

Contrast with *wide area network.*

Also see *bridge; gateway; network.*

loc•al var•i•a•ble

See *local*.

lock

(Security)

n. Exclusive ownership by one user or process of all or part of a multiuser database, for updating or some other operation. A lock prevents other users from performing a simultaneous, conflicting operation and in some cases from seeing obsolete data. The lock must provide adequate security during an operation without denying other users legitimate access to the remainder of the database. Sometimes a lock may allow others to read data but not change it. Database managers may provide locks with different extents, such as field locks, record locks, or file locks. Also, a file or disk protection method to prevent changing, erasing, or copying.

(dBASE)

The functions LOCK( ) and RLOCK( ) lock a record. FLOCK( ) locks a file.

In dBASE IV, the command SET LOCK ON causes locking of a file during use of the commands AVERAGE, CALCULATE, COPY, COPY STRUCTURE, COUNT, INDEX, JOIN, LABEL, REPORT, SORT, SUM, and TOTAL. The command CONVERT creates a hidden field _DBASELOCK, which contains information about locks in the file. The function CHANGE( ) tells whether a record has been changed; LKSYS( ) tells when and by whom a lock was applied.

Also see *field lock; file lock; record lock; unlock.*

log

n. Record of transactions or occurrences, such as a ship's log. A log of database transactions is useful in data recovery.

v. To keep such a record.

(Data communications)

To **log in** or **log on** means to begin a session, for instance, for a user at one station to make contact with another station. The two phrases are synonyms, and preference for one is usually cultural or dictated by the application, such as the use of **login** by UNIX. **Log off** or **log out** is used to end a session.

log•i•cal

adj. According to logic or reason, in accordance with what seems reasonable or natural. By extension, independent of the physical environment and its restrictions, specifics, and local idiosyncrasies.

(Computer operations; Data communications; Data management)

The theory and design on which an actual or physical machine, program, or database is built. For example, a logical database model or schema consists of the definition of data types, relationships, and rules under which it can be used. The physical database is the actual data that is put into the model (through a process called instantiation).

Similarly, a logical communications network is the model that the actual connection of hardware and software follows. And a computer's (logical) architecture is the model on which the machine is built.

Contrast with *physical*.

Also see *virtual*.

log•i•cal ac•cess map

See *data navigation diagram*.

log•i•cal ad•di•tion

(Logic)

Use of the Boolean operator OR. For example, with two binary digits, if either is one, the result is one.

$$1 + 0 = 1$$

$$1 + 1 = 1$$

If both operands are zero, the result is zero.

$$0 + 0 = 0$$

An alternative is to use the EXCLUSIVE OR operator, which differs from OR only in that it produces a zero result when both operands are one. It is thus equivalent to binary addition without a carry.

Also see *Boolean operator*.

log•i•cal da•ta in•de•pen•dence

See *independence, data*.

log•i•cal op•er•a•tor

See *Boolean operator*.

log•i•cal to•pol•o•gy

See *topology*.

log•ic da•ta•base

See *database, logic*.

log in

See *log*.

log•in

See *log*.

log off

See *log*.

log on

See *log*.

log out

See *log*.

long word

(Computer operations)

A unit of data that exceeds a word in length. The next higher unit, may be the same as a dou•ble word.

Also see *word*.

"look and feel"

(Hardware; Software)

Visual, tactile, and aesthetic characteristics of a brand of computer and its operating software that distinguish it from other brands and software. Though largely subjective, it is sufficiently integral to the basic design of a computer system to be copyrighted.

look•up

See *lookup table*.

look•up ta•ble

(Data management)

A set of values stored in memory, often sequentially or as an array. Examples are numeric values, as an alternative to being calculated as required, or data locations, as an alternative to the use of pointers. The accessing of a specific value is called **lookup** or **table lookup**.

loose cou•pling

See *coupling*.

lost up•date

See *update*.

Lo•tus 1-2-3

(Applications)

A spreadsheet program with built-in graphics and data management features (Lotus Development Corp).

"low•er case"

(Software)

Informal reference to stages of software design (software life cycle) involving implementation and support (coding, debugging, testing, documentation, extension, and re-design). For complementary functions, see *upper case*, though the boundary is not rigid. May be a play on words, since the function can be automated with CASE tools.

low-level language

See *language, low-level*.

LU 6.2

(Data communications)

Logical Unit 6.2. IBM's protocol for software that performs the session layer connection (ISO/OSI Layer 5) within the Advanced Program-to-Program Communications (APPC). Performs peer-to-peer communications, and addresses the host for terminal-mainframe connections.

Also see *advanced program-to-program communications*.

M

mac•ro

(Programming)

n. From the Greek, meaning large. A named or labeled sequence of commands or keystrokes that can be entered into a program or executed within an application as a single command. For example, in R:BASE's Application EXPRESS, an ASCII command file can be added to an application file as a command block by selecting Macro from the menu, then entering the file name.

(dBASE)

In dBASE IV, a macro menu (displayed with Shift-F10) permits creation of macros and saving them in a file. After retrieval with the command RESTORE, the macro can be executed with PLAY MACRO or Alt-F10, or from the macro menu.

A **macro li•brary** is a set of macros.

A **macro fa•cil•i•ty** or **macro lan•guage** aids in the creation of macros. Macros can also be created from the IBM PC keyboard with programs such as ProKey and SuperKey. Such macros, called **key•board macros**, are also used in programs such as Lotus 1-2-3.

mac•ro•as•sem•bler

See *language, assembly*.

mac•ro fa•cil•i•ty

See *macro*.

macro language

See *macro*.

macro library

See *macro*.

mail merge

See *form letter*.

main•frame
(Hardware)

n. Large computer of traditional design, consisting of one or more processing units (CPU), memory, and an input/output section capable of handling remote terminals, workstations, and other devices. A mainframe can handle the large-scale data processing needs of an entire corporation, government agency, or institution such as a university or hospital. Typically has a large memory and independent I/O processors (channels). IBM is the primary vendor. Other vendors were once known as the BUNCH (after the initials for Burroughs, Univac, NCR, Control Data, and Honeywell). The term persists, despite mergers, name changes, shifts in ownership, and the emergence of Asian and European manufacturers.

The term was originally main frame referring to the case that held the CPU, which usually took up an entire room. It was later synonymous with central processing unit.

Contrast with *midframe; minicomputer; minisupercomputer; personal computer; supercomputer; superminicomputer; workstation.*

Also see *central processing unit.*

main in•dex

See *index.*

main store
(British usage)

See *store.*

make
(Programming)

n. Utility program that allows for the generation of programs from multiple modules. When changes are made, it recompiles and relinks only those modules that have been affected.

The user must specify the dependencies in a so-called **make file**. The idea is to reduce the time required to recompile and relink a large application.

Also used (jargon) to describe the operation of using the make utility and as a verb to mean its application.

make file

See *make*.

man•age•ment in•for•ma•tion sys•tem
(Data management)

Abbreviated **MIS**. Method of organizing data so that reports provide managers with the information they require for day-to-day operations. In large businesses, often the function of centralized departments. May also be implemented directly by managers using workstations or networks.

man•ag•er

See *server*.

man•da•to•ry ac•cess con•trol

See *access control, mandatory*.

man•tis•sa

See *floating point*.

Man•u•fac•tur•ing Au•to•ma•tion Pro•to•col
(Data communications)

Abbreviated **MAP**. Specification developed by General Motors Corp. for a token-passing local area network that supports the operation of an automated manufacturing plant. Encompasses Layers 3-7 of the ISO/OSI Reference Model. Transmits at 5 and 10 Mbps on broadband cable. Specified by IEEE Standard 802.4.

Often used in conjunction with **TOP**, as **MAP/TOP**.

Also see *MAP/TOP; Technical and Office Protocol*.

many-to-many
(Data management)

Relationship between entities, each of which has other relationships at the same time. For example, a person may have a home telephone number and also a work number, which several people use. The person and the work number have a many-to-many relationship, as the person has other telephone numbers and other people use the work number.

Contrast with *one-to-many; one-to-one*.

map

n. A graphical representation of a geographic area, usually two-dimensional, to fit on a printed page or computer screen.

Also, such a representation stored in digital form as part of a computerized geographic information system (GIS), which can be manipulated or combined with other types of data.

Also see *geographic information system.*

Also a transformation of logical addresses (as used by a program) into actual or physical addresses. May apply to both memory and I/O addresses.

v. To make such a representation.

(Data communications)

n. A graphical representation of a network, cable, or segment.

v. To make such a representation.

(Data management)

n. A one-to-one representation of an address space. If on a per-bit basis, called a **bit map**. Each bit in the representation then corresponds to a unit in the actual space. For example, a bit map may indicate whether a point (pixel) on a screen is on or off, or whether a unit of memory is available or allocated.

v. To transfer code or data to or from memory, as between a disk and RAM.

Also a graphical representation of a data structure.

Also see *raster graphics.*

MAP

See *Manufacturing Automation Protocol.*

MAPSE

See *Ada; Ada Program Support Environment.*

MAP/TOP

Communications protocols that may be used complementarily for automated manufacturing (MAP) and office and technical management (TOP). The two share Layers 3-7 of the ISO/OSI Reference Model. Pronounced "map-top."

Also see *Manufacturing Automation Protocol; Technical and Office Protocol.*

map•ping

(Data management)

n. Transferring code or data to or from memory, as between a disk and RAM.

Di•rect mapping is the storage of each data item in a unique memory location. A direct-mapped high-speed memory (cache) can thus be accessed by address without any associative searching. It is easy to implement, but produces fewer matches than an associative cache.

Also see *cache*.

(Graphics)

Tex•ture mapping is the placing of a two-dimensional texture on a three-dimensional shape.

mas•sive•ly par•al•lel pro•cess•ing

See *parallel processing*.

mas•ter

See *host*.

mas•ter con•trol pro•gram

See *operating system*.

ma•te•ri•al•ized

adj. Having substance; being tangible, an object, or in a finished form.

(Data management)

Said of the placement of data in a logical field, either directly from stored memory or in a view, for example, as the result of a join.

ma•te•ri•als, bill of

See *bill of materials*.

math chip

See *floating point processor*.

math co•pro•ces•sor

See *floating point processor*.

max

(Mathematics)

Abbreviation for maximum. The largest of a series of numbers or numeric expression.

A function in many database and spreadsheet programs that returns the largest value in a list of numbers or expressions.

(dBASE)

MAX( ) returns the higher of two values. This is useful in determining whether each in a series of values is higher than a specified value. For example, a student is permitted a maximum of 18 semester hours' worth of courses per semester. In a file with fields STUDENT and CURRENTHOURS, to determine whether a student may sign up for a 2 semester-hour course, use

.LIST student, MAX(18, currenthours)

In dBASE IV, MAX( ) also compares dates.

The dBASE IV command CALCULATE has a MAX function that returns the largest value in a character, date, or numeric field.

Also see *min.*

MDA

See *monochrome display adapter*.

mean

(Mathematics)

adj. The average of a set of values. That is, their sum divided by the number of values. Usually used in statistics as a synonym for arithmetic mean. Other means exist, such as the geometric mean, the nth root of the product of n values.

A way of evaluating the reliability of computer systems and other hardware, as in **mean time be•tween fail•ures**. Data transmission reliability can be evaluated by calculating the **mean time be•tween er•rors.**

mean time be•tween er•rors

See *mean.*

mean time be•tween fail•ures (MTBF)

See *mean.*

mem•ber

n. A representative of a group. An element of a set.

(Programming languages)

In object oriented programming, an example or instance of a class.

In the C language, an element (called a field in most languages) within a structure (called a record in most languages).

mem•o•ry

n. Retention of what has been acquired or learned, and its availability for recall or recreation.

Section of a computer used to hold programs and data. Also called **pri•mary stor•age.**

mem•o•ry band•width

See *bandwidth.*

mem•o•ry dump

See *core dump.*

mem•o•ry im•age

Copy of a file in memory.

mem•o•ry res•i•dent

Part of a program or data that remains in the computer's memory during normal operation. May refer to a kernel or resident part of operating systems or to programs kept in memory to increase access speed.

mem•o•ry va•ri•able

Named location or area of computer memory where data is stored temporarily during program execution. Abbreviation **mem•var.**

Typical contents in dBASE are screen prompts, user commands, buffers for data entry, and results of calculations.

Gives special purpose languages such as dBASE some of the flexibility of general purpose languages.

mem•var

See *memory variable.*

menu

(Computer environment)

n. A list of options from which the user selects one for execution. A menu may be at the operating environment level, letting the user select an application to open (as in Windows), or within an application, to choose a command for execution. A system may have several levels of menus, organized hierarchically.

(R:BASE)

Application EXPRESS presents a menu with three options:

> (1) Define a new application

> (2) Modify an existing application

> (3) Exit

It also permits creation of menus allowing the use or modification of databases.

A menu-driven program is one with which the user interacts by selecting items from a menu, in contrast to a command-driven program. A **pop•up menu** is displayed on the screen as a result of a request, a error, or a previous command, such as a printing status menu with options to pause or cancel. A **pull•down menu** appears under its title when selected, perhaps with a mouse or by entering a keyboard command. A **pop-out menu** is an extension of a pulldown menu; it appears on the screen as a result of selecting an item. A **sub-menu** is a menu presented as the result of a selection from a main menu. A **tear-off menu** can be moved around the screen at the user's convenience, for instance, a menu of graphics tools in HyperCard.

Also see *dialog box*.

mes•sage

n. A communication.

(Programming)

In object oriented programming, a procedure-like method by which objects communicate and perform operations.

Also see *object oriented*.

(Data communications)

Unit of communications between processes, computers, or nodes. Message-based operating systems use a formal communications system (like a postal service) for interprocess communications, rather than shared memory or other ad hoc methods.

meta•char•ac•ter

(Data management)

Character with a special meaning that stands for any digit, any vowel, a designated number of characters, options, alternatives, or other specified groupings.

For example, ? might be defined as any digit, so that searching for 19?? would return any number between 1900 and 1999.

Popularly called a **wild card**, after the special role of certain cards (such as jokers) to serve as substitutes for any card in some games.

meta•class

(Programming)

n. In some object oriented programming languages, including Smalltalk, a class that is an instance of a class.

meta•da•ta

(Data management)

n. Data contained in a data dictionary. That is, data that describes the "real" data in the database.

Also see *dictionary*.

meth•od

See *object oriented*.

met•rics

n. Numerical measurements. Used in many fields, from music and poetry to engineering. A metric gives a specific number for use as a measure.

(Software)

Refers to methods for measuring the qualities of computer programs, such as power, speed, portability, and maintainability.

met•ri•fi•ca•tion

n. Process of defining mathematical measures to express a subjective or qualitative concept.

mi•cro•com•put•er

(Hardware)

n. See *personal computer*, but also refers to small computers used in embedded systems.

mi•cro•pro•gram

See *firmware.*

mid•frame

(Hardware)

n. A computer designed like a mainframe, but smaller, positioned between a mainframe and a workstation or a minicomputer.

mi•grate

(Software)

v. To adapt an application developed for one brand or model of computer or operating system to additional ones. Grammatically an intransitive verb, it is often used within the computer industry as a transitive verb. For example, one might say, "The company will migrate its application from VAX to Macintosh."

min

(Mathematics)

Abbreviation for minimum. The smallest of a series of numbers or numeric expressions.

A function in many database and spreadsheet programs that returns the smallest value in a list of numbers or expressions.

(dBASE)

MIN ( ) returns the lower of two values. This is useful in determining whether each in a series of values is lower than a specified value. For example, a student must have a grade-point average of 2.5 to be eligible for athletics. In a file with fields STUDENT and GRADEAVERAGE, to determine whether a student is eligible, use

.LIST student, MIN (2.5, gradeaverage)

The dBASE IV command CALCULATE has a MIN function that returns the smallest value in a character, date, or numeric field.

Also see *max.*

Min•i•mal Ada Pro•gram Sup•port En•vi•ron•ment (MAPSE)

See *Ada*.

mini•su•per•com•put•er
(Hardware)

n. Computer with the characteristics of a supercomputer, but on a smaller scale. Its speed in MIPS or FLOPS is typically higher than that of a superminicomputer.

Also see *supercomputer*.

MIPS
(Computer operations)

Acronym for Million Instructions Per Second. Pronounced "mipps." A measure of the speed of computers.

Also see *instructions per second*.

MIS

See *management information system*.

mod•el

v. To create a pattern for or representation of something. Model-based techniques thus differ from heuristic methods.

Also see *heuristic*.

n. A pattern or representation so created. A type or archetype. Also the basis for a computer simulation.

Also see *simulation*.

(Data management)

A design (conceptual model) or logical structure (physical model) of a database or data structure from which an actual database will be created and used.

Also see *model, conceptual; model, physical*.

(Graphics)

Three-dimensional graphic embodying design attributes, allowing analysis and change. Can appear solid (showing underlying structure as well as surface features), wire-frame (showing structure), or surface. Used in engineering design and CAD/CAM.

Also see *computer aided design; computer aided manufacturing.*

mod•el, con•cep•tu•al

(Data management)

Sche•ma or design on which a database is constructed, taking the users' needs into account. A description of data objects and their relationships. May use a data description or definition language. Sometimes called an **en•ter•prise model.**

Used to create a physical model.

Also see *database; data description language; model; model, physical; three schema model.*

mo•del, en•ter•prise

See *model, conceptual.*

mod•el, phys•i•cal

(Data management)

Logical database structure or format into which data will be placed and from which it will be used, plus the methods by which this will be done. For example, the database type may be hierarchical, network, or relational. May include a data manipulation language.

Based on the conceptual model.
Also called **in•ter•nal model** or **physical struc•ture.**

Also see *database; data manipulation language; model; model, conceptual; three schema model.*

mo•dem

(Data communications)

n. A device that enables computers to communicate over telephone lines by translating between digital and sound signals. Originally an abbreviation of modulator/demodulator; now generally used as a word.

mo•dem, call-back

(Security)

Add-on security feature to prevent unauthorized access to a computer system. A modem intercepts an incoming user request for access, requests a password, verifies the password, and instructs the user to hang up. The modem then calls the user back at a previously identified telephone number, allowing access.

mod•i•fi•ca•tion anom•a•ly

(Data management)

Unexpected consequence of changing data in a relational database.

mod•u•lar•i•ty

n. To divide or partition into units (modules).

(Programming languages)

The extent to which a system is or can be divided into modules or sections that can function independently.

Also see *modular programming.*

mod•ul•ar pro•gram•ming

(Programming languages)

Creation of an overall program as a set of independent sub-units or modules.

mod•u•late

(Data communications)

v. To convert analog or digital data to an electromagnetic wave for transmission. This may be done by varying the wave's height (amplitude modulation), frequency (frequency modulation), or polarity (phase modulation).

Also see *modem.*

Modula-2

(Programming languages)

General purpose procedure-oriented high-level language for programming and system implementation. Features modules, each of which contains a definition and an implementation; procedures, which can be assigned to variables; and data structures. Developed by N. Wirth in 1970s, as an outgrowth of Pascal and an earlier language named Modula. Allows separate compilation of modules.

Defined in N. Wirth, *Modula-2*, 3rd Corrected Ed. (New York: Springer-Verlag, 1985).

Also see *Pascal.*

mod•ule

n. Self-contained unit.

(Programming)

A self-contained unit of a program. A group of commands or lines of code in a procedural language that performs a particular operation, such as finding a record in a database. A module is treated as a single group of instructions. Modules can be internal to a program, and can be added to it or removed from it without disturbing the rest of it. They can also be external, or self-contained, and linked to each other or to programs. An object module contains compiled or assembled machine code that is directly usable by the computer.

(dBASE)

As an example of a module, here are the commands to create a series of options for a user to select from a menu:

DO CASE

        CASE (option 1)

        CASE (option 2)

ENDCASE

mod•ule lan•guage

See *Network Database Language*.

mod•u•lus

(Mathematics)

n. Remainder after division of one integer (whole number) by another, as in

$$28/3 = 9 \text{ with modulus (or mod) } 1$$

Used, for example, in checksum algorithms.

    Sometimes mistakenly called modulo, which is a related concept.

(dBASE)

dBASE provides the function MOD( ), useful for converting numbers from one set of units to another, as from minutes to hours and minutes. It presents the whole hours as integers, ITS, and any remaining minutes as the modulus, MOD. For example,

        total minutes = 471

        hours = ITS (total min/60)

        minutes = MOD (total min/60)

returns 7 hours and 51 minutes.

mon•i•tor

See *operating system; video monitor*.

mon•i•tor, ref•er•ence

See *reference monitor*.

mon•i•tor, vid•eo

See *video monitor*.

mono•chrome dis•play adapt•er
(Hardware)

Abbreviated **MDA**. Video display standard for IBM PCs, developed by IBM. For text only, it provides 720 x 350 pixel resolution (9 x 14 dot-matrix characters). Not used on PS/2 computers. For other video display standards, see *color/graphics adapter* (CGA); *enhanced graphics adapter* (EGA); *video graphics array* (VGA).

mouse
(Hardware)

n. Roller-driven device for moving a pointer or cursor on the screen and issuing commands. It is connected to the computer by a long, thin cord. Moving the mouse on a surface moves the pointer/cursor. Depressing and releasing a key on top of the device issues a command. (Some brands have one key, others have two or three.)

The size and shape of early devices vaguely resembled a common rodent, with switches as eyes and the cord as a tail, hence the name. First used at Stanford Research Institute (SRI) and (later) at Xerox Palo Alto Research Center (Xerox PARC) by D. Engelbart in the 1960s and 1970s as a pointing device to control systems using graphical interfaces (particularly the Bravo editing system).

mov•ing av•er•age

See *average, moving*.

MS-DOS
(Computer environment)

Common single-user, single tasking operating system for personal computers (IBM PCs, compatibles, clones, and related systems), developed by Microsoft Corporation in the early 1980s. Originally provided minimal features for a single-user, single-tasking floppy-disk based computer. Later versions offer a hierarchical file structure, pipes, filters, and support for a wide variety of floppy disks, hard disks, and networks. Most versions have a minimal user interface, showing only the current disk drive. Includes simple file and disk operations, I/O control, memory management, and command or procedure files (called **batch files**). So widely used that it is often referred to by the generic term **DOS**. **PC-DOS** is the official IBM version.

mul•ti•lev•el se••cu•ri•ty
(Security)

Abbreviated **MLS**. U.S. Department of Defense security policy, as implemented on a computer system. Consists of the simple security condition and the star or confinement property. Defined in various models, such as the Bell-LaPadula model.

Also see *Bell-LaPadula model; simple security condition; star property; Trusted Computer System Evaluation Criteria.*

mul•ti•ple in•dex

See *index.*

mul•ti•ple in•her•i•tance

See *child; parent; tree.*

Mul•ti•ple Vir•tu•al Stor•age, En•ter•prise Sys•tems Ar•chi•tec•ture
(Computer operations)

Abbreviated **MVS/ESA**. IBM operating system for older mainframes that have been upgraded to Enterprise Systems Architecture (ESA).

Multiple Virtual Storage, Extended Architecture
(Computer operations)

Abbreviated **MVS/XA**. Widely used IBM operating system for mainframes.

mul•ti•plex•ing
(Data communications)

n. Sending of several data streams over the same line, cable, or channel at the same time, either by alternating ("interleaving") in time or simultaneously, but at different frequencies. Data may be interleaved by bit, character, or message. Speed is lower than if a single stream were sent, but it provides greater economy, signal complexity, or both.

There are four types of multiplexing: synchronous, or fixed time periods; asynchronous (or statistical), using only active channels; polling, in which nodes are addressed in turn; and contention, in which a node wishing to transmit seizes an unused line.

mul•ti•pro••cess•ing

(Computer architecture)

n. The use of multiple processors in a computer. The computer is then called a mul•ti•pro••cess•or.

Also see *multiprogramming* and *multitasking* for distinct but often confused concepts.

mul•ti•pro••cess•or

See *multiprocessing.*

mul•ti•pro•gram•ming

(Computer operations)

n. Having several programs active in memory at the same time.

Also see *multiprocessing* and *multitasking* for distinct but often confused concepts.

mul•ti•sync mon•i•tor

(Hardware)

A video monitor (computer screen) that adjusts to the synchronization (clock) frequencies (lines per second) sent by the video circuit. Can be adapted to as high a resolution as 1,024 x 768 pixels, for use in CAD/CAE applications. Used with a variety of IBM PC display adapters, including CGA, EGA, and VGA.

mul•ti•task•ing

(Computer operations)

n. The performance by a computer of several different tasks or operations at the same time. May be performed by several processors or nodes, by interleaving tasks on a single node, or both.

For distinct but often confused concepts, also see *multiprocessing; multiprogramming; multiuser.*

mul•ti•user

(Computer operations)

adj. Capable of handling several users at the same time. Each user may have many tasks running (multitasking). Applied to both computers and software, such as operating systems and databases.

MUMPS
(Data management; Programming languages)

Database management system and high-level programming language developed for medical record keeping in 1970s. Originally an acronym for Massachusetts General Hospital Utility Multi-Programming System, after the initial sponsoring organization. Now controlled by the MUMPS Development Committee. 1989 version features structured programming and calls to external functions.

Defined in American National Standard X11.1.

MVS/ESA

See *Multiple Virtual Storage, Enterprise Systems Architecture.*

MVS/XA

See *Multiple Virtual Storage, Extended Architecture.*

N

n

Character used to represent an indefinite number.

NAK

See *negative acknowledge.*

n-ary

adj. Relating to the indefinite number represented by **n**. For example, a relation with *n* attributes is said to be n-ary.

Nas•si-Shneid•er•man chart

(Software development tools)

Chart for structured procedures featuring a vertical series of contiguous boxes, each of which contains a process, a selection and options (IF-THEN-ELSE), or an execution sequence (DO WHILE).

Described in I. Nassi and B. Shneiderman, "Flowchart Techniques for Structured Programming," *ACM SIGPLAN Notices,* 8 (8), August 1973, p. 12.

Sometimes called a **Chap•in chart,** a similar diagram developed at about the same time. Described in N. Chapin et al., "Structured Programming Simplified," *Computer Decisions,* 6 (6), June 1974, p. 28.

name

See *identifier.*

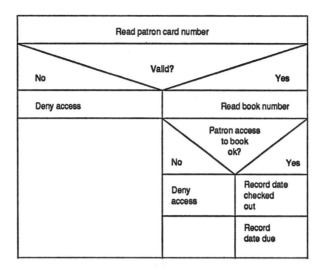

Nassi-Shneiderman Chart

Na•tion•al Bu•reau of Stan•dards (NBS)

See *National Institute of Standards and Technology*.

Na•tion•al Ins•ti•tute of Stan•dards and Tech•nol•o•gy

U.S. government agency that oversees the standardization of technological systems and assists in their development. Abbreviated **NIST**. Formerly called the National Bureau of Standards (NBS).

nat•u•ral lan•guage in•ter•face

See *interface; language, natural*.

nat•u•ral join

See *join*.

nav•i•gate

v. To follow a charted route or path from one location to another.

(Computer operations)

To follow a logical path through a data structure, menu, file, or dialog box.

(Data management)

To follow a path through a database's hierarchical organization.

Also see *tree.*

nav•i•ga•tion di•a•gram

See *data navigation diagram.*

NBS

See *National Institute of Standards and Technology.*

n-cube

See *hypercube.*

NDL

See *Network Database Language.*

neg•a•tive ac•knowl•edge
(Data communications)

An error signal by a system that has received data from a sender. For computers that use ASCII (not all do), the signal is the ASCII control character NAK. See table under *ASCII.*

Also see *acknowledge; ASCII.*

nest

v. To place one inside another.

(Data management)

To create a hierarchy of blocks.

nest•ed

adj. Placed one inside another.

(Programming)

Often applied to subroutines that call other subroutines. The **nest•ing lev•el** is the number of calls that have been made without corresponding returns.

(Data management)

Said of a block containing other blocks, such as subqueries or subroutines that must be executed before execution of the main block is completed. Often indicated in written form by indentations.

NetWare
(Data communications)

Network operating system from Novell, Inc., for communications among mainframes, minicomputers, workstations, and personal computers. Uses application programming interfaces (APIs).

net•work
(Data communications)

n. A group of computers, terminals, printers, and other devices connected by communications equipment for the purpose of sharing data and resources. Network devices may be connected by cables, telephone lines (with modems), or a combination.

net•work an•a•lyz•er

See *protocol analyzer*.

net•work da•ta•base
(Data management)

Database model in which the record is the basic unit of manipulation, with each one defined by a unique database key. A set is a relationship between two or more records, one of which is the owner, the others members. Each set has a unique identification. A single record set is also permitted – one that is owned by the system. In a recursive set, the same record is both the owner and a member (a cyclic relationship).

One-to-many, one-to-one, and many-to-many relationships are permitted. The multiple relationships permitted make this a flexible method of data management, but they also can cause slow response time.

Examples include DBMS-11 (DEC), DMS 1100 (Unisys), IDMS/R (Cullinet), and KnowledgeMan/2 (Micro Data Base Systems).

Also see *CODASYL; database; Network Database Language*.

Net•work Da•ta•base Lan•guage
(Data management)

Language that defines the logical structures and basic operations for a network database. Includes conditions, operands, identifiers, literals (logical representation of values), and data types. Supports character, fixed (numeric), integer, float, real, and double precision data types. Provides four languages for schema (logical) and subschema (view) definition, module, and data manipulation.

Defined in American National Standard X3.133-1986.

- **sche•ma def•i•ni•tion lan•guage** provides a logical description of a database, consisting of schema, record, and set types and names.

- **sub•sche•ma lan•guage** describes views.

- **mod•ule lan•guage** defines names, temporary set specifications, and procedures.

- **da•ta ma•nip•u•la•tion lan•guage** provides user commands, including commit, connect, disconnect, erase, find, get, modify, nullify, reconnect, rollback, store, and key identifier.

May be used with COBOL, FORTRAN, Pascal, and PL/I.

Also see *network database*.

net•work serv•er

See *server*.

NIST

See *National Institute of Standards and Technology*.

node

n. A thickening. A point of junction, intersection, ending, or branching.

(Hardware)

A computer, terminal, or other device on a network. Synonym: *station.*

A place where an electrical connection is made.

Also a computer processor that is connected to other processors; a term used in multiprocessing and parallel processing.

Also see *hypercube*.

(Applications)

A data point on a graph; a branching place in a data tree; an event or occurrence in a simulation. A place where a function is performed.

(Data management)

In a tree data structure, the location of a key value and its pointer. The place for the storage of data or information about data location. Nodes are connected by branches, beginning with the root node and ending with leaf nodes. There is only one path to each node. Also see *tree*.

(Data communications)

A computer, terminal, workstation, or other device on a network. Also a place where a network connection is made.

(Programming)

A predicate in structured programming.

Also see *flowchart; function; predicate.*

node name
(Data communications)

The unique identification of a device or node on a computer network, by which connections are made for sending or receiving data. Synonym: *address.*

Also see *identification.*

non-ded•i•cat•ed serv•er
(Data communications)

A network node that performs communications tasks as well as handling its own user tasks. Contrast with *dedicated server.*

Also see *dedicated; server.*

non•in•ter•laced dis•play
(Hardware)

Video display in which each complete pass of the electron beam across the screen excites ("refreshes") every line of pixels, providing a more flicker-free display than other patterns. Contrast with *interlaced display.*

non•pro•ce•dur•al lan•guage

See *language, 4th generation.*

nor•mal form

See *first normal form.*

nor•mal•ize

v. To adjust a value so that it falls within a specified range.

(Data management)

In a relational table, to place only one value per row under each column heading. Conversion of a table with several values in each cell (an **un•nor•mal•ized ta•ble**) into a table with only one value per cell is called **nor•mal•i•za•tion.**

Also see *instantiation; polyinstantiation.*

unnormalized table				normalized table	
No.	Value			No.	Value
1	a, b, c			1	a
2	d, e			1	b
				1	c
				2	d
				3	e

This table structure is called **nor•mal form** or **first nor•mal** form (1NF).

Normalization may require several stages before all ambiguities in the table structure are resolved. The stages, as defined, are: first normal form, second normal form (2NF), third normal form (3NF), Boyce/Codd normal form (BCNF), fourth normal form (4NF), and fifth (5NF) or projection-join normal form (PJ/NF).

Also see *Boyce-Codd normal form; fifth normal form; fourth normal form; second normal form; third normal form.*

(Programming languages)

To make certain that data is defined and used consistently and correctly.

(Mathematics)

To adjust the exponent and mantissa of a floating point number so that the mantissa lies within a prescribed range (often with its most significant digit being non-zero). The normalized form simplifies arithmetic operations and allows for more significant digits. Normalization does not change the number being represented.

Also see *floating point.*

NPL (non•pro•ce•dur•al lan•guage)

See *language, 4th generation.*

nroff

(UNIX)

n. Routine for text formatting and printing on dot-matrix and daisywheel printers. Pronounced "en-roff." Originally developed by J. Ossanna at Bell Telephone Laboratories in the early 1970s. Its functions include line fill, justification, hyphenation, footnotes, headers, footers, page numbering, list numbering, and centering.

Also see *troff.*

n-tuple

See *tuple.*

null char•ac•ter

(Data management)

A character that operations treat as indicating no information or referring to nothing, often used to indicate uninitialized, unused, or non-matching fields or parts of fields. ASCII has a non-printing null character with value 0, not to be confused with the printing zero character.

null field

(Data management)

An empty field, in contrast to one containing zero. Not all database programs differentiate, but the distinction is important. Null means lack of information, whereas zero is a value. For instance, during column averaging, null fields will not be included; however, if all empty fields are presumed to contain zero, they will be included. Null fields often mean that information such as age, year of birth, address, or price is not available or not reported. Taking the value to be zero is then obviously incorrect and will make statistics and comparisons unrealistic.

The distinction between nulls and zeros may be the subject of a policy decision. For example, one might decide to treat failure to take or complete a test (a null value) as equivalent to a score of zero for the calculation of an overall rating, although not for computing test statistics.

Also see *field*.

null state•ment

See *statement*.

null string

(Programming)

A string that contains no data, although it may include a terminator (such as a null character in the C language) or a length indicator (in Pascal).

Also see *string*.

nu•mer•ic

(Data management; Programming)

adj. Consisting of numbers or containing a number. A numeric field or variable could specify, for example, a person's age, weight, height, or number of children. Sometimes used to describe data that can be operated on arithmetically, unlike identification numbers, telephone numbers, street numbers, or postal zones (such as U.S. Zip Codes).

Also see *alphanumeric; alphabetic*.

nu•mer•ic op•er•a•tor

(Data management)

An operator that performs a mathematical function, such as addition (+), subtraction (-), multiplication (*), division (/), modulus or remainder (% or mod), or exponentiation (^ or **).

Also see *Boolean operator; character operator; relational operator.*

nu•mer•ic pro•ces•sor

See *floating point processor.*

ob•ject

n. That which is owned or controlled.

(Data management)

Data or a data structure. Synonym: as•set. That which is owned or manipulated by a sub•ject or own•er.

Also see *object oriented*.

ob•ject code

See *binary code*.

ob•ject file

(Programming)

File containing object or machine executable code. Produced by a compiler or assembler. MS-DOS object files use the extension **OBJ**. Those in UNIX use the extension **o**.

ob•ject mod•ule

(Programming)

A program module that is assembled or compiled for computer execution. The form is not human-readable. Synonym: **ob•ject pro•gram.**

ob•ject or•i•ent•ed

(Programming)

A type of programming in which code refers to complex objects rather than simple data forms. Objects may include data structures and procedures (called **meth•ods**). For example, an object might be a queue with procedures to enter and remove data, as well as a data structure. Objects that use the same methods are part of the same **class**. A new object or class that is derived from an existing class **in•her•its its** methods. Objects communicate and carry out operations by means of **mes•sages**, which are similar to procedures.

There are many object oriented languages and variants of languages. Among the most popular are Smalltalk and C++. Others include Actor (The Whitewater Group) and Eiffel (Interactive Software Engineering, Inc.). Object-oriented programming is also supported in languages such as Ada and LISP.

Objects often conceal the details of the structures and procedures within them (called **en•cap•su•la•tion**). The precise implementations are thus hidden from outside users and may be changed without affecting the external interface.

Some characteristics of object-oriented programming are present in the HyperCard language HyperTalk. For example, HyperCard stacks, backgrounds, cards, buttons, and fields are objects whose HyperTalk scripts (descriptions) contain method-like **han•dlers** that are functional or cause an action. In a stack PHYSICIANS, to change the format of field 1 on a card from Dr. Jane Doe to Jane Doe, M.D., create the handler

```
on mouseUp

    delete first word of field 1

    put ", M.D." after field 1

end mouseUp
```

HyperTalk objects are not grouped in classes, although cards can share backgrounds.

Also see *HyperTalk*.

ob•ject or•i•ent•ed da•ta•base

See *database, object oriented*.

ob•ject pro•gram

See *object module*.

OBJ file

See *object file*.

OCR

See *optical character recognition*.

oc•tal

(Mathematics)

adj. A number system with base 8. Used in computer programming as an alternative to writing binary numbers; each octal digit represents a group of three binary digits. The valid digits are 0 through 7. Hand calculators and desktop utilities are widely available for octal arithmetic. In recent years, octal has been largely superseded by hexadecimal as a representation method.

Note in the following table that octal and decimal numbers are equivalent through 7, but octal 10 is decimal 8. 8 and 9 are invalid digits in octal.

Decimal	Octal
0	0
1	1
2	2
3	3
4	4
5	5
6	6
7	7
8	10
9	11
10	12

odd par•i•ty

See *parity*.

of•fice doc•u•ment ar•chi•tec•ture and inter-change format

(Data communications)

Standard defining a structure for documents, making them portable among document or text processing systems.

Defined in ISO Standard 8613, and specified in National Institute of Science and Technology (NIST) Applications Portability Profile for U.S. government computer systems.

OLTP

See *on-line transaction processing*.

1NF

See *first normal form*.

one-to-many

adj. Relation in which an element has several values of another element associated with it at any one time, such as a company name that has several associated telephone numbers. Contrast with *many-to-many; one-to-one*.

one-to-one

adj. Unique pairing of elements in a set. A relationship in which each of two values are associated only with each other at any one time. An example is a name and employee number. Contrast with *many-to-many; one-to-many*.

on-line trans•ac•tion pro•cess•ing
(Data management)

Interactive data processing in distributed systems. Abbreviated **OLTP**. Contrast with *batch processing*.

Also see *interactive processing; transaction processing*.

OODBMS

See *database, object oriented*.

OOPS

Object-oriented programming system. See *object-oriented.*

op code

See *operation code*.

op•code

See *operation code*.

open ar•chi•tec•ture
(Computer architecture)

A computer architecture that provides for the easy attachment of add-ons or expansion facilities. The IBM PC and PS/2 lines are typical examples of open architectures in that they have standard buses and card slots for adding new functions or expanding existing ones.

Also a hardware or software design that has been published and is available for public use, although perhaps under licensing agreements.

Also see *architecture; bus.*

open se•cu•ri•ty en•vi•ron•ment

See *security environment.*

open sys•tem
(Computer operations)

Computer system each of whose components can be selected from among many makes and brands. Depends on conformity with standards, such as those for operating systems, ports, interfaces, cables, buses, communications, and printers and other devices.

Also see *connectivity; interoperability.*

op•er•and
(Mathematics)

n. An entity that is operated on, such as an arithmetic or logical quantity or data item.

Also see *operation.*

op•er•at•ing sys•tem
(Computer operations)

Abbreviated **OS**. Software that performs the basic procedures for operating a computer and on which applications software depends for execution. An operating system's kernel or core program assigns memory to applications and data, controls input and output, handles job scheduling, and performs other basic tasks. The OS may also include a file manager and built-in support for graphics, communications, databases, sound production, software development, and other functions. Other names for an operating system (including older terms) are **con•trol pro•gram, ex•ec•u•tive, mas•ter con•trol pro•gram, su•per•vi•sor,** and **mon•i•tor** (usually a simple OS with limited features).

Examples are PC-DOS (IBM PC), MS-DOS (IBM PC compatibles), MVS (IBM mainframes), OS/2 (IBM PS/2), Pick (with a modular format and incorporating database management), VM (IBM mainframes), VMS (VAX), UNIX, and the Macintosh System.

Also see *kernel; utility.*

(MS-DOS)

MS-DOS functions include specifying and managing files, partitioning and formatting a hard disk, formatting floppy disks, configuring the system, organizing directories, directing input and output, and providing commands to run utilities and debug programs.

op•er•a•tion

(Computer operations)

n. A computer action defined by an instruction. May involve moving data from one place to another or performing an arithmetic or logical function. The most common operations are LOAD, MOVE, and STORE.

Also see *operand.*

(Data communications)

A transmission mode, such as full duplex or half duplex, or synchronous or asynchronous.

op•er•a•tion code

(Computer operations)

The part of an assembly or machine language instruction that indicates what function the computer will perform. In assembly language, it is usually indicated by a short mnemonic, such as LD for load, SUB for subtract, or ST for store. Abbreviated as **op code** or **op•code**. Synonym: **in•struc•tion code.**

op•ti•cal char•ac•ter rec•og•ni•tion

(Hardware; Software)

The process of identifying typed or printed alphanumeric characters by viewing them. A common approach is for the program to compare a scanned character to an idealized outline of the character or a map of a specific type style. Some programs allow the user to "teach" them type characteristics, which they store and use. The universality of the outline determines how many different type styles and fonts will be correctly recognized. Abbreviated **OCR.**

Or•a•cle

(Data management)

A distributed relational database management program (Oracle Corporation) primarily intended for minicomputers and UNIX-based workstations. Uses SQL. Includes a forms generator called SQL*Forms.

Versions exist for personal computers (MS-DOS and Macintosh), but primarily so they can be used as stations in distributed systems. Accessible by using shells of several DBMSs as front ends.

Or•ange Book

See *Trusted Computer System Evaluation Criteria.*

ord•er en•try

(Accounting)

Method of keeping track of materials ordered by customers and preparing the accompanying papers, such as packing lists, shipping labels, and summary reports of orders received and sent.

Computerized packages usually require consecutive numbering and other constraints to prevent lost orders, duplication, and other errors and perform automatic cross-checking before a transaction can be committed.

or•thog•o•nal

adj. Literally, at an angle (from the Greek); intersecting. In modern usage, at right angles. Loosely, anything that connects with another, such as an idea, without overlapping it.

Refers to architectures in which design features (such as instruction sets, registers, and addressing modes) can be specified independently.

(Mathematics)

Describing functions or vectors whose sum is zero. Also a linear transformation that leaves distance and length unchanged.

(Graphics)

A three-dimensional view in which one face is parallel to the drawing or screen plane and the others are perpendicular (orthogonal) to it.

(Statistics)

Something that is independent.

(Data management)

Independent, as in the independence of data. A feature of a language that describes the degree of data independence, for example, the greater the independence or or•thog•o•nal•i•ty, the more efficient and powerful the language.

Also see *independence, data.*

OSI Ref•er•ence Mod•el

See *ISO/OSI Reference Model.*

OS/2
(Computer environment)

Operating system developed by Microsoft Corp. in the late 1980s for advanced IBM personal computers (PS/2 series) and compatibles. Single-user, multitasking system that provides a hierarchical file structure, environment control, I/O management, and interprocess communications. Supports more memory and larger disks than MS-DOS, with which it provides limited compatibility through a special feature called the **DOS com•pat•i•bil•i•ty box.** Has a graphical user interface called Presentation Manager that supports multiple windows. Regarded as a successor to MS-DOS for larger, more complex applications running on advanced personal computers.

out•put
(Data communications)

n. Data transmitted.

v. (Jargon)   To transmit data.

adj. Referring to data transmitted, as "output port" or "output procedure."

over•lay
(Data management)

v. To transfer into memory only that part of a program or data needed for immediate execution. Portions are added to memory or replaced as operations demand. Used when the entire program or data exceeds the computer's available memory.

(Data management)

n. A part of a program or data so handled. The programmer must specifically divide the program into overlays and describe how the operating system is to manage them. An alternative is a virtual memory scheme in which the operating system manages units of code and data without programmer intervention.

(Graphics)

n. A line drawing superimposed on another.

overt chan•nel

See *channel, overt.*

own•er

See *object; subject.*

own•er, da•ta•base

See *database administrator.*

PACK

(dBASE)

n. Command that permanently removes from a file all records marked for deletion (that is, ones marked with an asterisk). PACK also reindexes open index files.

A related command is ZAP, which is equivalent to DELETE ALL, followed by PACK. ZAP leaves only the file header, erasing all records.

(R:BASE)

Command that compresses a database to reduce the amount of space it occupies on a disk. PACK frees space allocated to data that was later deleted. Works row by row.

pack•age

(Programming languages)

n. In Ada, a program unit consisting of a declaration, which includes entities that can be used outside of the package, and a body, which contains program implementations, including other packages. The package is a basic unit in which procedures and data structures can be encapsulated.

Also see *Ada; encapsulation.*

pack•ag•ing

n. To put into final form, as a routine or message for execution or transmission.

pack•et

(Data communications)

n. A subdivision of data into uniform-sized blocks for efficient transmission from one computer or communications device to another. Each packet includes data as well as addressing, control, and error detection information. The data is divided into packets at the sending computer or at an intermediate exchange and reassembled at the receiving device. Packets must also contain sequencing information, as they may be received in an order different from that in which they were sent.

The amount of data in a packet depends on the communications protocol being used. For instance, the XModem protocol transmits 128 data bytes per packet, whereas YModem sends 1024 bytes.

Pack•et switch•ing is the routing of packets over communications channels that are dedicated only during the actual transmission. That is, the channels may serve different connections at different times, like a telephone network. The purpose is to increase transmission efficiency.

A network using this method is called a **packet-switched da•ta net•work (PSDN)**.

Also see *frame; ISO/OSI Reference Model; packet-switched data network.*

pack•et as•sem•bler/dis•as•semb•ler

(Data communications)

Abbreviated **PAD**. Software that divides data into packets for transmission on a packet switched data network and combines received data packets.

Also see *packet; packet-switched data network.*

pack•et-switched da•ta net•work

(Data communications)

Abbreviated **PSDN**. A network using packet-switching according to CCITT Standard X.25. An example is Telenet (US Sprint).

Also see *packet; X.25.*

pack•et switch•ing

See *packet.*

PAD

See *packet assembler/disassembler.*

page de•scrip•tion lan•guage
(Output formatting)

Language used to describe a page of text, illustrations, or a combination to a printer. Examples are PostScript and Standard Generalized Markup Language (SGML).

Some applications programs, such as word processors, provide formats for writing the text file in such a language. Or the language commands may be added manually to a text file.

page frame

See *frame*.

page lay•out pro•gram
(Output formatting)

An application that combines word processing with manipulation of large blocks of imported text and graphics to produce camera ready copy for publishing. Examples include Ventura Publisher (Xerox) and PageMaker (Aldus). Commonly used to produce newsletters, reports, technical articles, brochures, catalogs, advertisements, slides, magazines, and books.

Typically provides a blank page form, rulers, drawing tools, text editing commands, master pages (for basic formatting), tools for changing the size of a graphic (sizing) or using only part of one (cropping), and typesetting tools (such as kerning, the moving of individual letters by very small distances to the left or right for aesthetic reasons). Allows importing of formatted text and illustrations, and preparation for printing on laser printers and typesetting equipment.

Clear distinctions between word processors and page layout programs have blurred as some word processors have added desktop publishing features.

Also see *desktop publishing*.

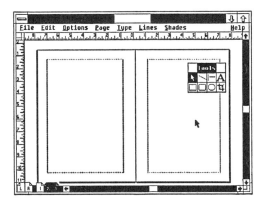

page•set
(Data management)

n. In DB2, the physical structure or data set for storage of tables and indexes.

Also see *tablespace.*

paint pro•gram
(Graphics)

An application for producing graphic images filled with colors, shades of grey, textures, or a combination, the equivalent of a painting. Used for producing commercial and artistic works other than line drawings.

The image consists of pixels (picture elements) or cells into which the screen is divided, a process known as raster or bit-mapped graphics. The color, grey shade, or texture assigned by the user during painting to each pixel can be stored in memory. The smaller the pixels, the higher an image's resolution or the sharper and more distinct it is.

For a different method of placing images on the screen and in memory, contrast with *draw program.*

Also see *raster graphics.*

par•a•digm

n. An extraordinarily clear or comprehensive example of a class; an archetype. Synonym: *model*, though paradigm may have greater cachet, because its use has been less widespread. Often appears in the form "programming paradigms."

Par•a•dox
(Data management)

A relational database management program (Borland International) for personal computers. Provides an application language, and permits creation of templates and scripts. Permits querying by example through the use of check-off boxes.

(See illustration under *query by example.*)

par•al•lel in•ter•face
(Data communications)

Hardware used to connect devices that transfer data in parallel, that is, more than one data bit at a time. Contrast with *serial interface.*

par•al•lel port

(Data communications)

An I/O port used for parallel data transmission. For example, the IBM PC's LPT1 (PRN), LPT2, and LPT3 devices are often called parallel ports.

Contrast with *serial port*.

par•al•lel pro•cess•ing

(Computer operations)

The use of multiple processors to simultaneously perform different sequences of instructions or operate on different sets of data. There are many different approaches and classifications. For example, systems may be classified as single-instruction, multiple-data (SIMD); multiple-instruction, single-data (MISD); or multiple-instruction, multiple-data (MIMD). Other approaches include array processors, data flow systems, and pipeline systems.

Some computers use a few processors, each of which operates relatively independently, on a large segment of the program; this approach is called coarse granularity. Others use many closely communicating processors, each of which completes a small part of the program. Referred to as massively parallel processing or fine granularity. One common architecture is called distributed memory, or cube based, because of the way the processors are connected, in the geometric shape of a **hy•per•cube**.

Also see *hypercube*.

par•al•lel trans•mis•sion

(Data communications)

Transmission in which more than one data bit is sent at a time. Contrast with *serial transmission*.

The method of data transmission within a computer. Also a common method of communication between a personal computer and a printer.

pa•ram•e•ter

n. Quantity or value on which measurement or decisions can be based. For example, the size of a computer memory may determine how much data will be loaded at one time.

par•ent

(Data management)

n. In a tree data structure, a node connected by branches to a node or nodes below it (child nodes).

Also in an alternative to indexing, a database file used to organize the response to a query for data from another (child) file through the use of pointers.

Also a process that creates another process.

Also see *branch; child; node; tree.*

par•i•ty
(Computer operations)

n. An error-checking method involving an extra bit that makes the number of binary ones in a set of bits either even (**even parity**) or odd (**odd parity**). This extra bit is called the **parity bit.** Parity allows for the detection (but not correction) of single-bit errors.

Common terminology is to refer to determining the value of the parity bit as **parity gen•er•a•tion** and to the testing of its value as **parity check•ing.** Incorrect parity is reported as a **parity er•ror.** Also sometimes called a **re•dun•dan•cy check.** Parity can be applied either by bytes (**hor•i•zon•tal**) or to the same bit position in a group of bytes (**ver•ti•cal**).

par•i•ty bit

See *bit; parity.*

par•i•ty check•ing

See *parity.*

par•i•ty er•ror

See *parity.*

par•i•ty gen•er•a•tion

See *parity.*

parse

v. To analyze or divide something into its structural or functional components. For example, to divide a sentence into its verb, subject, object, prepositional phrases, or other parts of speech and grammatical structures. Applied to text input to programs.

(Programming languages)

To analyze a program, such as during compilation.

n. Such an analysis or division.

pars•er
(Programming languages)

n. A program or routine that analyzes or parses a program.

par•ti•tion

v. To divide a whole into independent elements or sections.

n. An independent section of a whole. Also a barrier or wall between independent elements or sections.

(Data management)

Often used to refer to an area of memory dedicated to a specific purpose. For example, in DB2, a part of a data set containing between one and four gigabytes of data.

Also refers to an area of a hard disk set aside for use by a particular operating system, such as MS-DOS or UNIX.

par•ti•tioned ta•ble•space

See *tablespace*.

part•ner•ship

n. A cooperative relationship defined by law or rules.

(Data management)

An entity relationship.

Pas•cal
(Computer languages)

n. Structured high-level programming language developed by Niklaus Wirth (ETH-Zurich) in the 1960s and early 1970s for the systematic teaching of programming. Features include error-checking, diverse data types, strong typing, and programming structures. A descendent of ALGOL (ALGOrithmic Language). A particularly popular version is Turbo Pascal for personal computers (Borland International).

Also see *ALGOL; language, procedure-oriented*.

Defined in ISO Standard 7185 and American National Standard X3.97-1983.

Named for Blaise Pascal, 17th century French mathematician and developer of a calculating machine.

Extensions include Concurrent Pascal for concurrent systems and Extended Pascal.

pass•ive da•ta dic•tion•ar•y

See *data dictionary*.

pass•word

n. An agreed-upon set of alphanumeric characters required for entry to a facility or passage through an area.

(Security)

A character string required to verify a user's identification before access to a computer system, file, or data is granted. For example, most electronic mail systems require both an identification name or number and a password as part of the log-on procedure before allowing someone to send or receive messages.

Also see *identification; log*.

path

(Data management)

n. In a tree data structure, the unique route to a node.

Also see *node; tree*.

In tree-structured directories, the chain of directories from a starting point (usually the root directory) to a specific directory or file. For example, the PATH specification determines where MS-DOS will search for files, as in

PATH = \USR; \USR\BIN; \USR\FILES

PATH tells the computer how to find specified executable files. Here the root directory is USR, and the executable files are located in the subdirectories BIN and FILES.

MS-DOS applies PATH only to command or batch files, whereas UNIX and some DOS utilities apply it to data files also.

The term **path•ing** is sometimes used to describe the ability of programs to handle path specifications. They can then use files outside their own local directories.

Also see *directory*.

(Data communications)

The route over which a data packet is transmitted to its destination.

PC

See *personal computer*.

PC-DOS

(Computer environment)

IBM's version of MS-DOS (Microsoft Corp.) for personal computers.

Also see *MS-DOS*.

PDES

(File formats; Graphics)

Product Data Exchange Specification. Standard file format primarily for CAD/CAM product description. Records a product's shape and dimensions, materials, performance specifications, and finished form. Intended to be portable so it can accompany the product from design to maintenance during use. The format's development is controlled by PDES, Inc., which is owned by a group of industrial firms.

STEP is a similar European specification under development.

Also see *IGES*, of which PDES is an outgrowth.

PDL

See *page description language*. Also means *program design language* in software engineering.

peep•hole opti•miz•er

(Programming languages)

A compiler optimizer that works on basic blocks, making such improvements as eliminating unnecessary or redundant instructions, reorganizing loops, and optimizing register usage.

peer-to-peer

(Data management)

Application processing in a distributed system that moves from one processor to another, such as from a personal computer to a mainframe, as opposed to communication from a terminal to a mainframe.

Sometimes used imprecisely as a synonym for program-to-program, as in Advanced Program-to-Program Communications, IBM's session layer protocol.

per•mis•sion

See *grant*.

per•sis•tence

n. Continuation of something unchanged beyond a specified or expected time.

(Programming)

The ability of an object or relationship to last beyond program execution.

Considered a desirable characteristic of languages used in database management and in data models.

per•son•al com•put•er (PC)

(Hardware)

Small computer first developed in the middle to late 1970s, originally intended to be used for individual work, with all programs and data stored on small (floppy) disks over which the user could retain control. Philosophy of use was contrasted to that of mainframes, with centralized data storage and program control and with user access only through dropoff points or remote terminals.

Now able to work both individually and connected to other computers of all sizes. The market is dominated by MS-DOS compatible machines, such as those made by IBM and Compaq. Such machines are often called PC's, PC-compatibles, PC clones, or IBM (PC) compatibles. Specific models include PC's, XT's, AT's, and PS/2's. The other major family of personal computers is the Apple Macintosh series. An alternative term is **mi•cro•com•put•er.**

per•son•nel se•cu•ri•ty

See *security.*

phys•i•cal

adj. Relating to the actual, rather than the theoretical or logical.

(Computer environment)

Dependent on the local environment and its restrictions, specific hardware and software, policies, and idiosyncrasies.

(Computer operations; Data communications; Data management; Hardware)

The actual machine being used or data being entered and manipulated, in contrast to the theoretical or logical design for such hardware and software. For example, a physical database consists of the data entered into the designed or logical database structure (a process called instantiation). Also the physical machine is the actual hardware, whereas a virtual machine is the one the user sees.

Similarly, a physical communications network is the actual connection of hardware and software, based on the **logical network** design. And a computer is the embodiment of the design or computer architecture. Also a physical device or physical address is the actual device or memory address used, as opposed to the logical or virtual one referred to in the program.

Contrast with *logical*.

Also see *virtual*.

phys•i•cal ad•dress

See *physical*.

phys•i•cal da•ta in•de•pen•dence

See *independence, data*.

phys•i•cal de•vice

See *physical*.

phys•i•cal rec•ord

See *block*.

phys•i•cal se•cu•ri•ty

See *security*.

phys•i•cal struc•ture

See *model, physical*.

phys•i•cal to•pol•o•gy

See *topology*.

PIN num•ber

(Security)

Unique personal identification number allowing a user access to computer data. Common examples are user codes for automated teller machine transactions, electronic fund transfer, and checkwriting at supermarket checkout counters.

Also see *identifier*.

pipe
(MS-DOS; UNIX)

v. A facility that directs the output of one command to be the input of another. The operator is |. The two connected commands form a **pipe•line**. In practice, the operating system creates a temporary file to hold the intermediate results.

The operator may also be used with a filter command, so that the output from the first command is transformed.

Also see *filter*.

n. Diminutive of pipeline.

pipe•line
(UNIX)

n. Two commands linked by the operator |.

Also see *pipe*.

(Computer operations)

n. Operations in the process of being performed.

(Hardware)

adj. As in **pipe•line pro•ces•sor**, which performs several operations at once on different operands. The operations form part of an overall procedure, much like workstations on an assembly line. Compare with *parallel processor*.

pipe•lin•ing
(Computer operations)

n. Dividing an operation into several stages and performing them all at the same time on different operands in assembly-line fashion. Often refers specifically to instruction execution schemes that fetch, decode, and execute different instructions simultaneously. The result is much higher throughput as soon as the pipeline is filled initially, and as long as it can be kept filled.

Also a technique to increase a computer's speed by dividing complex operations into simpler ones that can be executed simultaneously, such as mathematical calculations. Many signal processing tasks (such as spectral analysis, image compression, and filtering) can be performed in this way.

pip•ing
(MS-DOS; UNIX)

n. Using the output from one command or operation as the input to another. Synonym: **chaining** (of programs).

PJ/NF

See *fifth normal form.*

PL/I

(Computer languages)

n. Acronym for Programming Language One, but uses the roman numeral I, meaning "one". A procedure-oriented, high-level programming language developed in the 1960s for the IBM System 360, based on characteristics of ALGOL, COBOL, and FORTRAN. Designed for use in both business and scientific computing. PL/M is a microcomputer version used in embedded systems. Little used otherwise, except on mainframes.

Also see *language, procedure-oriented.*

Defined in American National Standards X3.53-1976 and X3.74-1981.

plat•form

(Computer environment)

A brand or model of computer, operating system, or other underlying software and hardware. Software is said to run or require a particular platform, and a conversion is necessary to port it to another.

point

n. A place or location.

(Accounting)

A percentage, such as the interest rate on a loan. Also a fee calculated as a percentage of a loan. For example, a lender may charge two points (a 2% fee) to arrange a home mortgage.

(Mathematics)

A geometric location determined by a set of coordinates.

(Output formatting)

A measure of type height. In the American Point System, used in the United States, Canada, Mexico, and Great Britain, 1 point = 1/72 in. or about 0.35 mm. Other countries use the Didot point, which is minutely larger. Abbreviated as pt.

Also see *font.*

point-and-click

See *point-and shoot.*

point-and-shoot

(Computer environment)

Selection of a screen option by pointing at it with a mouse or other pointing device and clicking a button. An alternative to selection from a menu or via a keyboard command. Probably borrowed from photography. Synonym: *point-and-click*.

point•er

(Data management)

A storage location (disk, memory, or register) that contains an address, rather than data. For example, a disk block number in an index may point to the memory location of a record. There may be multiple levels of pointers, as well as pointers to complex data structures or functions.

point-of-sale (POS) system

(Applications)

A system of computer hardware and software for retail sales. Each transaction at a sales terminal is automatically entered into a central computer, credited to or debited from accounting ledgers, and used to adjust inventory. Often used in conjunction with universal product codes marked on items.

Also see *universal product code*.

poll

(Data communications)

n. Request for current status. For example, a network controller may request a node's identification and status at specified intervals. Polling permits the node to send or receive data. Polling refers to methods requiring a computer or controller to request or examine the status of devices, rather than having it communicated directly.

Also see *network*.

poly•gon

(Mathematics)

n. A multisided two-dimensional shape, such as a triangle, rectangle, or hexagon.

(Graphics)

A multisided object that can be saved and manipulated as an entity. For example, it may be handled as a layer, filled, moved, or combined with other objects.

poly•in•stan•ti•a•tion

n. Derived from instantiation (a concrete example of a universal or an abstraction) plus poly (more than one).

(Security)

Multiple sets of facts with the same key. For example, a secure database may have a Top Secret entry and a conflicting Secret entry. Technically a failure of data integrity and an inconsistency with the relational model.

po•ly•mor•phism

n. The ability to take different shapes or forms.

(Programming languages)

In object oriented programming, the ability of objects from different classes to respond to the same message.

pop-out menu

See *menu*.

pop•up menu

See *menu*.

port

(Data communications)

n. A hardware connection between a computer or central processing unit and a peripheral device, such as a printer. The basic addressable unit of the computer's I/O section.

(Computer operations)

v. Referring to an application, to move it from one computer to another or to make it capable of running on a different computer or in a different environment.

Also see *platform; portable*.

por•ta•ble

(Computer operations)

n. Capable of running on different computer systems or in different environments. For example, operating systems such as MS-DOS and UNIX can run on many different models of computers from many different manufacturers. The same applies to some database management systems, such as Oracle.

Also see *platform*.

POSIX
(Computer environment)

UNIX-like operating system defined for portability among platforms. Name is derived from Portable Operating System + UNIX.

Defined in IEEE Std. 1003.1 - 1988.

An enhancement, Extended POSIX, is used by the U.S. government.

Also see *Extended POSIX; UNIX.*

post
(Accounting)

n. To enter a transaction into an account or ledger. Unposted transactions may be deleted, modified, or corrected without affecting permanent records or causing audit trail entries.

pre•ci•sion
(Computer operations)

n. The length of the data string that can be maintained accurately during floating point mathematical operations.

pred•i•cate

n. In a logical proposition, a property, characteristic, or relation of a subject. For example, hardness of a chair in "the chair is hard."

Also see *subject.*

pred•i•cate cal•cu•lus
(Logic)

A symbolic system for analysis of logical propositions. Can be used in constructing database management systems and knowledge-based systems.

pre•pro•ces•sor
(Data management; Programming languages)

n. Routine used to prepare a program for compilation. Often allows features such as defined variables, conditional compilation, and macros. Serves as a convenience and time-saver for the programmer, adding features the compiler lacks. The preprocessor generally does direct text substitution without involving actual syntactic analysis.

(DB2)

Used to convert a query written in an application language to a style that can be executed by the database manager, such as converting SQL statements into comments and creating a database request module.

(C)

The symbol # plus a command at the beginning of a line invokes the preprocessor for defining constants, inserting macros, and including file constants. For example,

    #include <stdio.h>

causes the current program to find a header file named stdio.h, which is located either in the current or other directories, and to substitute it for the line. This saves the programmer from having to enter a long list of definitions.

Conditional compilation is also possible with

    #if
    #else
    #endif

or

    #if
    #endif

pre•view
(Output formatting)

n. A feature that allows the user to examine output on the screen before commiting it to final form, such as an actual printed copy. Common in desktop publishing packages, report writers, spreadsheets, and word processors.

pri•ma•ry col•ors
(Graphics)

Basic colors of which all others are composed.

The primary colors of light are red, green, and blue, which are combined to produce images or displayed on a television set or **RGB mon•i•tor.** These are called **add•i•tive colors,** since others are obtained by adding them together and white is the sum of all three.

To make negatives for color printing, the primary colors are yellow, magenta, cyan (blue-green), and black. A separate negative is made for each, and each is printed separately; the quality of the final version depends on the accuracy with which the ink layers are superimposed. These are called **sub•trac•tive colors,** since others are obtained by removing them and white is the absence of all three.

For pigments, the primary colors are red, yellow, and blue.

pri•ma•ry in•dex

See *index*.

pri•ma•ry key

See *key*.

pri•ma•ry stor•age

See *memory*.

prim•i•tive

(Graphics)

n. A basic form, such as a point, character, or line. Also a basic operation, such as drawing a line, placing a point on the screen, or setting a color.

(Data management; Programming)

A single letter, symbol, pseudocode element, or other unit of data that cannot be divided. A term derived from the field of linguistics. Also refers to a basic operation that cannot be divided or interrupted; it often does one step in a complex function such as a graphics, data structure manipulation, database, operating system, or string manipulation task.

Also see *data type*.

prin•ci•pal

See *subject*.

print•er font

See *font*.

print serv•er

See *server*.

priv•i•lege

(Security)

n. Degree of access. A user or subject is usually granted the least amount of access (called **least privilege**) to the system required to perform authorized operations.

Also see *access; access control; access permission; grant; granularity; isolation*.

prob•a•bi•lis•tic

See *stochastic*.

prob•a•bi•lis•tic da•ta•base

(Data management)

Database model that permits relational, probabilistic (uncertain), and "fuzzy" (vague) data. A set of probabilistic systems or distributions. Also a generalization of a relational database.

prob•a•bil•i•ty

(Mathematics)

The likelihood that an event will occur, measured in terms of the ratio of the number of expected occurrences to the total number of possible occurrences.

pro•ce•dur•al lan•guage

See *language, procedure oriented*.

pro•ce•dur•al security

See *security*.

pro•ce•dure

n. Organized method of accomplishing something, for example, step by step.

(Programming)

Routine or function that performs a given task. May be built in, such as mathematical functions, or written by the programmer. Often refers specifically to a routine (such as a sort or string operation) that does not return a single result, as opposed to a function (such as a mathematical operation or search) that does.

Also see *language, procedure oriented; method*.

pro•ce•dure file

(Programming)

A file consisting of commands to be submitted to a program for execution. Sometimes a direct substitute for submission from an input device (such as a keyboard). May involve more advanced language facilities, such as conditional and loop statements. Also called a **batch file** (MS-DOS), **com•mand file**, or **script** (UNIX).

pro•ce•dure or•i•ent•ed lan•guage

See *language, procedure oriented*.

pro•cess

n. A series of steps, actions, or events leading to a conclusion.

(Computer operations)

A program in a state ready for execution. But note that the term multiprocessing refers to multiple **processors**, not to multiple processes (which is **multitasking**).

Pro•duct Da•ta Ex•change Spe•ci•fi•ca•tion

See *PDES*.

pro•gram

(Programming)

n. A sequence of instructions to be executed by a computer, producing a desired result.

v. To write computer instructions. Also to enter operating instructions into a computer's memory.

Also used adjectivally, as in "program development" or "program design."

pro•gram flow•chart

See *flowchart*.

pro•gram•mer

(Programming)

A person who develops a solution to a problem or a routine for another activity that can be executed on a computer, then describes it in a language that a computer can understand and execute.

The term **soft•ware en•gi•neer** is also used, sometimes to indicate a person who handles all aspects of software development rather than just coding. Software engineer is more often applied to those working on embedded or large-scale systems.

Also a device for fixing the contents of read-only memories (a PROM programmer). This usage means that hardware-oriented sources often refer to a software developer by the seemingly redundant term "software programmer."

pro•gram•ming by mod•i•fi•ca•tion

See *differential programming*.

pro•gram stub

See *top-down.*

pro•gram test•ing

Synonym: soft•ware testing (the usual term). See *validation.*

pro•gram ver•i•fi•ca•tion

See *debugging.*

pro•jec•tion

n. A throwing outward. A representation of something in another form.

(Data management)

A relational operator that decomposes a relation or table into specified sets of columns or attributes. Selection performs the same operation for tuples or rows.

pro•jec•tion-join nor•mal form

See *fifth normal form.*

PRO•LOG

(Programming languages)

Contraction of PROgramming in LOGic. Programming language based on relational calculus that uses logic rules to prove relationships among objects by backward chaining. Developed in the early 1970s by A. Colmerauer and others. Programs are composed of terms. Each term may be a constant, either an integer or an atom (non-integer); a structure, an object composed of other objects or components; or a variable. PROLOG is used in relational database management, various areas of artificial intelligence, mathematical and other logical problem solving, biochemistry, and design automation. Many versions are available.

Described by A. Colmerauer and others in "Etude et realisation d'un système PROLOG." Convention de Recherche IRIA-Sesori No. 77030, 1973. A standard reference is W. F. Clocksin and C.S. Mellish, *Programming in Prolog*, 3rd ed. (New York, Springer-Verlag, 1987).

Also see *backward chaining; predicate calculus; relational calculus.*

pro•to•col

n. A set of rules or specifications.

(Data communications)

A set of conventions governing the format and timing of data transfers.

Hardware protocols may include modem compatibility and, for networks, type of wire or cable.

Popular software protocols include binary synchronous communication (BSC), HDLC, and SDLC. The term **da•ta-link con•trol** is older but equivalent. Protocols for use on networks include Transmission Control Program/Internet Program (TCP/IP) and Manufacturing Automation Protocol (MAP).

Software protocols for modem transmissions usually include the transmission rate (baud), whether transmission is one-way or two-way (half or full duplex), parity, character length in bits, and number of stop bits.

Software protocols for networks must cover every aspect of the interaction between sending and receiving devices, including creating data units of the proper length, network requirements, establishment and termination of transmission paths, error checking, and addressing. Examples include TCP/IP and the ISO/OSI Reference Model.

pro•to•col an•a•lyz•er

(Data communications)

Diagnostic tool for local area networks, permitting traffic monitoring to improve network efficiency and detection of causes of error packets and other faulty data transmission. Also called **net•work analyzer.**

Also see *local area network.*

pro•to•typ•ing

(Data management; Hardware; Software)

Creation of a first version of a machine or piece of software based on a completed design or logical structure.

Rap•id prototyping is the interactive creation of the design and the first version, permitting experience based on actual use to be included in the design. This process is meant to produce an error-free finished product faster than traditional methods. Can also be used in creating information or other systems. See *information engineering; information systems.*

PSDN

See *packet-switched data network.*

pseu•do•code
(Programming)
n. An outline of a computer program that states the purpose of each module or line of code. Pseudocode is useful in designing a program and as documentation. It often resembles a computer language (most frequently ALGOL or Pascal), but cannot actually be translated by a compiler. A formalized pseudocode is called a program design language (PDL).

pub•lish•ing, desktop
See *desktop publishing*.

pseu•do table
See *view*.

pub•lic key en•cryp•tion
See *encryption*.

pull•down menu
(Computer environment)
A screen menu that appears under its title when selected, perhaps with a mouse or by entering a keyboard command.

Also see *menu*.

QBE

See *query by example*.

QMF

See *Query Management Facility*.

qual•i•ty as•sur•ance

The probability that a device, system, or object will perform as intended during testing.

Also see *reliability*.

QUEL

See *Ingres*.

que•ry
(Data management)

n. A request for information from a database user. The information may include instructions, status, or data. The query must specify the limits on the information and criteria needed to find and display it.

Queries may be structured before execution (fixed logic; programming style), formulated through a series of questions and answers (cue-response or promoting; English language style), derived from examples, or specified by a combination or variation of these techniques.

v. To request information from a database.

(dBASE)

For example:

> @...SAY displays user-formatted data.
>
> @...GET displays variables for editing and accepts input.
>
> CREATE QUERY creates a filter condition and stores it in a query (qry) file.

Also see *browse; query by example*.

(Data communications)

n. A request for current status.

Also see *poll*.

que•ry, ad hoc

(Data management)

A database query initiated directly by a user, rather than indirectly through an application that provides menus or other structures for formulating it.

que•ry by ex•am•ple (QBE)

(Data management)

Query-by-Example is a 4th generation language developed by M. Zloof of IBM in the late 1970s. It allows a user to request information (query) from a database by means of an example record rather than a command. The basis for the application QBE (IBM). Defined in Zloof's paper, "Query-by-Example: A Data Base Language." *IBM Sys. J. 16*, 324 (1978).

Also used generically to describe similar interfaces. dBASE IV and Paradox are among databases that provide interfaces in the QBE style.

(Paradox)

For example, the user selects ASK from the main menu and enters a table name to display a query form showing all the fields. The user then checks off the ones to be displayed and fills in examples of the information wanted. A query form for a table ADDRESSES that asks for the names and addresses of people with telephone numbers in area code 415 would look like this:

ADDRESSES	Name	Address	Area Code	Phone No.	Occupation
	✔	✔	✔ 415		

Query Management Facility

(Data management)

Abbreviated **QMF**. IBM software for querying and report writing with the relational database management systems DB2 and SQL/DS.

query op•ti•mi•za•tion

(Data management)

Making efficient use of computer time during database queries, especially in relational and multiuser systems. Effective strategies depend on the nature, size, and design of the data, system, and queries. But they may include stored queries, timing of updates, use of an appropriate query language, and in relational systems, the extent to which the actual relations embody the conceptual model.

queue

n. A waiting line organized so that items are removed in the same order in which they were entered.

Also called a first-in, first-out (FIFO) buffer. See *first-in, first-out*.

(Mathematics)

Branch of mathematics dedicated to the analysis of such systems is **queu•ing the•ory**. It is often used to analyze networks, operating systems, and shared databases.

(Computer operations)

Items such as processes, data, or transactions waiting in line to be processed in order of receipt or entry.

(Data communications)

A series of messages waiting to be transmitted in order of receipt, such as text files to a printer or data across a network.

v. To place data in such waiting lines. The term **en•queue** is also used.

queu•ing the•ory

See *queue*.

RAM

n. Memory that can be both read and changed in normal operation. Originally an acronym for random-access memory, meaning all locations could be accessed in the same amount of time, as opposed to the serial access of a tape. Now refers simply to ordinary memory. A **RAM disk** is an area of RAM that special software treats as though it were a (very fast) disk.

RAM disk

See *RAM*.

RAMP

See *Risk Analysis and Management Program.*

rap•id pro•to•typ•ing

See *prototyping*.

ras•ter graph•ics
(Graphics)

Method of representing a graphic image on a screen by designating its position on a grid, pixel by pixel, with bits representing each pixel. The smaller the pixels and the more bits per pixel, the higher the image resolution and the more detail that can be included. However, when they are defined by specific screen positions, images are difficult to modify in size, attitude, and shape. The creation of sharp edges usually requires the image to be modified (traced) by a vector graphics program.

Also called **bit mapped graphics.**

The type of graphics produced by paint programs.

Contrast with *vector graphics*.

Also see *paint program*.

raw

adj. Unprocessed or uncooked.

(Data management; Statistics)

Unprocessed or unsystematized data. An example is partial election returns reported before all polling places have completed their tallies.

Also data converted from analog to digital, but otherwise unprocessed.

(UNIX)

Mode of terminal data processing in which bytes are not assembled into lines (called cooked), but are handled one-by-one. Raw mode is a synonym for unbuffered mode.

Also see *buffer; cooked*.

R:BASE

(Data management)

A relational database management program for personal computers (Microrim). Characterized by extensive use of menus to create databases and enter commands. Permits query by example. Provides a command language based on SQL. Derived from the RIM database developed at Boeing Aircraft Co. for use on large computers.

RDBMS

See *relational database management system*.

read

(Computer operations)

v. To copy data from secondary storage or an input device into the computer's memory. Synonym: *load*.

Also see *write*.

read ac•cess

See *access; grant*.

read lock

Synonym: *read access*. See *access; grant*.

read-mod•i•fy-write cy•cle

See *update*.

realm

See *area*.

re•al-time

In synchronization with the actual occurrence of events.

re•al-time con•trol

Control of operations in synchronization with the occurrence of events, as in guidance, power plant or chemical plant management, robotics, or military systems (fire control or communications).

(Computer operations)

Execution of instructions by a computer as they are issued, especially the processing of data as soon as it is entered, rather than storing it for later processing.

Also the ability of a user to intervene in the execution of a series of instructions without stopping the process.

rec•ord

(Data management)

n. A grouping of associated data fields in a database file. For example, each record in a file ADDRESS BOOK may contain fields for name, address, and telephone number. Several records comprise a flat file or a relational database table. Synonym: *row*.

rec•ord lock

(Security)

Exclusive ownership by one user or process of a file in a multiuser database for updating or some other operation. A lock prevents other users from performing a simultaneous conflicting operation or reading obsolete data. In dBASE III PLUS, for record modification, the locking process requires the read-modify-write sequence to be a single operation.

Also see *field lock; file lock; lock; unlock*.

re•cov•er•a•bi•li•ty

(Computer operations; Data management)

Provision within a system for restoring functionality without loss of applications or data in case of failure or error. May include backing up of data (secure storage of duplicates) and methods of reconstructing damaged or destroyed data from earlier versions.

re•cov•ery, da•ta

(Data management)

The process of salvaging or restoring data after a system crash, disk damage or failure, or user error.

Also see *integrity, data.*

re•cur•sion

n. A process in which an operation is performed using its own previous result. Repetition.

An example is repeated calculation of a mathematical function, such as

$$x + 2 = x$$

If the initial value of x is 3, the first operation is

$$3 + 2 = 5$$

giving x a new value of 5. The second operation is

$$5 + 2 = 7$$

and so on.

This type of process may be used in programming and database models. Often refers specifically to a subroutine that calls itself as part of its execution; typical uses are in sorts, searches, and probability functions.

Also see *recursive.*

re•cur•sive

adj. Referring to a repetitive process that calls itself as part of its execution, such as an algorithm, program, routine, or query. Differs from **it•er•a•tive,** which is repetitive but not self-defined.

Also see *recursion.*

(Programming)

A recursive routine may be **di•rect,** calling itself from a subroutine, or **in•di•rect,** calling another routine that in turn calls the original routine.

(Data management)

A cyclic relationship in network databases, in which a record is both the owner of a set and a member of it.

Also see *Network Database Language*.

re•di•rec•tion
(Data management; Programming)

The ability to switch the input or output of a process from its standard source or destination to another. For example, one may redirect a process to obtain its input from a disk file or remote communications line, rather than from the keyboard. Similarly, one may redirect its output to a disk file or printer, rather than to the screen.

re•duced in•struc•tion set com•put•er

See *RISC*.

re•dun•dan•cy check

See *parity*.

ref•er•ence mon•i•tor
(Security)

Concept of an operating system that controls subjects' access to objects, checking whether each use or entry is permitted by the security policy. It may be implemented as a security kernel. To be successful, it must be foolproof, tamperproof, and verifiable.

The actual implementation is called a reference validation mechanism (RVM).

Also see *completeness; isolation; kernel; reference validation mechanism; risk assessment; verification*.

ref•er•ence val•i•da•tion mech•a•nism (RVM)
(Security)

Component of a security system that implements a reference monitor. Implementation can be centralized, through a security kernel, or through a state machine, which passes a use request or entry to the next state if it meets specified conditions.

Also see *reference monitor; security kernel; state machine*.

ref•er•en•tial con•straint

See *constraint*.

ref•er•en•tial in•teg•ri•ty

See *integrity, data.*

reg•is•ter

n. High-speed local storage unit within a CPU or I/O device. A group of registers is a register set or register file.

re•gis•ter file

See *register.*

re•gis•ter set

See *register.*

reg•is•ter win•dows

See *SPARC.*

re•in•dex

(Data management)

To rebuild an index after changes to the database.

(dBASE)

The REINDEX command rebuilds the indexes to an open file, using the original keys and specifications.

In dBASE IV, REINDEX also rebuilds multiple indexes.

Also see *index.*

re•la•tion

n. An association or connection specified qualitatively or quantitatively.

(Data management)

A link. An association between data items or groups of data (such as tables, rows, tuples, records, or key fields). May be specified in the data model or created with relational operators, such as join, union, and intersection.

Though the term is often identified with the relational database model, it is characteristic of all types.

Also see *database.*

re•la•tion•al al•ge•bra

(Data management)

Algebraic method of devising and characterizing logical relations for relational databases. Uses the logical operators union, intersection, difference, projection, selection, natural join, and Cartesian product.

Defined in C. Parent and S. Spaccapietra, "An Algebra for a General Entity-Relationship Model." *IEEE Trans. on Software Engineering,* 11 (7), July 1985, p. 634.

re•la•tion•al cal•cu•lus

(Data management)

Version of predicate calculus used to define logical relations for relational databases. Languages based on relational calculus include PROLOG, QBE (IBM), QUEL for Ingres, and Structured Query Language (SQL).

Proposed by E. F. Codd in "A Relational Model of Data for Large Shared Data Banks," *CACM,* 13 (6), June 1970.

re•la•tion•al da•ta•base

(Data management)

Database model composed of flat files, associated through established links, called relations. Tables consist of unordered tuples (in the logical model), which are called rows in the physical model. Designed to allow efficient use of many types of data during queries. One means of developing the model and organizing access to the data is by using Structured Query Language (SQL).

The model is characterized by rigorous rules designed to allow unambiguous definition of data and relations. First presented by E.F. Codd in his article, "A Relational Model of Data for Large Shared Data Banks." *CACM,* 13 (6), June 1970. Reprinted in Michael Stonebraker, ed. *Readings in Database Systems* (Palo Alto, CA.: Morgan-Kaufmann, 1988).

Examples are dBASE (Ashton-Tate) and DB2 (IBM).

A modification of the relational model to improve connections and relations among data elements is the **extended relational database** or **entity relationship database.**

Also see *database; entity relationship database; relation; Structured Query Language.*

re•la•tion•al da•ta•base man•age•ment sys•tem

(Data management)

Abbreviated **RDBMS.** Management system for databases built on the relational model.

Also see *database management system; relational database.*

re•la•tion•al op•er•a•tor

(Data management)

An operator that compares values, yielding a true or false (Boolean) result. Typical operators are less than (<), less than or equal to (≤), equal to (=), not equal to (≠), greater than or equal to (≥), and greater than (>). For example:

> 5 ≤ 6 is true

> 9 = 8 is false

Synonym: *comparison operator.*

Also see *Boolean operator; character operator; numeric operator.*

(dBASE)

The structured commands IF, CASE, and DO WHILE use conditions involving relational operators with character, date, and numeric data. For example,

> IF Total ≥ 5000

NOTE: Symbols in languages vary. For example, not equal to is # in dBASE, < > in Pascal, and != in C. Equal to is == in C.

Also see *Appendix A.*

re•la•tion•ship

n. That which connects or provides commonality for individual things, objects, or concepts.

(Data management)

A data object that associates entities.

re•li•a•bil•i•ty

n. The probability that a device, system, or object will perform as intended during a specified time period of normal operations. Often expressed as mean time between failures (MTBF).

Also see *quality assurance.*

re•port

(Data interpretation)

n. Information resulting from a user's manipulation of data, presented in a format offered by the DBMS or one created by the user. For example, the data may be presented in rows or columns or like address labels. A report does not necessarily contain supplementary text, so it may often more closely resemble a table than a business report. The report may be printed, exported to another application, or stored in permanent memory.

Also see *columns format; labels format; rows format.*

Many database programs incorporate report writing. In some cases, add on software called a **report writer** supplements the database program's abilities by providing custom formats or more flexibility in selecting data.

re•port writ•er

See *report.*

re•pos•i•to•ry

(Data management)

An expanded dictionary for distributed DBMSs that includes information about alphanumeric, visual, sound, and other types of data and about the application, which may include an object oriented or graphical user interface. May be specific to a single brand or line of database systems, such as DB2 (IBM).

re•quest•or-serv•er ar•chi•tec•ture

See *client-server architecture.*

re•store

(File management)

n. The loading of an archival file back into the source computer.

Also see *backup.*

(dBASE)

To retrieve variables and erase existing ones. For example, to change to a different set of printer codes, use

        RESTORE FROM newprinterfile

To preserve the existing variables, use

        RESTORE FROM newprinterfile ADDITIVE

re•sults ta•ble

(Data management)

In a relational database management system, a table containing information sought in a query. May be arranged for output as a report and may be restricted as a view.

Also see *report; table; view.*

re•voke

(Security)

v. Withdrawal by the database administrator of an individual's permission to use a database. For specifics, see *grant.*

RGB mon•i•tor

(Hardware)

Analog or digital video monitor that receives separate computer signals for the primary colors red, green, and blue.

Also see *primary colors.*

ring net•work

(Data communications)

A network configuration in which nodes are connected logically in a circular pattern, without a central station.

RISC

(Hardware)

Acronym for Reduced Instruction Set Computer. A computer architecture designed for faster processing through the use of fewer and less complex instructions than conventional processors (called **CISC**, Complex Instruction Set Computer). Additional functions must be performed with software.

RISC processors typically have large register sets, orthogonal structures, and load/store architectures in which only load and store instructions refer to memory addresses (other instructions operate on registers only).

risk

(Statistics)

The chance or probability that a given event will occur. Risks are classified for many different purposes. For example, there are two types of economic risk: speculative, one that can result in profit or loss or neither one, and pure, one that can result only in loss.

(Security)

Computer security risks are pure risks, meaning that the purpose of a security system is to quantify possible losses and minimize the probability of their occurring.

Also see *risk assessment; risk management.*

risk anal•y•sis

Calculation of the vulnerability of a person, group, place, or thing to a hazard or threat. Consists of two elements: the size or severity of each threat, measured in dollars or other relative scale, and the probability that it will occur. Also called **risk as•sess•ment.**

Such quantitative measures are considered superior to qualitative descriptions, such as likely or low, since they mean different orders of magnitude to different people.

Quantitative risk assessment for computer systems, developed by Robert Courtney (then with IBM), is defined in FIPS 65.

(Security)

Enumeration of the possible threats to a computer system and data and their vulnerability to the threats. A requirement for the design of effective computer security.

Also see *security.*

risk anal•y•sis and man•age•ment pro•gram

(Security)

Acronym is **RAMP.** A methodology for performing quantitative risk assessment. Available commercially as IST/RAMP (International Security Technology, Inc.). Evaluates losses from delay, physical damage, fraud, unauthorized disclosure, and theft; also quantifies file sensitivity and the cost of backup.

Also see *risk analysis.*

risk as•sess•ment

See *risk analysis.*

risk man•age•ment

Techniques used to minimize the possibility of losses due to the occurrence of unacceptable risks.

Also see *risk; risk assessment.*

roll•back

(Data management)

A return to the last saved version of a file, because of an uncompleted transaction. For example, the user of an open file may decide not to save a change, or may encounter problems, such as locks, errors, overflows, disk errors, deadlock, or starvation. Rollback obviously requires that the system retain all intermediate results or states.

(dBASE)

In dBASE IV, ROLLBACK negates updates and other changes made during the aborted transaction.

Also see *transaction.*

roll for•ward

(Data management)

After a system failure or data loss, the updating of a backup copy with entries from a transaction log that occurred after the last backup. Synonym: *forward recovery.*

root

(Data management)

The base node of a tree data structure, such as a file directory. The node from which all branches ultimately originate.

Also see *directory; node; tree.*

In MS-DOS, the symbol \ by itself indicates the root directory.

root di•rec•tory

See *directory; root.*

root node

(Data management)

The node on which a data tree is based.

Also see *node; tree.*

rou•tine

(Programming)

n. A computer program or part of a program that accomplishes a task. Also an often used or common set of commands.

Also see *subroutine.*

row

(Data management)

n. In a flat file, a horizontal grouping of associated data fields, such as name, address, and telephone number. In relational databases, the logical form is called a **tu•ple.** Synonym: *record.*

rows for•mat

(Data management)

A report style that presents each record as a row, for example,

Jefferson	Thomas	died 1826
Madison	James	died 1836

Contrast with *columns format; labels format.*

Also see *report.*

RSA en•cryp•tion

See *encryption.*

R*

(Data management)

Pronounced "R-star." Prototype distributed database management system (IBM) for server-to-server operations.

Also see *Starburst.*

RS-232C

(Data communications)

A common serial interface defined by the Electronic Industries Association (EIA). It uses a 25-pin connector. Often used to connect modems, printers, terminals, and other peripheral devices to computers.

rule base

See *knowledge base*.

run time

(Computer operations)

The time at which a program or routine is executed.

run-time li•cense

See *license*.

run-time pack•age

(Applications)

A set of routines that is linked into a user program at run time. It usually includes I/O, mathematical, and other standard functions that most programs need. An important factor is that it often makes the object module much larger than one might expect.

run-time soft•ware

(Applications)

A version of software used as part of an application. For example, an accounting application based on dBASE IV might contain a special run-time version of the base software. Run-time versions often omit program or application development features and other features (such as the user interface) that are assumed by the application.

Also see *license*.

run unit

(Programming)

In COBOL, one or more object programs (executable instructions) that work as a unit during execution.

S

SAA

See *Systems Application Architecture*.

san•i•tize

v. To cleanse or make more acceptable.

(Security)

To prevent unauthorized data from reaching a user. May be performed by a guard processor, sometimes with human assistance.

To filter a data stream or transmission, preventing systems or users from obtaining unauthorized data.

Also see *filter; guard.*

Also to completely delete data from a storage medium.

save

(Computer operations)

v. To copy data from the computer's memory to secondary storage. Synonym: *write.*

Also see *load.*

Also to move data from temporary status into permanent storage after it has been edited or otherwise modified.

scal•able pro•ces•sor ar•chi•tec•ture

See *SPARC*.

sche•ma

n. A conceptual organization, framework, or outline.

(Data management)

Definition of a database, usually in a data description language. A description of its attributes. Synonyms: **ab•stract syn•tax, con•cep•tu•al mod•el, en•ter•prise mod•el.**

A **sub•sche•ma** similarly describes a view.

Also see *database; model; view.*

sche•ma def•i•ni•tion lan•guage

See *Network Database Language.*

sci•en•tif•ic vi•su•al•i•za•tion

See *visualization.*

screen

(Hardware)

n. Video monitor on which computer data is displayed.

Also see *video monitor.*

Also the data that can fit on the screen at one time. Extended to mean a memory array or disk file containing a screen's worth of data (sometimes called a **screen im•age**).

(Graphics)

Shading that can be overlayed on a graphic image or text area, usually represented in terms of percentage of opaqueness.

screen cap•ture

(Computer operations)

Saving the contents of a screen either in printed form or in a disk file.

screen de•scrip•tion lan•guage

See *screen generator.*

screen font

See *font.*

screen gen•er•a•tor

(Data management)

A program that allows a developer to design computer screens for an application. Also called a **screen han•dler**. Screen elements may include aesthetic design, graphics, query or alternative menus, or other ways to make the application more functional for a user.

Contains a **screen-de•scrip•tion lan•guage** for creating the screens and a **screen ma•nip•u•la•tion language** for communicating the user's queries or selections to the application.

Synonym: **screen paint•er**.

screen han•dler

See *screen*.

screen im•age

See *screen*.

screen ma•nip•u•la•tion lan•guage

See *screen generator*.

screen paint•er

See *screen generator*.

script

(Programming)

n. In object-oriented programming, the written description of an object's methods, roughly the equivalent of a program in procedural language. For example, HyperTalk scripts comprise the methods or handlers by which the HyperCard stack responds to messages.

Also see *HyperTalk; object oriented*.

(Artificial intelligence)

Schank's alternative to a rule-based system. An event based knowledge system organized in frames, with links between sequential events.

(UNIX)

In the C shell, the name for the equivalent of a batch file, command file, or procedure file. C shell scripts use a syntax resembling the C language, but are not compiled.

Also see *procedure file*.

SDLC

See *synchronous data link control*.

SDM

See *semantic data model*.

search

(Data management)

n. Examination of data to find items that satisfy specified criteria.

Also see *query*.

v. To conduct such an examination.

sec•ond nor•mal form

(Data management)

Method of removing anomalies from data in first normal form (1NF). Data must be both in 1NF and functionally dependent on the primary key. Abbreviated **2NF**.

For example, if the primary key is a combination of several columns, one or more nonkey columns may not be dependent on all of them. The table LIBRARY USE is in 1NF, with the column headings:

Card Number	Patron Name	Expiration Date	Fines Owed	Books Reserved	Books Overdue

Here the primary key is a combination of Card Number and Patron Name. However, Expiration Date is functionally dependent only on Card Number. To put this data in 2NF, it is necessary to make two tables:

Card Number	Expiration Date

whose primary key is Card Number and

Card Number	Patron Name	Fines Owed	Books Reserved	Books Overdue

whose primary key is a combination of Card Number and Patron Name.

First, second, and third normal forms are sufficient for most data management tasks. However, more advanced and theoretical normalizations are possible.

Also see *Boyce/Codd normal form; fifth normal form; first normal form; fourth normal form; normalize; third normal form*.

se•cu•ri•ty

n. Being safe from danger or harm.

(Security)

The preservation of a computer system and its data by preventing unauthorized entry or use.

Effective computer security involves determining appropriate kinds of access and interaction by legitimate users (such as reading, writing, and erasing data), excluding unauthorized users, preventing corruption of data and operations by viruses and other harmful programs, and maintaining hardware and software entry controls (such as filters and passwords). It may require human guards and physical access control.

Overall computer security should include attention to the special needs of subsystems, such as databases or communications.

Data or systems operated for the U.S. government require special security provisions. For example, the U.S. Department of Defense publishes evaluation criteria for trusted computer systems (DOD S200.28-STD) and trusted networks (NCSC-TG-005).

Also see *access; authorization; grant; integrity; trusted; validation; verification.*

Most databases for personal computers omit elaborate security procedures. However, several distributed DBMSs provide them. SQL-compatible data managers (such as DB2) allow creation of views for individual users. Ingres automatically modifies queries, including data changes, according to the degree of access defined for the user.

A se•cu•ri•ty mod•el, which formally defines the methods for defending the system, may be implemented on an existing system or used in the design of a new system. It can also be the basis for instructing system users.

Also see *Bell-LaPadula model; kernel; view.*

se•cu•ri•ty clas•si•fi•ca•tion

(Security)

Level of security assigned to data or another object. For example, in the U.S. Department of Defense, objects are classified as Unclassified, Confidential, Secret, and Top Secret. Compare with *security clearance.*

se•cu•ri•ty clear•ance

(Security)

Level of access granted to a system's user or subject. Compare with *security classification.*

se•cu•ri•ty, com•put•er

(Security)

An approach to data management that involves protecting data from accidental or intentional destruction, alteration, augmentation, and dissemination. Usually accomplished by a sequence of controls on access to and use of both hardware and software.

In•ter•nal security involves preservation of data privacy and integrity by means of, for example, locks, defined views, passwords, encryption, and protection against viruses, Trojan horses, and creation of covert channels.

Ex•ter•nal security involves controlling physical access to the system (phys•i•cal security), allowing each individual access to only a certain level of system use or only certain data (pro•ce•dur•al security), and screening people before allowing them to use the system (per•son•nel security).

Successful security systems depend on careful analysis of the degree to which the system and the data must be secured in relation to the uses to which the data is put. This must be embodied in the security policy, which is carried out at the external, operating system, and application levels.

Also see *access; authentication; covert channel; encryption; grant; integrity; Trojan horse; trusted.*

se•cu•ri•ty en•vi•ron•ment

(Security)

The degree of security of a computer system and the circumstances of its maintenance.

A closed security environment is one in which both the system's design and the users can guarantee the integrity of operation. In defense-related systems, for example, developers must have the same or higher security clearance as the data.

An open security environment is one in which either the system's design or a user fails to guarantee the integrity of operation.

Also see *clearance; environment; integrity; security.*

se•cu•ri•ty ker•nel

See *kernel.*

se•lec•tion

n. Something that is chosen.

(Data management)

A relational operator that decomposes a relation or table into specified sets of tuples or rows. Sometimes called re•stric•tion. The opposite of a join.

Projection performs the same operation for columns or attributes.

The command SELECT, though similar in name, actually encompasses all the permitted algebraic functions.

se•man•tic da•ta mod•el

(Data management)

Model that incorporates meaning as well as the structure of data. Abbreviated SDM. The purpose is to make the system more intelligent. Though semantic modeling is at an early stage, the existing concept entity contains a degree of meaning by its properties (description), relationships to other entities, and type. Chen's entity/relationship model is an example.

Also see *entity; entity/relationship model.*

sen•si•tiv•i•ty

(Security)

n. A measure of the value of data or another system object and the degree to which it must be protected.

A **sensitivity la•bel** is the classification assigned to the object.

Also see *classification.*

sen•si•tiv•i•ty la•bel

See *sensitivity.*

se•quen•tial

adj. Arrangement and processing in consecutive order with no direct way to reach later elements. The term **sequential ac•cess** is applied to a file or peripheral (such as a tape or disk) organized in this way.

(Data management)

A sequential search of a database could examine records in the order in which they were entered. For example, in dBASE, the current record pointer moves sequentially with the commands LOCATE and CONTINUE. With LOCATE, each record is searched, beginning with the first one, until a match is found or until the end of the file. CONTINUE proceeds with a search begun with LOCATE.

Or records may be stored in contiguous memory locations, and searched in that sequence. A sequence may be defined in an index.

se•quen•tial ac•cess

(Data management)

Storage of data records in linear sequence, so that individual records cannot be retrieved directly. A feature of tape backup storage and simple disk systems. Contrast with *direct access; indexed sequential access*.

se•ri•al in•ter•face

(Data communications)

A connection between two devices in which data is transferred one bit at a time. Contrast with *parallel interface*.

se•ri•al port

(Data communications)

An I/O port for serial data transmission. For example, the IBM PC ports COM1 (AUX) and COM2. Contrast with *parallel port*.

se•ri•al trans•mis•sion

(Data communications)

Transmission of data characters one bit at a time. Contrast with *parallel transmission*.

serv•er

(Data communications; Data management)

n. A network node that makes services available to other nodes, such as file management or printing. In some cases, a computer acts solely as a server (a **dedicated server**). In others, it also functions as an independent node (a **non-dedicated server**). Synonym: **net•work serv•er**. Contrast with *client*.

A **file server** stores files in shared and private subdirectories.
A primary or **network server** keeps track of node names and network resources.
A **print server** handles printing needs.
Also refers to the software required to manage distributed databases on networks, such as SQL Server (pronounced se'kwal sur'ver, a product of Ashton-Tate, Microsoft, and Sybase).

Also see *database server*.

Also called an **en•gine** or **back-end**.

(Computer operations)

A "manager" that performs a specific set of functions within an operating system (client-server architecture). For example, an OS might contain servers or managers for graphics, file handling, communications, and input/output.

ser•vice bu•reau

(Applications)

Commercial vendor that provides specialized computer services on a fee basis. Usually charges only for services provided or usage fees, rather than actually selling software or hardware. Examples of services include payroll handling, billing, and publishing services, such as producing camera ready copy for printing, presentation graphics, and other finished materials.

May also handle overflow work, end-of-period functions, or specialized requirements. Before the advent of low-cost personal computers and workstations, service bureaus often handled all the computing needs of smaller organizations.

ses•sion

(Data communications)

n. The connection between computers or network nodes during a data transmission.

SGML

See *Standard Generalized Markup Language.*

share•ware

(Software)

n. Computer software that is sold outside of ordinary commercial distribution, usually by the author. The usual sales method is for the author to make the program available (by disk or computer bulletin boards) to users without requiring advance payment; users pay only if they find the program useful. Examples include PC File (ButtonWare) and various utilities for dBASE.

The system is based on trust between author and buyer. Shareware has largely replaced **free•ware,** which was distributed in a similar manner, but at no cost.

sheet-or•i•ent•ed GIS

See *geographic information system.*

shell

n. An outer layer, case, or covering.

(Programming languages)

A front-end or user interface, the part of a program that responds to user commands.

(UNIX)

UNIX has several alternative user interfaces, the most popular of which are the Bourne, C, and Korn shells. The **Bourne shell**, developed by S.R. Bourne, is used primarily for writing scripts (command files). The **C shell**, developed by W. Joy for Berkeley UNIX, contains both C language-like and UNIX commands and is used for interactive data manipulation. The **Korn shell**, developed by D. Korn, extends the Bourne shell by allowing greater flexibility in using variables.

shroud•ed source

(Programming languages)

Computer code provided in an easily compiled form, but one that is difficult to copy. A form of software protection.

signed file

(Security)

A file containing a unique checksum.

Also see *encryption; fingerprint.*

sig•nif•i•cand

See *floating point.*

sim•ple net•work re•la•tion•ship

See *database, network.*

sim•ple se•cu•ri•ty con•di•tion

(Security)

Permission to read only at a particular security level or lower levels.

Sometimes called a "no read up" condition, as users may not read information classified above their level.

Also see *access; grant; permission.*

sim•plex

(Data communications)

n. A simple send-receive connection in a fixed direction, such as from a remote reporting station to a computer.

Also see *duplex.*

Sim•u•la 67

(Programming languages)

n. A procedure-oriented structured high-level language, developed in Norway in the 1960s. Features a class-based structure and inheritance. A derivative of ALGOL and a precursor to Ada and object-oriented languages. Important historically, despite limited use in practice. Oriented toward simulation applications.

Described in O.J. Dahl, B. Myrhaug, and K. Nygaard, *Simula 67 Common Base Language* (Norwegian Computing Center, 1984).

sim•u•la•tion

(Application)

n. A model of a natural or engineered phenomemon created and operated on a computer to produce behavior like that of the original system. Example systems that are often simulated include economies, biosystems, communications and computer networks, emergency services, corporations, vehicles (such as airplanes, helicopters, and ships), biological organs, factories, hospitals, power plants, weapons, and computers.

The computer model may be constructed to operate in real time or in compressed or expanded time. Operation may be represented symbolically or graphically. Simulations may also only consider the times at which events occur (**dis•crete simulation**), as opposed to operating continuously in time (**con•tin•u•ous simulation**). Discrete simulations are often used in business and social science applications; continuous simulations are used in scientific and engineering applications.

sin•gle-pre•ci•sion float•ing point

(Computer operations)

Floating point numbers stored with the standard precision. In IEEE Standard 754, defined as a 32-bit number with a 24-bit significand or mantissa, an 8-bit exponent, and an exponent bias of 127.

Also see *double-precision floating point; floating point; precision.*

sin•gle task•ing

adj. Capable of working on only one task at a time. For example, MS-DOS is a common single tasking operating system.

sin•gle-user

adj. Capable of supporting only a single user, but perhaps multiple tasks. Applied both to computers and to software such as operating systems and databases. For example, OS/2 is a single-user, multitasking operating system.

site li•cense

See *license*.

skel•e•tal

adj. Acting as a skeleton or supporting structure.

(Data management)

A **skeletal struc•ture** is the physical description of a database. Once a physical model has been designed or selected, the specifications for files, records, tables, rows (or tuples), or columns in which data will be entered.

slave

See *guest*.

Small•talk

(Computer languages)

The first object-oriented programming language, developed at the Xerox Palo Alto Research Center in the 1970s. The Smalltalk system consists of the Virtual Machine, with an interpreter, data storage manager, and I/O handling; and Virtual Image, objects to describe text, graphics, and data manipulation.

Smalltalk was the inspiration for the Apple Macintosh desktop.

Also see *object oriented*.

smash

v. To disintegrate or go to pieces.

(Graphics)

To disassemble an object into more primitive forms, such as a polygon into lines. Synonym: *unjoin*. Compare with *ungroup*.

SMFAs

See *system management functional areas.*

smooth

n. Without irregularities.

adj. Having no irregularities.

v. To remove irregularities, as to smooth a data curve.

SNA

See *Systems Network Architecture.*

snap

n. A fastening or lock.

(Graphics)

A tool that attracts or connects a new object to an already drawn object or to a predefined position. Besides CAD and other graphics programs, the snap feature is used in page layout programs to position text and graphics.

snap•shot

(Data management)

In distributed systems, a read-only version of part of the database, updated only at specified intervals, that is stored at user sites. A method of making more efficient use of the actual database. A feature of R*.

Similar to Ingres's de•fer•red up•date.

Also see query; R*.

soft lim•it

(Computer operations)

An operating limit, such as memory size, set by software, rather than hardware. It can thus be changed by instructions to the controlling software. Contrast with *hard limit.*

soft•ware

n. Computer programs.

soft•ware driv•er

See *driver.*

soft•ware en•gi•neer

See *programmer*.

soft•ware en•gi•neer•ing

(Software)

Development and writing of software using engineering discipline and practices, rather than the inclinations of the individual programmer.

Also see *computer aided software engineering* (CASE).

soft•ware in•ter•rupt

See *exception*.

soft•ware life cy•cle

(Software)

The process of software development, including problem definition or requirements analysis, program design, coding, debugging (verification), testing (validation), documentation, and maintenance (including extension and re-design). May involve an individual program or a system, such as a database. The names of the stages vary, depending on application and orientation.

Also see *computer aided software engineering* (CASE).

soft•ware test•ing

See *validation*.

sort

v. To arrange in rank order, such as numerical or alphabetical.

(Data management)

A command in many applications that automatically arranges data in predetermined or user-defined rank order. In spreadsheets and databases, the sort may involve several fields and may be performed on several levels.

For example, the sort may be alphabetical, with field A as the primary key; if it has the same value for several records, they may be sorted with field B as a secondary key.

n. The arranging of data in the order determined by criteria based on its contents. For example, the listing of database records alphabetically according to a name field. Within a primary sort, secondary sorts may use other criteria. For example, mailing labels may be sorted by state, then by city, then by Zip Code.

(dBASE)

SORT creates a new file, sorted on one or more key fields. The sort may be alphabetical, numerical, or chronological. To create a new sorted file MAILINGS with all fields from the file NAMES, sorted by Zip Code, enter

.SORT ON zip TO mailings

The command SORT TO works similarly, but uses only selected fields, as in

.SORT TO mailings ON name; zip

The SORT command can use as many as ten alphabetic, numeric, or date fields. The ordering may be ascending or descending, and may be case-sensitive for alphabetic fields. The sorted data is placed in a new file. For example, to sort an open file containing names and addresses by the fields STATE and ZIPCODE, and put the result in a file STATEL-IST, use

.SORT ON state, zipcode TO statelist

Both fields are automatically sorted in ascending order. To have ZIPCODE sorted in descending order, place /D after the field name:

zipcode/D

source code
(Programming)

Program written in a human-readable language, such as a high-level language or assembly language. Requires translation to run on a computer.

SPARC
(Hardware)

Acronym for Scalable Processor ARChitecture. A RISC microprocessor developed by Sun Microsystems, but manufactured by many sources. The design specification has been published, so it is considered an open architecture.

The term "scalable" comes from an effort to allow the architecture to be implemented in many different technologies in which components may have different sizes. The architecture allows for varying numbers of largely independent but overlapping register sets (called **reg•is•ter win•dows**).

(Note: This acronym is unrelated to the ANSI/SPARC involved in the development of CODASYL.)

spa•tial da•ta

(Graphics)

Data identified with a specific location, such as a flat map or globe, or a point in three-dimensional space. A type of data associated with computer aided design, geographic information systems, and scientific visualization.

spline

(Graphics)

n. Loosely, an arc or curve. More precisely, a smooth curve connecting data points defined by a polynomial. A form drawn by a tool in some graphics programs.

 Also a common method of fitting a curve to a given set of data points (called **spline in•ter•po•la•tion**).

spline in•ter•po•la•tion

See *spline*.

spoof•ing

n. Deceiving or contriving a hoax. From Spoof, a game invented by Arthur Roberts, 19th century English comedian.

(Security)

Creating a program that resembles another program such as a network or computer entry screen, deceiving the user into entering his or her name and password. The false program then records this information for later retrieval, and presents the user with an "incorrect password" message, returning to the true log-on program.

spread•sheet

(Applications)

A program based on a grid of rows and columns that permits entry into cells of numbers, numerical formulas for mathematical manipulation, and text for documentation. Works like an array of interconnected calculators that propagate results automatically along rows and columns. Examples are Excel (Microsoft) and 1-2-3 (Lotus Development).

 Computer spreadsheets continue the format and terminology traditionally used by accountants for hand-entered and -manipulated data.

SQL

See *Structured Query Language*.

SQL/DS

(Data management)

General purpose distributed relational database management system using SQL (IBM). Querying and report writing are performed with the Query Management Facility (QMF). SQL/DS runs on IBM mainframes under the VM/CMS and DOS/VSE operating systems.

SQL* Forms

See *Oracle*.

stack

(Data management)

n. In HyperCard, a group of cards (records), the equivalent of a table or file in other database systems.

Also see *HyperCard*.

(Programming)

A data structure organized in a last-in, first-out (LIFO) manner. Computers often use stacks to save subroutine return addresses, parameters, intermediate values, and results, allowing routines to call one another in a hierarchical manner.

stack frame

See *frame*.

Stan•dard Gen•er•al•ized Mark•up Lan•guage (SGML)

(Word processing)

A uniform way of describing text for computerized formatting, including style, fonts, placement of headings, arrangement of illustrations, and other aspects of document publication. Permits use of computerized document storage and management.

Defined by ISO standard 8879-1986/A1-1988 and two U.S. government standards – Mil Std 28001 and FIPS 152. SGML has been specified in the U.S. National Institute of Standards and Technology Applications Portability Profile for U.S. Government use.

Stan•ford (Hen•nes•sy) bench•mark

(Programming)

A benchmark suite that computes permutations, solves puzzles, multiplies matrixes, computes a floating-point fast Fourier transform, and does sorts.

Star•burst

(Data management)

Prototype distributed database management system (IBM) for workstation-server operations.

Also see *R**.

star net•work

(Data communications)

A network configuration in which all nodes are connected to a central station, logically like the arms of a star. All communications between nodes are routed through the central station.

star prop•er•ty

(Security)

Permission to write only at a particular security level or higher levels. Also called ***-property** or **con•fine•ment property**.

Sometimes called a "no write down" condition, as users may not reduce the classification level of information. Such a reduction could lead to security violations, as it would allow users with less privilege to access the information.

Also see *access; grant; permission*.

start bit

(Data communications)

A data bit that precedes a character in asynchronous serial transmission to indicate the start of transmission.

Also see *serial transmission; stop bit*.

start-stop trans•mis•sion

See *asynchronous transmission*.

star•va•tion

(Data management)

n. Condition in which a user or process never receives the resources it needs because of its low priority, low speed, or constant preemption.

state

n. A situation or condition related to circumstances or surroundings.

(Computer operations)

The value of a storage bit, either 0 or 1 or logical true or false. Also the collective value of all storage bits. Also the values of a set of system functions that define future behavior upon input.

state di•a•gram
(Software development tools)

Graph that depicts the state of a system, represented by nodes, and the transitions or changes of state, represented by edges. Also called **state-trans•i•tion diagram.**

state ma•chine mod•el

A model based on a finite number of defined states and rules for passing from one to another. Described by a state table or state diagram.

state•ment
(Programming)

n. An executable unit written in a programming language. It usually contains keywords, operands, and delimiters, although it may contain nothing (a **null statement**). A sequence of statements that make a computer perform a particular task is a **pro•gram.**

Also see *program.*

(dBASE)

A command verb and a character, date, numeric, or logical expression. An example is locating the next instance in an open database of the name Lincoln with

.FIND Lincoln

More commonly called a **com•mand line.**

state ta•ble
(Software development tools)

Table listing all of a system's possible inputs, current states, next states, and outputs.

Also see *state diagram,* of which it is a tabular equivalent.

state trans•i•tion di•a•gram

See *state diagram.*

stat•ic

adj. Unchanging; at rest.

A **static var•i•able** is one that retains its value in-between invocations of the routine in which it is defined. This permits its use to transfer status information (such as a count or the state of a data structure) from one invocation to the next. Note that a static variable need not be visible externally. Arrays and records (or structures in C) may also be static. **Static link•ing** is performed before a program is started. **Static mem•o•ry al•lo•ca•tion** remains for the life of the program, rather than only as long as it is needed or the routine in which it occurs is active.

Contrast with *dynamic*.

stat•ic link•ing

See *static*.

stat•ic mem•o•ry al•lo•ca•tion

See *static*.

stat•ic var•i•able

See *static*.

stat•us

n. Current condition.

(Computer operations)

The current state or condition of a computer or register.

(Data communications)

The ability or readiness of a network node to send or receive data.

STEP

See *PDES*.

sto•chas•tic

(Communications)

adj. Describing a process in which imprecise or random events affect the values of variables, so that results can be given only in terms of probabilities. Used mainly in communications to describe the behavior of channels. Synonym: *probabilistic*.

stop bit
(Data communications)
A bit that follows a character in serial transmission, indicating the end of transmission. A protocol may require more than one bit. Some older formats even require fractional stop bits. Lack of the proper number of stop bits is called a **fram•ing error.**

Also see *asynchronous transmission; serial transmission; start bit.*

stor•age chan•nel
See *channel, covert.*

store
(File management)
v. To place data in memory or on a storage device. Synonym: *save.*

Also see *load.*

(dBASE)
The command STORE creates or specifies a memory variable and stores data in it.

n. British term for a storage device. The term was first used by the 19th century conceptualizer of the computer, Charles Babbage. Memory is referred to as the **computer's store** or **main store;** secondary storage devices, such as disks or tapes, are referred to as **backup store** or **backing store.**

Also refers to memory that contains the information used to actually execute the computer instructions (a **control store**).

stored pro•gram com•put•er
See *computer.*

stored query
(Data management)
A response to an anticipated query that is prepared within the system from current data so that it is available when requested. When frequently entered queries are anticipated, the system may be more efficient than if a response must be prepared for each query.

Also see *query optimization*, of which this is often a part.

straight AS•CII file
See *ASCII file.*

stream
(Data communications)
n. A continuous transmission of data, such as text or voice, rather than a recurring format such as records. In UNIX, a stream is anything that serves as a continuous source or destination for data; it may be a device or a file.

stream•ing
(Data communications)
n. Method of data transmission in which an ACK is returned only when transfer is complete. Used in the protocol ZModem.

> Also see *ZModem*.

> Also a continuous backup storage method, usually to tape (called **streaming tape**).

string
(Computer programming)
n. A series of characters (or characters and symbols) treated as a unit of data. Common string operations (or **string pri•mi•tives**) include concatenation, insertion, deletion, copying, moving, length determination, and identification of substrings. Sometimes also used to refer to a series of data items of other types, such as integers, real numbers, decimal numbers, or even complex structures.

string pri•mi•tive
See *string*.

struc•tured
(Computer languages)
adj. Refers to programming methods based on a limited but complete set of structures, including a continuation facility, a simple conditional statement (of the if-then type), and a simple conditional loop (of the do-while type). The structure may consist of **sequences** of instructions, **decisions** that depend on the data (if –, then –, else –), **loops** or repetitions of instructions or sequences (do, do while, repeat until, or while), or **procedures** that substitute one instruction for a series of instructions.

Languages such as Ada, C, Modula-2, PL/I, and Pascal support structured methods directly. Assembly language, BASIC, COBOL, and FORTRAN support them only with additions or extensions.

struc•tured anal•y•sis

(Software development tools)

A top-down method of analyzing the logical and physical design of systems or programs. Used to define requirements and produce error-free operations or executable code. Features abstraction, functional decomposition, and hierarchical organization. Also called **structured sys•tems analysis.** Described by E. Yourdon, *Modern Structured Data Analysis* (Englewood Cliffs, NJ: Prentice-Hall, 1989).

The same methods, if applied beforehand, are called **struc•tur•ed de•sign.**

Also see *decomposition; top-down.*

struc•tur•ed de•sign

See *structured analysis.*

Struc•tured Query Lan•guage (SQL)

(Data management)

A nonprocedural computer language that provides standard commands for accessing relational databases. Abbreviated as SQL (sometimes pronounced "sequel"). SQL was developed by IBM and was a model for its DB2. It has been adopted in DB2, Oracle, Ingres, dBASE IV, and many other databases.

Defined by American National Standard X3.135-1986 and Document X3H2-86-61, ISO standard 9075:1989, ISO TC97/SC21/WG3N117 and 143, and FIPS 127.

Standardization permits network access to databases in personal computers, minicomputers, and mainframes. For example, an IBM PC user can obtain information from a database held on a DEC VAX, IBM mainframe, or network server. SQL lets PC database users import data from other computers or databases. It is also intended to let users of spreadsheets, word processing, and CAD applications import database information. However, enhancements and other variations from the standard may hamper SQL's unrestricted use.

"Structured" refers to the rules that govern the language's use. For instance, SQL queries employ recursion.

Em•bed•ded SQL is the incorporation of SQL in other languages.

SQL routines manipulate, define, control, secure, and manage the transfer of data. There are three types of commands:

• **da•ta def•i•ni•tion lan•guage** permits creation of tables and indexes. For example, the following sets up a table ADDRESSES with fields that specify the type and, if appropriate, the number of characters:

CREATE TABLE addresses

(name char(30), address char(25), area_code number,

phone_no. number, occupation char(20))

• **da•ta ma•nip•u•la•tion lan•guage** is used to query the database and to add and delete data. For example, the following determines how many entries are in the table AD-DRESSES:

> SELECT COUNT(*)

> FROM addresses

• **da•ta con•trol lan•guage** allows and withholds access to the database, with the commands GRANT and REVOKE.

Users can issue SQL commands directly to enter databases on other computers, or indirectly through a "friendly" host database interface, such as Query By Example or natural language. An example is a HyperCard interface to use a mainframe version of Oracle.

(dBASE)

In dBASE IV, the command SET SQL ON substitutes SQL commands for dBASE file-handling commands and functions within a program.

stub

See *top-down*.

sub•di•rec•to•ry

See *directory*.

sub•ject

n. Someone or something that can be controlled, acted upon, or operated upon.

> In logic, the entity in a proposition, such as a chair in "the chair is hard."

Also see *predicate*.

(Computer operations)

A person or process using a computer system.

(Data management)

Computer operation on behalf of a user performed on an object. For example, a program that is processing data is a subject; the data is an object.

Also called the **own•er** of the object. Synonym: *principal*.

(Security)

A capability list that indicates what a subject may access.

Also see *capability list*.

sub-menu

See *menu.*

sub•rou•tine

(Programming)

n. A part of a routine that performs an operation. Also a routine nested in or executed from another routine. When the subroutine is completed, the main routine or program resumes execution. The process of transferring control to a subroutine is a **call** and the restoration of control to the caller is a **return**. Items the subroutine needs to execute are **parameters**; the caller must pass them to it.

(dBASE)

The command LOAD places a machine language subroutine in memory. It can be executed from a program with CALL.

sub•sche•ma

See *schema.*

sub•sche•ma def•i•ni•tion lan•guage

See *Network Database Language.*

sub•trac•tive col•ors

See *primary colors.*

suite

n. A group or coordinated grouping.

(Hardware; Software)

Sometimes used to refer to a group of devices.

Also used to mean a set of software applications, programs, or tools. For example, a test suite is a complete set of test cases.

su•per•com•put•er

(Hardware)

n. A computer that processes very large amounts of data in very long data words at very high speeds, often using parallel processing. Has the highest ranking in MIPS or FLOPS. Generally used only for massive arithmetic calculations in applications such as fluid flow, weather prediction, signal processing, and simulation. A leading manufacturer is Cray Computer.

Also see *parallel processing.*

su•per•mini•com•put•er
(Hardware)

n. A model of a minicomputer extended to produce high performance in terms of MIPS or FLOPS. Usually still below a minisupercomputer in capabilities.

Also see *minicomputer; minisupercomputer; supercomputer.*

Super VGA

See *video graphics array.*

su•per•vis•or

See *operating system.* Often refers to a special mode in which privileged instructions (such as I/O or system configuaration) can be executed. The ordinary mode is called **user mode.**

su•per•vis•or call

See *exception; system call.* Often abbreviated **SVC.**

SVC

See *exception; system call.*

swap•ping

See *virtual memory.*

sym•bol•ic de•bug•ger

See *debugger, symbolic.*

sym•bol•ic link
(Data management)

In an open file, a record consisting of the name of another file that serves as a pointer to that file. When the link is invoked, the file is opened.

For example, the Berkeley UNIX command **ln** creates a symbolic link.

sym•bol•o•gy

n. Data in symbolic form, for example, a bar coding system or a magnetic stripe.

Also see *bar code*.

synch•point

See *synchronization point*.

syn•chro•ni•za•tion point

(Data management)

The boundary of a transaction. Abbreviated **synch•point**. A synchpoint is established at the beginning of a transaction and at the conclusion of one that ends with a commit. A rollback moves activity back to the beginning synchpoint. Either a commit or a rollback releases any lock placed during the transaction. In the event of errors or deadlock, the process need only be rolled back to the most recent synchronization point, not all the way back to its beginning. Synonym: **check•point**.

Also see *transaction*.

syn•chron•ous ac•cess

See *access, synchronous*.

syn•chron•ous da•ta link con•trol

(Data communications)

Abbreviated **SDLC**. IBM's protocol for synchronous data transmission under SNA. Moves data of any length and in any code serially, using either full or half duplex.

Also see *Systems Network Architecture*.

syn•chro•nous trans•mis•sion

(Data communications)

A mode of data communications that transfers data continuously at a constant rate of speed. The method used within a computer. Also used for high speed transfer, particularly on mainframe computers.

For example, on IBM mainframes, SDLC (synchronous data link control) is used to send data serially. BSC (binary synchronous communication) controls data sent in blocks using either ASCII or EBCDIC characters. It requires a means of synchronization, such as a header or a synchronization (sync) character (often ASCII SYN).

Contrast with *asynchronous transmission*.

syn•onyms

(Data management)

Different names or keys referring to an identical address. Produced, for example, by a hashing routine.

Also see *hashing; key.*

syn•tax

n. Grammatical structure of a language. The relationships among words in sentences, paragraphs, or other structures.

(Computer languages)

The organization of expressions of a computer language, especially the rules governing the use of commands. High level languages follow grammatical rules similar to those for natural languages.

dBASE, for example, uses a command line or "sentence" read left to right. It begins with a verb (such as CREATE, JOIN, or SET) and may be followed by an adverb, object, and prepositional phrase. The sentence

> FIND January

contains a verb and an object. The sentence

> SET FIELDS TO name, address

contains a verb, object, and preposition.

There is no standard format for displaying syntax. For applications with their own languages, the user's manual generally contains a vocabulary, syntax description, or list of commands. One common convention puts optional words or phrases in brackets ([ ]) and variables in angle brackets (< >).

For example, in dBASE, the syntax for HELP is

> .HELP [<keyword>]

meaning the user can simply enter

> .HELP

or also include a specific key word. To obtain information on the command EDIT, enter

> .HELP edit

Standard computer languages are described in BNF (Backus normal form or Backus-Naur form).

sys•tem

n. A complex collection of specialized elements functioning to accomplish a goal not possible for an individual element.

For example, a **com•put•er system** might consist of a computer or processor, a monitor or terminal, other I/O devices, and operating and applications software. Often, however, just a longer term for computer, used to promote unreadability.

sys•tem boot

See *bootstrap loader*.

sys•tem call
(Programming)

A transfer of control to an operating system routine, typically to perform a low-level function such as I/O, timing, or system configuration. Sometimes referred to as a **su•per•vis•or call** (SVC). Sometimes uses the same mechanism as an **exception** or **trap**.

Also see *exception*.

sys•tem flow•chart

See *flowchart*.

sys•tem life cy•cle

See *software life cycle*.

sys•tem man•age•ment func•tion•al areas
(Data communications)

Types of effort required to control, monitor, and manage a computer network. These include:

• **con•fig•u•ra•tion** – mapping the network's physical structure, beginning and ending operation, and monitoring its status,

• **fault man•age•ment** – detecting, repairing, and preventing transmission errors,

• **per•for•mance man•age•ment** – measuring its efficiency, availability, and accuracy, and

• **se•cu•ri•ty man•age•ment** – maintaining access control and recording possible violations.

Sys•tems Ap•pli•ca•tion Ar•chi•tec•ture (SAA)
(Computer operations)

IBM's standard design for interconnecting mainframes, minicomputers, and PS/2 personal computers. Includes communications protocols and hardware and software interfaces.

Sys•tems Net•work Ar•chi•tec•ture (SNA)
(Computer operations)

IBM's description of data communications within a distributed mainframe computer system. Composed of physical units (host, terminals, communications controllers) and logical units (function-oriented software). It includes formats, logical structure, protocols, and operations.

The architecture has three layers – application, function management, and transmission (control of data link, path, and transmission). Synchronous transmission uses the IBM protocol SDLC. The communications program VTAM manages access, connects nodes, moves data, and permits networking operations, such as line and device sharing.

Also see *LU6.2; Systems Application Architecture (SAA); virtual telecommunications access method (VTAM).*

T

ta•ble
(Data management)

n. A group of records, the equivalent of a flat file. A relational database consists of multiple tables.

Also see *database; flat file; relational database.*

ta•ble look•up

See *lookup table.*

ta•ble, look•up

See *lookup table.*

tab•leau
(Data management)

n. A relation with variables.

ta•ble•space
(Data management)

n. In DB2, the pageset (physical structure) containing table records and index data.

Also see *pageset.*

Par•ti•tioned tablespace is a tablespace divided into independent parts based on a key range. Each part can be reorganized individually.

tag

n. An indicator of attributes of an associated object, such as its meaning, type, size, structure, state, appearance, ownership, or addressing mechanism.

Tagged Im•age File For•mat

(Graphics)

Abbreviated **TIFF**. Protocol for storage and transfer of image data, including black and white bit-mapped graphics, halftones (mixture of black and white pixels to represent gray), and gray scale (shades of gray). Developed by software publishers (Aldus, Microsoft) and scanner manufacturers.

Used in page layout programs (such as PageMaker), printers (PostScript and non-PostScript), three-dimensional and paint programs, scanning, and data transmission.

TCB

See *trusted; trusted computing base.*

TCP/IP

(Data communications)

Abbreviation for Transmission Control Program/Internet Program. A set or suite of protocols for Internet, Ethernet, and other large networks at research institutions, usable by personal computers, minicomputers, and mainframes. TCP checks data integrity and meets the requirements of Layer 4, Transport Layer, of the ISO/OSI Reference Model. IP determines the data path, under the requirements of Layer 3, Network Layer.

Also see *ISO/OSI Reference Model.*

TDI

See *trusted database interpretation.*

TDR

See *time domain reflectometer.*

tear-off menu

See *menu.*

Tech•ni•cal and Of•fice Pro•to•col

(Data communications)

Abbreviated **TOP** (pronounced "top"). Specification developed by Boeing Computer Services for an Ethernet-like local area network that supports an automated office and technical system, including order taking, manufacturing status, and file servers. Encompasses Layers 3-7 of the ISO/OSI Reference Model. Physical layer uses CSMA/CD baseband (10 Mbps) cabling and signaling as specified by IEEE Standard 802.3.

Often used in conjunction with **MAP**, as **MAP/TOP**.

Also see *Carrier Sense Multiple Access/Collision Detection; Manufacturing Automation Protocol; MAP/TOP*.

Tem•pest

(Security)

n. Hardware specifications that limit the release of low-level electromagnetic radiation from computer operations that can be picked up by clandestine data monitors. Required for computer equipment to be used in the U.S. Department of Defense and other federal agencies. Equipment that meets Tempest requirements is certified by the U.S. National Security Agency (NSA).

tem•plate

A pattern for a finished product.

(Graphics)

A pattern for a drawing, for example, a sketch scanned into a draw program that the user may trace into a line drawing.

Also see *draw program.*

(Software)

A master style sheet or page layout for a spreadsheet, database report, or published document. Also a layout for a record (or structure in C) or a function call.

tem•plate lan•guage

(Data management)

A set of commands allowing creation of macros.

Also see *macro.*

ter•mi•nal

(Hardware)

n. A screen or printer and keyboard that is connected to a remote computer or central processor. Need not contain local processing power. Called a **dumb terminal** if it does not.

Also see *workstation.*

A personal computer or workstation may act as a terminal through the running of a *terminal emulation* package.

ter•mi•nate and stay res•i•dent

(Applications)

Abbreviated **TSR.** A program for an IBM PC or compatible that remains in memory after it is loaded and can be activated at any time (usually through a special combination of keys), without affecting another application that is currently in use. For example, someone might use a TSR calculator while working with a word processor, a TSR notepad while working with a database or spreadsheet, or a TSR database while working with a graphics program. TSRs provide a primitive form of multitasking in the single-tasking MS-DOS environment.

Among the most popular PC TSR's is SideKick (Borland International). It includes a calculator, notepad, editor, autodialer, calendar, telephone directory, and datebook.

Macintosh synonym: *desk accessory* (DA).

ter•mi•na•tor

(Programming)

n. An ending marker for a string, file, record, or other data grouping. Examples are the null character that ends a string in C and the stop bit or bits that follow a character in asynchronous communications. dBASE files use the ASCII line feed character (1A hexadecimal = 26 decimal) as a terminator.

(Hardware)

A resistor on each end of a network transmission cable that suppresses error-causing reflections.

ter•nary

adj. Relating to the number three, for example, a relation with three attributes.

text file

See *ASCII file.*

tex•ture mapping

See *mapping*.

third-generation language

See *language, 3rd generation.*

third nor•mal form

(Data management)

A method of removing anomalies from data in second normal form (2NF). Data must be both in 2NF and also have no nonkey attribute (or data item) with functional dependency on another nonkey attribute or that can be derived from another nonkey attribute (called a tran•si•tive de•pen•den•cy). Abbreviated 3NF.

For example, a table LIBRARYUSE is in 2NF with column headings

Card Number	Patron Name	Fines Owed	Books Reserved	Books Overdue

where the primary key is the combination of Card Number and Patron Name. However, the column Fines Owed can be derived from the nonkey column Books Overdue. To put this data in 3NF, it is necessary to make two tables:

Card Number	Patron Name	Fines Owed

and

Card Number	Patron Name	Books Reserved	Books Overdue

Devised by E.F. Codd for relational databases, but also used in other database types.

First, second, and third normal forms are sufficient for most data management. However, more advanced and theoretical normalizations are possible, such as *Boyce/Codd normal form, fifth normal form, and fourth normal form* (also called pro•jec•tion-join nor•mal form).

Also see *first normal form; normalize; second normal form; third normal form.*

3NF

See *third normal form.*

three sche•ma mod•el
(Data management)

Ambiguous phrase that may refer to one of two database models developed during the 1970s – one by the CODASYL organization and the other by the X3 committee of the American National Standards Institute (ANSI). Each is based on three schemas.

The two sets of schemas are roughly comparable.

ANSI SCHEMAS	CODASYL SCHEMAS
conceptual	logical
internal	storage structure
external	application subschemas

Also see *ANSI/X3/SPARC; CODASYL.*

tick•et
(Security)

n. An unforgeable pattern of bits designating an object to which a user or subject has access. Some security systems require a list of such tickets for each subject. For a subject to gain access to an object, all it must do is present the proper ticket; no lists need to be searched.

Synonym: *capability.*

Also see *access control list.*

TIFF

See *Tagged Image File Format.*

TIGER

See *topographically integrated geographic encoding and referencing system.*

tight cou•pling

See *coupling.*

time bomb
(Security)

A method of overriding a computer system's security provisions (a **trap door**) that goes into effect upon a specific set or time sequence of circumstances. May be either hardware or software.

time di•vi•sion mul•ti•plex•ing

(Data communications)

Transmission line or channel for high speed digital transmission of voice and data simultaneously by alternating bits from each data stream on the same path. Several types are currently in use, including **T-1**, which transmits at 1.544 megabits per second, and **T-3**, which transmits at 44.736 megabits per second.

Contrast with *frequency-division multiplexing.*

Also see *multiplexing.*

time do•main re•flec•tom•e•ter

(Data communications)

Electronic measuring tool to detect line errors. Also used to measure local area network (LAN) segments. Abbreviated **TDR**.

time stamp

(Data management)

The time at which data or a relation is added or changed, or the time interval during which it is effective. Sometimes entered into a database as a way of preserving data integrity and as part of an audit trail. In multiuser systems, used for controlling concurrent use.

Also means to mark the date and time of creation or change on an object, such as a file.

Also written **time•stamp.**

time•stamp

See *time stamp.*

tim•ing chan•nel

See *channel, covert.*

to•ken

See *token passing.*

to•ken pass•ing

(Data communications)

A network configuration in which a node can transmit data only after taking control of a data pattern called the **to•ken** that circulates through the network. A protocol of token-ring networks. Contrast with *poll.*

to•ken ring net•work

(Data communications)

A ring network in which a node can transmit only when it controls a token. The data message is attached to the token and removed at the receiving node. The configuration gives each node an opportunity to transmit, and eliminates the possibility of data collisions when several nodes try to transmit at the same time. A widely used configuration for local area networks, supported by IBM and described in IEEE Standard 802.5.

T-1

See *time division multiplexing*.

tool

n. An object or instrument designed or consciously adapted to perform a function. Toolmaking is a characteristic ability of people and other primates.

(Software)

A system program or routine, usually one of a set, designed to perform a specific task. For example, a graphics **tool•box** may contain a tool for drawing rectangles and another for drawing circles. A CASE program may contain tools for use in writing an application. Some 4GL language tools help a user design queries for a distributed database. Debuggers and compilers are other examples. Tools are aids in producing working applications.

tool•box

See *tool*.

TOP

See *Technical and Office Protocol*.

top-down

(Data management; Programming languages)

adj. Method of system or program design characterized by decomposition. Produces a hierarchical, modular structure, in which design begins with the overall structure and proceeds to lower levels that contain subfunctions. Ideally, each level or module is designed, written, and tested before the next one is begun. Modules that have not yet been written must be replaced by **stubs** that mimic their behavior.

Also see *decomposition*.

Contrast with *bottom-up*, noting that most designs and analyses use both.

to•po•graph•ic•ally in•te•grat•ed geo•graph•ic en•cod•ing and ref•er•enc•ing sys•tem

(Graphics)

Acronym: TIGER. Digitized map base developed by the U.S. Bureau of the Census for use in geographic information systems. Other data can be incorporated for manipulation and display by means of vendor- or user-supplied interfaces.

to•pol•o•gy

(Data communications)

n. Design of a computer network.

Phys•i•cal to•pol•o•gy is the design by which computers, printers, terminals, cables, and other equipment are joined into a network (via data transmission paths).

Log•i•cal to•pol•o•gy is the set of protocols by which data is sent and received over a network, such as token ring, star, or token passing.

trans•ac•tion

(Data management)

n. A sequence of operations that must be handled as a unit. That is, it is all-or-nothing. Either all the operations are performed, or everything is rolled back to the previously saved versions. For example, in an open database, a user might access a record, add, change, update, or delete data, and save the change. Could involve many databases. The boundaries of the transaction are called synchronization points or **synch•points.**

Also see *synchronization point.*

The user's decision to save the change is called a **com•mit.** If the user decides not to save the change, or if problems are encountered (such as locks, errors, overflows, disk errors, deadlock, or starvation), the transaction ends with a **roll•back** to the last saved version of the file. The system obviously must save all intermediate results or states.

(dBASE)

In dBASE IV, a transaction starts with the command BEGIN TRANSACTION. The user commits with the command END TRANSACTION, which also releases any lock on the record or file. UNLOCK does not work during an open transaction. ROLLBACK negates updates and other changes made during the aborted transaction.

Also see *lock; rollback.*

trans•ac•tion anal•y•sis

(Data management)

Method of structured system or program design that organizes by transaction type, each in a separate module. Execution is directed to the appropriate module by a **transaction cen•ter**. Contrast with *transform analysis*.

trans•ac•tion band•width

See *bandwidth*.

trans•ac•tion cen•ter

See *transaction anlysis*.

trans•ac•tion pro•cess•ing

(Data management)

Performance of specified repetitive operations, such as making reservations or checking credit, on a sequence of distinct and unrelated requests. Each request is treated as a separate unit, to be completed as a whole or not at all.

On-line transaction processing (OLTP) makes real-world up-to-date information available to system users. Contrast with **batch processing** and **in•ter•ac•tive processing**.

trans•form anal•y•sis

(Data management)

Method of structured system or program design that changes data from physical to logical form for processing level by level, then returns it to physical form for execution. The logical processing furthest removed from the physical layer is called the **cen•tral transform**. Contrast with *transaction analysis*.

tran•si•tive de•pen•den•cy

(Data management)

Functional dependency of a nonkey attribute that can be derived from another nonkey attribute. Forbidden in 3NF data.

Also see *third normal form*.

trans•la•tor

(Computer languages)

n. A program that converts a routine or program from one computer language into its equivalent in another language. A general term encompassing assemblers, compilers, and interpreters.

Trans•mis•sion Con•trol Pro•gram/In•ter•net Pro•gram

See *TCP/IP*.

trans•mis•sion er•ror

(Data communications)

The incorrect transmission of data, so that what is received differs from what was sent. Errors may be caused by electrical current variations, signal attentuation, faulty cables, signal reflection, nuclear radiation, or environmental conditions, such as excessive heat, high humidity, or electrical storms.

Error checking, performed automatically by some communications protocols, verifies accurate transmission.

Also see *error checking; error correction; error detection.*

trap

See *exception.*

trap door

(Security)

A hidden routine or piece of hardware that allows the overriding of a computer system's security provisions.

tree

(Data management)

n. An organizational structure that resembles an upside-down tree, used in many hierarchical situations, including menus, databases, and operating systems. A tree begins with **a root** and **branches** to **nodes**. There is only one path to each node.

Many operating systems, such as MS-DOS and UNIX, have their file directories organized this way. The base is a root directory and other directories and subdirectories are subordinate to it, with the files being the nodes. The Macintosh operating system employs the metaphors of desktop, folders, and files, but the concept is the same.

Databases also use tree structures in searching for and sorting data. The root is a root node and the final nodes are called **leaf nodes**. These are called **binary trees**, because each branch has just two nodes, each of which may have two branches, and so on. The program begins a search by comparing the query data to the key value, which becomes the root node. If there is no match, the search moves along branches according to a preset routine until a match is made. Useful for databases entirely in the computer's active memory.

An example of such a hierarchical structure is IMS (Information Management System) from IBM.

Also see *B tree; B+ tree; branch; leaf node; node; directory.*

tree-struc•tured di•rec•to•ry sys•tem

See *directory.*

troff

(UNIX)

n. A routine for text formatting, typesetting, and printing. Designed for use on typesetting machines, rather than dot-matrix or daisywheel printers. Pronounced "tee-roff." One implementation is Device Independent troff (AT&T). An extension of nroff originally developed at Bell Telephone Laboratories in the early 1970s. It includes commands to change type size and style.

Also see *nroff.*

Tro•jan horse

A deadly agent secretly introduced into a place or situation where it can do harm. Derived from Greek mythology (in Homer's Iliad). During a long war between Greece and Troy, a large, ostensibly harmless wooden horse found outside Troy's walls and taken into the city actually concealed Greek soldiers. The maneuver led to Troy's defeat.

(Security)

An ostensibly useful program containing unauthorized routines that harm a computer system's data or operations.

Also see *virus; worm.*

trust•ed

adj. Having faith or confidence in.

(Security)

A program, other system component, or system that is guaranteed not to allow a breach of security, even though its privileges could make this possible. For example, a **trust•ed com•put•ing base (TCB)**, which relies on a combination of internal design and accurate administrative data, a **trust•ed front end**, **trust•ed sub•ject**, or a **trust•ed pro•cess.**

Trust•ed Com•put•er Sys•tem Eval•u•a•tion Cri•te•ria

(Security)

Seven-level rating of trusted computing bases defined for computer systems and networks by the U.S. Department of Defense. The National Computer Security Center's Evaluated Products List rates computer systems according to the criteria.

Commonly called the **Or•ange Book.**

The seven cumulative levels are, in order of increasing security:

D	Minimal Protection
C1	Discretionary Security Protection
C2	Controlled Access Protection
B1	Labeled Security Protection
B2	Structured Protection
B3	Security Domains
A1	Verified Design

Also see *trusted.*

trust•ed com•put•ing base

(Security)

Computer system concept employed by the U.S. Department of Defense that defines security in terms of trusted and untrusted users. Abbreviated **TCB.** The basis of the Trusted Computer System Evaluation Criteria.

Also see *trusted; Trusted Computer System Evaluation Criteria.*

trust•ed da•ta•base in•ter•pre•ta•tion

(Security)

U.S. Department of Defense application of Trusted Computer System Evaluation Criteria for database systems. Abbreviated **TDI**. A set of evaluation criteria is under development.

Also see *Trusted Computer System Evaluation Criteria.*

trust•ed front end

See *trusted.*

trust•ed ker•nel

See *kernel.*

trust•ed net•work in•ter•pre•ta•tion

(Security)

U.S. Department of Defense application of Trusted Computer System Evaluation Criteria for communications networks.

Also see *Trusted Computer System Evaluation Criteria.*

trust•ed pro•cess

See *trusted.*

trust•ed soft•ware

(Security)

An application or operating system that will not allow or cause a breach of security. One developed by trusted people who have demonstrated its correctness by such means as using standard coding and verification techniques.

Also see *trusted.*

trust•ed sub•ject

See *trusted.*

TSR

See *terminate and stay resident.*

T-3

See *time division multiplexing*.

tuple

(Data management)

n. A component of a data relation, a set whose concrete representation is a record or row. Pronounced as in "quintuple."

A tuple, as a mathematical set, is unordered, meaning that it can be rearranged. And it is unique within the relation.

Also see *relation*.

2NF

See *second normal form*.

two-phase commit

(Data management)

Protocol for committing after a transaction update in multiple entirely separate databases. In this situation, the commit process must be satisfactorily concluded in each database, or it is cancelled for all of them. In such cases, each one is rolled back to its last commit. The first phase involves informing all servers of the impending commit.

Also see *distributed database; transaction*.

type

See *data type*.

type dec•la•ra•tion

(Programming)

A character or statement that describes the type of a data variable and therefore how it is processed. For example, in BASIC dialects, an integer variable may be indicated by the character % or the statement DEFINT, and a string by $ or DEFSTR. Many languages, such as Ada, C, Modula-2, and Pascal, require all variables to be declared before they are used. In such languages, a type declaration consists simply of a type followed by a list of variables that are of that type, such as

```
int ndays, nmonths, nyears;
```

in C.

type•face

(Output formatting)

n. A design for a family of printing type that is executed in one or more styles and several sizes. For example, the Times typeface may be rendered in roman, italic, bold, condensed, and expanded styles, and in sizes from 6 to 64 points. Elements of a typeface include whether it is with or without (sans) serifs (short decorative lines at the top, bottom, and ends of letters and numbers), thickness, curve shapes, and other artistic and aesthetic considerations.

Also see *font; point.*

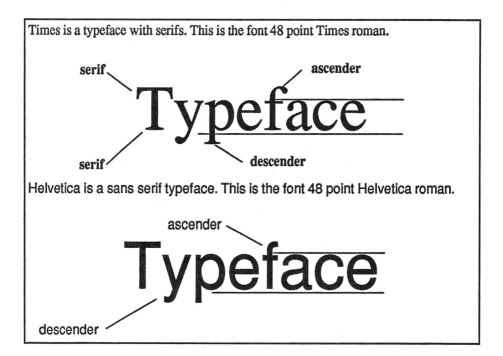

Times is a typeface with serifs. This is the font 48 point Times roman.

serif ascender

serif descender

Helvetica is a sans serif typeface. This is the font 48 point Helvetica roman.

ascender

descender

type•set•ting

n. The act of setting text in type by hand, hot metal machine, or computer, preparatory to printing.

(Word processing)

adj. A machine that produces very high quality printing from computerized text (1200 dots per inch), as distinguished from the output of a laser printer (perhaps 300 dots per inch). An example is the Linotronic series (Linotype Corp.).

U

UDF

See *user-defined function*.

unary

adj. Singleness. Relating to the number one.

(Mathematics)

A **unary op•er•a•tor** (such as - or + as leading signs) requires only one operand.

unary op•er•a•tor

See *unary*.

un•cer•tain•ty

(Statistics)

n. Relating to the limits on what is known about the problem under analysis. Consists of the degree of: confidence in the accuracy of the data sample; tolerance, or relevance of the data to the total problem; completeness and accuracy of the data; and ambiguity in the structuring of the problem.

un•group

(Graphics)

v. To disassemble several objects that had been combined into a more complex entity. Compare with *smash*.

un•in•ter•rupt•ible

adj. Must be done as a unit without interruptions.

Also see *atomic*.

union

(Data interpretation)

n. In relational databases, an operation that creates a new table composed of all records in each of two specified tables. For example, in R:BASE, the command UNION combines two tables with at least one column in common. An organization-wide table HOMEINFO, with columns NAME, STREET, CITY, STATE, and ZIP could be combined with the departmental table DEPTLIST, with columns NAME and MAILSTOP, to form CARD-LIST by

> R>UNION homeinfo WITH deptlist FORMING cardlist

CARDLIST contains all rows from both tables, with the columns NAME, STREET, CITY, STATE, ZIP, and MAILSTOP, that is, all rows with names from DEPTLIST. Fields with no matching values are filled with nulls.

Contrast with *intersection*.

(Programming)

C language facility for accessing the same data in multiple ways, for example, either as an integer or as characters. This lets the same field (member in C) serve different purposes in different records (structures in C). Similar to a variant record in Pascal. Unions can also allow access to the individual characters (or bytes) within larger data units.

A **dis•joint union** is one having no elements in common. It supports the data abstraction method called generalization.

Also see *disjoint; generalization*.

unique in•dex

See *index*.

unique•ness con•straint

(Data management)

In network databases, a restriction assuring that no two records of a given type or belonging to the same set have identical values for any specific component.

Uni•ver•sal Pro•duct Code

See *bar code*.

UNIX

(Computer environment)

Operating system developed by AT&T Bell Laboratories in the late 1960s. Popular environment for multiuser systems including many computer brands and types. Closely tied to the C language, in which it is largely written. Provides multitasking, a hierarchical file structure, file sharing and security, environment control, I/O management through standard devices and files, and interprocess communications. User access is through **shells** (front ends), such as the Bourne, C, and Korn shells. Emphasis is on providing integrated software tools for the full-time professional user working in a time-shared environment. Oriented toward systems applications, software development, and design aids rather than mathematical ("number crunching") or data processing applications.

There are two major versions, System V, supported by AT&T, and Berkeley (or BSD), supported by the University of California, Berkeley. Several manufacturers and users have developed specialized versions, such as AIX (IBM) and POSIX, and proprietary versions, such as Ultrix (DEC) and XENIX (Microsoft). There are also real-time and secure versions.

Described in the AT&T Information Systems' *UNIX System V Programmer's Reference Manual* and *Programmer's Guide* (two volumes, published by Prentice-Hall) and in many other books at a variety of levels.

Also see *C; shell.*

un•join

(Graphics)

v. To disassemble an object into more primitive forms, such as a polygon into lines. Synonym: *smash.* Compare with *ungroup.*

un•lim•it•ed run-time li•cense

See *license.*

un•lock

(Security)

v. To remove a lock from all or part of a multiuser database. That is, to release it from exclusive ownership once updating or some other operation has been performed.

(dBASE)

A lock may be released with the commands UNLOCK (dBASE III PLUS and IV) and SET LOCK OFF (dBASE IV), with the locking of another file or record, or by closing the file with CLEAR ALL, CLOSE, QUIT, or USE.

un•nor•mal•ized ta•ble

See *normalize*.

UPC

See *bar code*.

up•date

v. To make current. In a computer, this involves reading the current values from storage, changing them, and writing them back. The basic process is called a **read-modify-write cycle.**

(Data management)

To add, delete, or change data in a database. In multiuser databases, it must be done in a way that prevents conflicting changes to the same data (so-called **lost updates**) and also keeps other users from accessing old data while the updating is underway (so-called inconsistent analysis). This usually involves locking the file, record, or other portion of the data.

Also see *lock*.

(SQL)

The three updating commands are DELETE, INSERT, and UPDATE.

(dBASE)

UPDATE copies information from one file to another, as long as the two have one common or key field and field name. Also the updated file must be indexed on the key field, and the source file may be similarly indexed. An example is copying accumulated entries at the end of a day from a temporary file to a permanent or main file. At the dot prompt, enter

UPDATE ON name of file being updated FROM source file name

then describe the changes to be made.

For example, one might enter today's payments received into a temporary file, then update the acccounts receivable file from it. This avoids repeated opening and closing (and reindexing) of a large receivables file.

The commands APPEND, DELETE, and REPLACE can also be used to update records.

up•load

(Data communications)

v. To send data from one computer or device to another. Unlike export, upload has a strong hierarchical meaning, with the more complex unit (or central unit) at the receiving end. For example, one might upload data from a terminal or personal computer to a minicomputer or mainframe.

Also see *download*.

"up•per case"
(Software)

Informal reference to the definition (requirements analysis) and design stages of software development (software life cycle). For complementary functions, see *lower case*, though the boundary is not rigid. May be a play on words, since the function can be automated with CASE tools.

us•er
(Applications)

n. Individual or organization that employs a computer system and applications software to manage data, solve problems, or produce information or materials. The user, for instance, interacts with a distributed database management system through its front end.

Synonym: *end user*.

user-de•fined func•tion
(Software)

Option in some applications allowing the user to define a method or characteristics, such as those of a database report. Often refers to cases in which the user can replace a default function with one that he or she has coded. Abbreviation is **UDF**.

(dBASE)

In dBASE IV, the user may define popup and other menus and bars (with the commands DEFINE POPUP, DEFINE MENU, DEFINE BAR), report boxes (DEFINE BOX); selection options, such as prompt messages (DEFINE PAD); and windows (DEFINE WINDOW). These can be activated with the relevant ACTIVATE commands.

user ID

See *identifier*.

user mode

See *supervisor*.

user name

See *identifier*.

util•i•ty

(Computer operations)

n. A program or routine that performs a function required by an operating system, application, or user. Examples are sorting, compilation, data transfer, code conversion, print formatting, and file managment. Utilities may be part of the operating system or separate applications.

val•i•da•tion

(Data management)

n. A method of assuring that data entered in a field fulfills previously set conditions. For instance, entering a letter of the alphabet in a field that is reserved for numbers would trigger a rejection announcement.

(Programming)

Ensuring that a program produces correct output. Synonyms: **pro•gram test•ing, soft•ware test•ing** (the common term).

var•i•able

(Computer programming)

n. A named data element or string into which any value may be entered, as long as it meets type requirements. For example, a numerical element could accept any number, but not a city name. Also called a **mem•o•ry variable** in some databases, such as dBASE.

VAX

(Hardware)

A family of 32-bit minicomputers built by Digital Equipment Corp. (DEC). Their features include virtual memory, I/O channel processors, and multi-level priority interrupt systems. Models range from single-user systems often used in embedded applications (the MicroVAX line) to multiprocessor systems that rival mainframes in capacity and performance.

Also see *UNIX; VMS.*

vec•tor graph•ics

(Graphics)

Method of creating an outline graphic by defining its endpoints, edges, and curves mathematically. This type of representation allows images to be enlarged or reduced (resized), rotated, reversed, and distorted.

The type of graphics created by CAD, statistical, and draw programs.
Contrast with *raster graphics*.

Also see *draw program*.

ver•tex

(Graphics; Mathematics)

n. A point where a line or curve ends or where multiple lines or curves intersect. Some graphics programs permit joining of lines or curves at such a point.

ver•ti•cal par•i•ty

See *parity*. Also called a *vertical redundancy check (VRC)*.

ver•ti•ces

See *vertex*. The form vertexes is also used, as part of a trend doward dropping irregular Latin plurals (as with indexes instead of indices).

VGA

See *video graphics array*.

vid•eo graph•ics ar•ray

(Hardware)

Abbreviated **VGA**. Color standard for analog monitors developed by IBM, used on IBM PCs and PS/2s. Provides four levels of resolution; the highest for graphics is 640 x 480 pixels, and for text is 700 x 400. Capable of either 2 or 16 colors, but this can be expanded to as many as 256K colors.

As of 1990, the current IBM PC standard. Provides higher resolution and more colors than the previous standard, EGA.

The Super VGA variant (not supported by IBM) allows resolutions as high as 800 x 600 pixels.

For other standards, see *color/graphics adapter (CGA); enhanced graphics adapter (EGA); monochrome display adapter (MDA)*.

vid•eo mon•i•tor

(Hardware)

Computer screen.

view

(Data management)

n. A portion or subset of a data table created for a specific user or group of users. The purposes are to provide only the information required and to prevent access to the entire table. Queries and changes, which affect the entire database, may be permitted. May be restricted using a filter. Synonyms: *pseudo table, virtual table.*

(SQL)

For example, the database administrator can create a view MAILINFO from a five-column table ADDRESSES by selecting only the two columns containing names and addresses:

>   CREATE VIEW Mailinfo
>
>   AS SELECT Name, Address
>
>   FROM Addresses

(Output formatting)

An alternative presentation of text on the computer screen. For instance, in Microsoft Word, text can be displayed in outline form as a view of its document format. Additions and changes can be made in either format.

VINES

See *virtual network.*

vir•tu•al

adj. The quality of existing, but not being formally recognized.

(Hardware; Software)

A logical design that extends the size or attributes of a machine or piece of software without expanding it physically. For instance, **virtual mem•ory** creates memory addresses that do not exist physically in the computer, but permit data to be moved into and out of the physical memory as required for program execution. A **virtual tab•le** is a view, not part of the logical design of the database. A **virtual ma•chine** is the one the user sees; the physical machine is the actual hardware. The virtual machine may involve software, such as an operating system or interface program, or it may be an emulation or simulation.

vir•tu•al ad•dress

See *physical*.

vir•tu•al de•vice

See *physical*.

vir•tu•al ma•chine

See *virtual; VM*.

vir•tu•al mem•ory
(Data management)

Method of memory allocation that assigns logical addresses for use in programs to refer to both physical memory and secondary storage. References to secondary storage cause the memory manager to load the required information into memory (a process called swap•ping, as other information must be moved to secondary storage to make room). The memory manager handles the loading and storing without user intervention. Synonym: vir•tual stor•age.

vir•tu•al network
(Data communications)

Network connected to a larger network by software, rather than by a hardware gateway. An example of such software for personal computer and workstation local area networks using UNIX is VINES (VIrtual NEtworking Software) by Banyan Systems.

Also see *gateway; network*.

vir•tu•al stor•age

See *virtual memory*.

vir•tu•al stor•age ac•cess meth•od
(Data management)

Abbreviated VSAM (promounced "vee-sam"). IBM software that provides access to data files (called **data sets** in IBM terminology) on mainframes. Features data compression and B tree indexing.

vir•tu•al ta•ble

See *view*.

vir•tu•al tele••com••mu•ni•ca•tions ac••cess meth•od

(Data communications)

Abbreviated **VTAM** (pronounced "vee-tam"). IBM software that links terminals and applications programs on System/370 mainframe networks. Allocates resources, controls access, moves data, and provides network control and sharing.

Also see *Systems Network Architecture (SNA)*.

vir•tu•al user

See *capability*.

virus

(Programming; Security)

n. A program or routine that attaches itself to other programs and spreads by self-replication or infection of other programs. Usually loaded into a system by surreptitious means and may be either harmful or harmless. Some people divide viruses into two classes: those that are Trojan horses and must be copied to infect another system, and those that turn benign programs into Trojan horses or carriers.

Also see *Trojan horse; worm.*

vi•su•al•i•za•tion

n. The process of making an image or substance apparent to the eye; the creation or recreation of a visual object in the mind.

(Graphics)

Display of digital data as a graphic image, in gray scale or multicolor. Permits the user to grasp meanings and relationships more easily and intuitively than by reading the data in numerical format. Or may be used to supplement the data's numerical form. Also called **sci•en•tif•ic visualization**.

VM

(Computer environment)

Acronym for Virtual Machine. An operating system for large IBM mainframes that gives users the illusion of having their own machines with a choice of IBM operating systems.

Also see *virtual.*

VMS
(Computer environment)

Acronym for Virtual Memory System. An operating system for DEC VAX minicomputers that provides a hierarchical file system, memory management, process scheduling, I/O and mass storage management services, and interprocess communications. It offers extensive security, sharing, and synchronization facilities in a multiuser environment.

Also see *virtual*.

VSAM

See *virtual storage access method*.

VTAM

See *virtual telecommunications access method*.

W

WAN

See *wide area network.*

Warn•i•er-Orr di•a•gram

(Software development tools)

Hierarchical diagram based on set theory, but with vertical listing rather than horizontal, and using only the left brace. Hierarchy is horizontal, from left-to-right. Called "output oriented," because the output determines the structures of both the data and the program. Devised by J.D. Warnier (CII Honeywell Bull) in the 1950s; augmented by K. Orr in the 1970s. Described in K. Orr, *Structured Systems Development* (New York: Yourdon, Inc., 1977).

whet•stone pro•gram
(Computer operations)
Benchmark problem for comparing the speeds of floating point operations in computer systems.

white-col•lar crime
(Security)
Theft or other illegal activity committed without violence, the threat of weapons, or other direct person-to-person interaction. Usually committed by an office worker, such as a manager, professional person, salesperson, clerk, or secretary. Includes intentional breaches of computer security or other misuse of computer systems or data belonging to others. Also includes industrial espionage, forgery, embezzlement, bribery, concealing the sources of funds ("laundering"), false advertising, selling of information, securities fraud, violations of environmental or zoning regulations, election fraud, kickbacks, and other similar activities.

wide area net•work
(Data communications)
A network that covers a large geographic area, beyond the few miles usually allowed for a local area network (LAN). May be worldwide. Abbreviated **WAN.**

Also see *local area network.*

wild card
See *metacharacter.*

win•dow
(Computer environment)
n. An area of the computer screen assigned to a specific purpose and capable of being manipulated independently. Some systems, such as Microsoft Windows, allow different applications, such as a database and a word processor, in different windows.

Also see *Windows; X Window.*

(Programming)
During editing, the part of a program in the computer's main memory, the rest of it remaining in secondary storage. For assembly language programming, the memory locations are contiguous and specified.

(Graphics)
A part of the display area from which something has been cut or deleted.

Win•dow•ing is dividing the screen into windows. An **ac•tive win•dow** is one in which *data* may be added or changed. A **cur•rent win•dow** is one presently in use.

win•dowed pro•to•col

(Data communications)

Protocol that sends a specific number of packets, called the **window size**, before receiving an ACK or NAK. An example is Windowed XModem.

Also see *W/XModem*.

Win•dowed X•Mo•dem

See *W/XModem*.

win•dow•ing

See *window*.

Win•dows

(Computer environment)

Applications management program (a product of Microsoft Corporation) for IBM and compatible personal computers. It allows several applications or files to be open at the same time. The OS/2 Presentation Manager is a variation of this program.

Also see *window*.

word

(Computer operations)

n. The group of bits or characters comprising the basic unit of information handled by a computer at one time. Often taken to be a 16-bit unit (two bytes) when discussing personal computers. A 32-bit unit is then a **dou•ble word** or **long word.**

Word

(Word processing)

A word processor for MS-DOS and Apple Macintosh computers, has page layout features (Microsoft).

WordPer•fect

(Word processing)

A word processor for MS-DOS and Apple Macintosh computers, has page layout features (WordPerfect Corp.).

word pro•ces•sor

(Applications)

A program that manipulates text, performing such functions as text entry from the keyboard, importing of text from other programs, text editing, style definition, and importing of graphics and data or reports from database managers and spreadsheets. Examples for MS-DOS computers are Word (Microsoft) and WordPerfect (WordPerfect Corp.).

Some word processors run on dedicated machines, such as those made by Xerox.

Some word processors include desktop publishing features, overlapping with page layout programs.

Also see *desktop publishing; page layout program.*

(Hardware)

A computer used for word processing or a specialized machine dedicated to that purpose.

word wrap

(Output formatting)

Automatic placement of a word too long to fit at the end of one line at the beginning of the next line. A feature of word processors.

work•around

(Programming)

n. A routine that allows a user to bypass a weakness, error, or incompatibility in an application, so that it will work correctly, better, or faster.

work•sta•tion

(Hardware)

n. A computer with capabilities between those of a personal computer and those of a minicomputer, generally used by a single individual for relatively demanding tasks such as AI, CAD/CAM, graphics, or software development. There is no firm definition of the differences among personal computers, workstations, and minicomputers.

World Pro•duct Code

See *bar code*.

WORM
(File management)

Acronym for Write Once, Read Many times.

Also see *CD-ROM*.

worm
(Security)

n. A self-replicating program illegally entered into a computer or computer network whose only purpose is to tie up operations, destroy programs or data, or both.

Also see *virus*.

WPC

See *bar code*.

write
(Computer operations)

v. To copy data from the computer's memory to secondary storage. Synonym: *save*.

Also see *read*.

write ac•cess

See *access; grant*.

write-down
(Security)

n. The process of writing from one process into a file with a lower access classification. A breach of the star or confinement property within multilevel security. Often necessary in actual applications to change or correct classifications. Can only be performed by a trusted subject.

Also see *star property*.

write lock
(Data management; Security)

A lock that denies write access and, in some systems, read access as well.

Also see *access*.

Write Once, Read Many Times (WORM)

See *CD-ROM*

W/X•Mo•dem
(Data communications)

n. Windowed variation of the XModem protocol that allows a maximum of four packets of data to be transmitted before receiving a reply.

Also see *windowed protocol; XModem.*

WYS•I•WYG
(Computer environment)

Acronym for "what you see is what you get." (Pronounced wiz' e wig). Applied most often to word processors, it means text or graphics appear on the computer screen exactly the way they will be printed. In practice, there may be discrepancies because of differences between screen fonts and printer type fonts, margins, control characters, or other variables. Formatting commands are handled by menus and do not appear on-screen.

In contrast, other word processors resemble typesetting systems by requiring style and formatting commands to be embedded in the screen text, to be executed only in the printed form.

XCMD

See *command, external*.

XENIX

(Computer operations)

UNIX version developed by Microsoft for IBM personal computers and compatibles.

Also see *UNIX*.

XFCN

See *function, external*.

X.500

See *X.400*.

X.400

(Data communications)

n. ISO standard containing a protocol for electronic mail and the transmission of messages. Defines a gateway between different electronic mail networks, and includes error checking and encryption.

Future major upgrading of the standard, including user directories, will be called **X.500**.

X.25

(Communications)

CCITT communications protocol for data handling on packet-switched networks. An accepted standard for communications on wide area networks. It makes use of high-level data link control (HDLC). Used, for example, on MCI Mail (MCI) and Telenet (US Sprint).

Also see *high-level data link control*.

X Win•dow

(Computer environment)

A standard display system developed by the MIT Laboratory for Computer Science as part of Project Athena. It allows multiple windows on network workstations or terminals, regardless of operating system or brand of hardware. Applications may reside on different host computers.

Defined by American National Standard X3H3.6.

Also see *window*.

X•Mo•dem

(Data communications)

Communications protocol that transfers data in packets of 128 bytes. The receiver verifies each data packet for accuracy with a checksum byte and acknowledges the accuracy with ACK. The sender must receive the acknowledgment before sending the next packet.

Also see *acknowledge; checksum.*

Y

Y•Mo•dem

(Data communications)

A protocol designed to improve on XModem. It transfers data in 1 kilobyte blocks (1024 bytes) and supports multiple file or batch file transfers. A variation, called YModem-g, transmits without waiting for acknowledgment.

Also see *acknowledge; XModem.*

Y•Mo•dem-g

See *YModem.*

Your•don-Con•stan•tine struc•ture

(Software development tools)

Method of structured design featuring specifications and three stages of structure charts, leading to the final structure. Built around the process, rather than the data. Described in E. Yourdon and L. Constantine, *Structured Design* (Englewood Cliffs, NJ: Prentice-Hall, 1979).

Your•don-De•Mar•co diagram

(Software development tools)

Data flow diagram featuring a widely used method of notation. First used in DeMarco's method of structured analysis, featuring physical and logical models, costs and schedules for each model, model selection, and final structured specifications.

Described in T. DeMarco, *Structured Analysis and System Specification* (New York: Yourdon, Inc., 1978).

Z•Mo•dem
(Data communications)

n. Protocol designed to improve on XModem and YModem. ZModem is intended to reduce network-caused delays by using data streaming, in which an ACK is returned only when transfer is complete; however, a NAK is returned in case of a transmission error.

Also see *acknowledge; negative acknowledge; streaming; XModem; YModem.*

Appendix A
Common Mathematical, Logical, and Other Symbols

Language	Mathematical							String Concatenation	Substring	Logical					Comparison and Equality						
	add	subtract	multiply	divide	exponential	modulus	percent			and	or	not	not equal	grouping	less than	less than or eq to	equal to	gtr than or eq to	gtr than	not equal to	exact equality
BASIC	+	−	*	/	** or ↑	MOD (some versions)				and	or	not			< LT .LT	<= LE .LE	= EQ .EQ	>= GE .GE	> GT .GT	<> OR # , NE .NE	
C	+	−	*	/		%				&& &	= ¬ <	!	!=		∨	⇓	==	>=	>	!=	==
Clipper	+	−	*	/	** or ^	%		+ −	$	.AND.	.OR. or	.NOT. or !		( )	<	<=	=	>=	>	<> or #	==
COBOL	+	−	*	/	**	RE-MAIN DER		+ −							<	<=	=		>		
dBASE	+	−	*	/	** or <	MOD()		+ − { }(IV only)	$	.AND.	.OR. or	.NOT. or !		( )	<	<=	=	>=	>	<> or #	==
FORTRAN	+	−	*	/	**					.AND.	.OR.	.NOT.			.LT.	.LE.	.EQ.	.GE.	.GT.	.NE.	
HyperTalk	add or +	subtract or −	multiply or *	divide or /	^	mod		& &&		and	or	not	≠ or is not		<	<= or ≤	= or is	>= or ≥	>	≠ or is not	
Network Database Language																					
Pascal	+	−	*	DIV		MOD		+ &		AND	OR				<	≤	=	≥	>	≠	
R:BASE	+	−	*	/	**	MOD()	%	+ &		and	or				< or LT	<= or LE	= or EQ	>= or GE	> or GT	<> or NE	
Structured Query Language (SQL)	+	−	*	/						and	or	not			<	<=	=	>=	>	<> ^= !=	

APPENDIX B
COMPUTER DATABASE LANDMARKS

Chronology

late 1950s   IBM introduces the first random access disk file system, the RAMAC

late 1950s-   U.S. Department of Defense develops computerized command and con-
early 1960s   trol systems involving central databases, permitting user queries

1959   Conference on Data Systems Language (CODASYL) convened at U.S.
              Department of Defense headquarters; representatives of manufacturers
              and government and civilian computer users begin defining COBOL, the
              first widely used high-level computer language for business (database
              management) applications

1959   SHARE (IBM users group) defines the formatted file as an *entity* possess-
              ing *properties* to which *values* can be assigned

early 1960s   COBOL language defines *file* as a collection of similar *records*

1966   CODASYL Data Base Task Group (DBTG) begins defining a COBOL
              extension for database use

1967   J.L. Kuhns proposes relational calculus, an application of predicate cal-
              culus

1968   IBM introduces IMS, a hierarchical database

1969   W.C. McGee introduces the file *schema*, in which files are grouped by
              classes, each represented by a file *type* that defines *entries* and *fields*

1970   E.F. Codd defines the relational database

early 1970s   INGRES QUEL query language implements relational calculus

1970s   CODASYL specifications implemented in network databases, such as
              DMS 1100, DBMS, IDMS, and IDS

1971   CODASYL begins defining data description language

1972   E.F. Codd defines relational algebra

1972   E.F. Codd defines relational calculus

1973   IBM introduces the concept of the *data dictionary* and implements it in
              IMS

1974   D.D. Chamberlin and R.F. Boyce introduce Structured Query Language
              (SQL)

1975	ANSI/X3/SPARC defines the "ANSI three-schema standard" for database structure
1977	Oracle Corp. introduces Oracle, a relational database management system
1978	M. Zloof develops Query By Example, a 4th generation language, which becomes the basis for the application QBE (IBM)
1979	IBM introduces DB2, a relational database modeled on SQL
1980	Information Builders introduces Focus, a 4th generation language for use with DB2 and other mainframe database management systems
1981	Ashton-Tate introduces dBASE II, invented by C.W. Ratliff
1986	Structured Query Language defined in American National Standard X3.135-1986

Major Databases

Name	Publisher	Type	Date intro-duced	Computer platforms	Major features
dBASE	Ashton-Tate	relational	1981	IBM PC MS-DOS	procedural language, dot commands
DB2	IBM	relational	1979	IBM MVS/370 and MVS/XA mainframes	distributed QMF for queries and report writing
GemStone	Servio Logic Develop-ment Corp.	object oriented	late 1980s	servers: DEC RISC DEC VAX (VMS) IBM RT (AIX) Sun	client-server architecture, pro-gramming language OPAL, persistent objects
IMS	IBM	hierarchical	1968	mainframe BTAM OS	access methods: sequential indexed sequential direct indexed direct logical database secondary index-ing

Name	Publisher	Type	Date intro-duced	Computer platforms	Major features
Ingres	Relational Technology (Ingres Corp.)	relational	early 1970s	esp. minicomputers VMS (DEC) UNIX MVS/XA MS-DOS	QUEL query language, Query-By-Forms, user menus
IDMS	Cullinet	network	1960s	mainframe	supports CODASYL model
IDMS/R	Cullinet	relational network	1980s	mainframe	supports CODASYL model
Oracle	Oracle Corp.	relational distributed	1977	minicomputers workstations	SQL, SQL* Forms form generator
R*	IBM	hierarchical	1970s	server-to-server	prototype distributed
SQL/DS	IBM	relational	1970s	distributed systems System/370 VM/CMS DOS/VSE	SQL
Starburst	IBM	hierarchical	1970s	workstation-server	prototype distributed

APPENDIX C
STANDARDS

Ada

(U.S.) MIL-STD-1815A-1983

"ANSI three-schema standard"

ANSI/X3/SPARC DBMS Framework - Report of the Study Group on Database Management Systems (Montvale, NJ: AFIPS Press, 1977); also published in *Information Systems 3* (1978)

ASCII

American National Standard X3.4-1986; additions: ANSI X3.64-1979; extensions: ANSI X4.31-1974

BASIC

American National Standard X3.113-1987

C language

American National Standard X3.159

carrier sense multiple access/collision detection (CSMA/CD)

IEEE Standard 802.3

CD-ROM

ISO Standard 9660.

COBOL

American National Standard X3.23-1985

CODASYL

CODASYL Data Description Language Committee Journal of Development 1978 (Material Data Management Branch, Department of Supply and Services, 11 Laurier St., Hull, Quebec, Canada K1A 0S5)

Common Lisp Object System

ANSI X3J13 Document 88-002R

CSMA/CD

IEEE Standard 802.3

Data Encryption Standard (DES)

FIPS 46-1977 and American National Standards X3.92-1981 and X3.106-1983

electronic business data interchange (EDI)

American National Standards X12.1-12.16, 12.20, and 12.22, dated 1986 or 1987

electronic mail

ISO Standard X.400; future major upgrading will be ISO Standard X.500

encryption/decryption algorithm

See *data encryption standard*

Ethernet

(including 10BASE5 or Thick Cable; 10BASE2 or Thin Cable or Cheapernet; 10BASE36, broadband cable; and 1BASE5 or StarLAN, twisted-pair telephone wire)

IEEE Standard 802.3

Extended Pascal

ANSI X3J9/JPC Document 88-151

Extended POSIX

FIPS 151 (IEEE Standard 1003.1-1988) and proposed IEEE standards P1003.2 (draft 8) and P1003.7

floating point and double-precision floating point

IEEE Standard 754

flowcharting

American National Standard X3.5-1970

FORTRAN

American National Standard X3.9-1978

GOSIP

(U.S. Government Open Systems Interconnections Profile)
FIPS 146

high-level data link control (HDLC)

ISO Standards DIS 3309.5 and 4335

Information Resource Dictionary System (IRDS)

Being defined by the U.S. National Institute of Standards and Technology and ANSI Committee X3H4

initial graphics exchange specification (IGES)

American National Standard Y14.26M-1987

ISO/OSI Reference Model

ISO standard 7498

also:

Layer 1	CSMA/CD	IEEE 802.3
	Token bus	IEEE 802.4
	Token ring	IEEE 802.5
Layer 2	IEEE 802.2, CCITT DR X.212	
Layer 3	ISO 8348, 8473, 7777	
Layer 4	ISO 8072, 8073	
Layer 5	ISO 8326, 8327	
Layer 6	ISO DP 8822, DP 8823	
Layer 7	Common services	ISO DP 8649, DP 8650
	File transfer	ISO DP 8571
	Mail/Message	CCITT X.400 series
	Job transfer	ISO DP 8831, DP 8832
Wide Area Net, layers 1-3	CCITT X.25	

Manufacturing Automation Protocol (MAP)

Encompasses Layers 3-7 of the ISO/OSI Reference Model; transmits on broadband cable specified in IEEE Standard 802.4

MUMPS language

American National Standard X11.1

Network Database Language

American National Standard X3.133-1986

office document architecture and inter-change format

ISO Standard 8613

packet-switched data network (PSDN)

CCITT Standard X.25

Pascal

ISO Standard 7185 and American National Standard X3.97-1983

PL/I

American National Standards X3.53-1976 and X3.74-1981

POSIX

IEEE Standard 1003.1 - 1988

quantitative risk assessment for computer systems

FIPS 65

relational databases

See *Structured Query Language*

RS-232 serial interface

Electronic Industries Association (EIA) Standard RS-232C

Standard Generalized Markup Language (SGML)

ISO Standard 8879-1986/A1-1988, Mil Std 28001, and FIPS 152

Structured Query Language (SQL)

American National Standard X3.135-1986 and Document X3H2-86-61, ISO Standard 9075:1989/ ISO TC97/SC21/WG3N117 and 143, and FIPS 127

Technical and Office Protocol (TOP)

Encompasses Layers 3-7 of the ISO/OSI Reference Model; physical layer uses CSMA/CD baseband (10 Mbps) cabling and signaling as specified by IEEE Standard 802.3

token ring network

IEEE Standard 802.5

U.S. Department of Defense evaluation criteria for trusted computer systems

DOD S200.28-STD

U.S. Department of Defense evaluation criteria for trusted databases

Standard under development by National Computer Security Center

U.S. Department of Defense evaluation criteria for trusted networks

NCSC-TG-005

X Window

Being defined by American National Standards Institute Committee X3H3.6

APPENDIX D
BRITISH USAGES

Most database-related words are the same in British and American usages. Some common exceptions in spelling or terminology are listed here. "British" usage is also customary in other English-speaking or English-using countries such as Australia, Canada, Hong Kong, India, Ireland, Malaysia, New Zealand, Nigeria, Pakistan, Singapore, and South Africa.

British	American
analogue	analog
analyse	analyze
authorise	authorize
backing store	secondary storage
backup store	secondary storage
batch-mode	batch
centre	center
colour	color
computerised	computerized
defence	defense
diagramme	diagram
dialogue	dialog
digitising	digitizing
fount	font
formalisation	formalization
immediate access store (IAS)	main memory
indices	indexes
labour	labor
licence	license
matrices	matrixes
normalisation	normalization
optimisation	optimization
programme	program
recognise	recognize
schemata	schemas
store	storage or memory
text processor	word processor
transport	drive
vertices	vertexes
visual display unit (VDU)	video display terminal (VDT) or CRT terminal

APPENDIX E
MULTILINGUAL EQUIVALENTS
OF ENGLISH DATABASE TERMS

English	French	Italian	Spanish
access *n.*	accès	accesso	aceso
access *v.*	accéder	accedere	acceder
address *n.*	adresse	indirizzo	dirección
algorithm	algorithme	algoritmo	algoritmo
AND	ET	E	Y
argument	argument	argomento	artumento
array	tableau	tabella	table
assembly language	langage d'assemblage	linguaggio assemblatore	lenguaje ensemblador
attribute	attribut	attributo	atributo
baud	baud	baud	baudio
binary	binaire	binario	binario
bit	bit	bit	bit
block *n.*	bloc	blocco	bloque
Boolean	booléen	booleano	booleano
buffer *n.*	tampon memoire intermédiaire	memoria intermedaria	memoria intermedia
bug	défaut	difetto	defecto
byte (8 bit)	octet	ottetto	octeto
concatenate *v.*	enchaîner	concatenare	encadenar
checksum	total de contrôle	totale di controllo	total de control
code	code	codice	código
column	colonne	colonne	columna
communications network	réseau de communications	rete di comunicazione	enlace de communicaciones
compiler	compilateur	compilatore	compilador
computer	ordinateur	elaboratore	ordenador
data	données	dati	datos
database	base de données	base di dati	base de datos
data logging	enregistrement chronologique de données	registrazione cronologica di dati	registro cronológico de datos

English	French	Italian	Spanish
database management system	système de gestion de base de données	sistema di gestione di base di dati	sistema de gestión de base de datos
data description language	langage de description de données	linguaggio descrizione di dati	lenguaje de descripción de datos
data manipulation language	langage de manipulation de données	linguaggio manipolazione di dati	lenguaje de descripción de datos
delimiter	séparateur	separatore	separador
dictionary	dictionnaire	dizionario	diccionario
directory	répetoire	repertorio	repertorio
distributed	réparti	ripartita	repartado
exclusive OR	OU exclusif	O esclusivo	O exclusivo
fault tolerant	insensible aux défaillances	insensibile ai malfunziona-menti	insensible a los desfallecimientos
field	zone	zona	zona
file	fichier	archivio o flusso	fichero
floating point	virgule flottante	virgola mobile	coma flotante
function *n.*	fonction	funzione	función
hardware	equipment; matériel	attrezzatura; componenti di mecchina	equipo; componentes físicos; máquinas y equipo
heuristics	l'heuristique	la euristico	la heuristico
hexadecimal	hexacécimal	esadecimale	hexadecimal
hierarchical	hiérarchique	gerarchica	jerárquica
histogram	histogramme	istogramma	histograma
identifier	identificateur	identificatore	identificador
index *n.*	index	indice	indice
index *v.*	établir un index	ancorare a un indice	establecer un indice
indexed sequential access method (ISAM)	méthode d'accès séquentiel indexé	metodo di acceso sequenziale con indice	método de aceso secuencial indexado
information	information	informazione	información
input *n.*	entrée	entrata	entrada
integer	nombre entier	numero intero	numéro entero
interface	interface	interfaccia	acoplamiento mútuo

English	French	Italian	Spanish
invoice *n.*	facture	fattura	factura
input/output (I/O)	entrée/sortie (E/S)	entrata/uscita	entrada/salida
iteration	itération	iterazione	iteración
key	clé	chiave	clave
language	langage	linguaggio	lenguaje
layer *n.*	couche	stratto	capa
library	bibliothèque	libreria	biblioteca
lock *v.*	bloquer	bloccare	bloquear
logic, logical	logique	logico	lógico
model	modèle	modello	modelo
memory	memoire	memoria	memoria
modem	modem	modem	modem
module	module	modulo	módulo
natural	naturel	naturale	natural
nesting	emboîté	incastrato	encastrado
network	réseau	rete	red
node	nœud	nodo	nodo
normal	normale	normale	normal
null	nul	nullo	nulo
numeric	numérique	numerico	numérico
object *n.*	objet	scopo	objecto
object *adj.*	objet	oggetto	objecto
operand	opérande	operando	operando
operator	opérateur	operatore	operador
OR	OU	O	O
output *n.*	sortie	uscita	salida
parallel	(en) parallèle	(in) parallelo	(en) paralelo
parity	parité	parità	paridad
path	branche	ramo	rama
physical	physique	fisico	fisico
password	mot de passe	parola d'ordine	palabra de paso
procedure	procédure	procedimento	procedimiento
program *n.*	programme	programma	programa
query *v.*	interroger	interrogare	interrogar
queue	file d'attente	coda	fila de espera
read *v.*	lire	leggere	leer
real time	temps réel	tempo reale	tiempo real

English	French	Italian	Spanish
record *n.*	enregistrement	registrazione	registro
recursion	récurrence	ricorrenza	recurrencia
relation	rapport; relation	relazione	relación
report	état	prospetto	estado
rollback	reprise	ripartenza	reanudiación
routine	sous-programme	sottoprogramma	subprograma
row	rangée	riga	hilera
security	sécurité	sicurezza	seguridad
sequential	séquentiel	sequenziale	secuencial
serial	(en) série	(in) serie	(en) serie
software	programmes	programmi	programas
sort *v.*	trier	ordinare	ordenar
storage	mémoire	memoria	memoria
structure	structure	struttura	estructura
system	système	sistema	sistema
table	table	tabella	tabla
tree	arbre	albero	árbol
union	opération OU inclusif	operazione O inclusivo	operación O inclusivo
update *v.*	mettre à jour	aggiornare	actualizar
user	utilisateur	utilizzatore	utilizador
validation	validation	convalida	validación
variable	variable	veriabile	variable
verify	vérifier	verificare	verificar
virtual	virtuel	virtuale	virtual
word	mot	parola	palabra
write	écrire	scrivere	escribir

APPENDIX F
SOURCES OF INFORMATION

Organizations

ACM SIGMOD

> ACM
> 11 W. 42nd St.
> New York, NY 10036

American National Standards Institute (ANSI)

> 1430 Broadway
> New York, NY 10018

Data Processing Management Association

> 505 Busse Hwy.
> Park Ridge, IL 60068

IEEE Computer Society

> 1730 Massachusetts Ave. NW
> Washington, DC 20001

Institute of Electrical and Electronics Engineers (IEEE)

> United Engineering Center
> 345 E. 47th St.
> New York, NY 10017

Object Management Group [object-oriented programming]

> P.O. Box 395
> Westborough, MA 01581

U.S. National Institute of Standards and Technology (NIST) (formerly National Bureau of Standards, NBS)

> Bldg. 233
> Room B107
> Gaithersburg, MD 20899

Publications

ACM Transactions on Database Systems

> 11 W. 42nd St.
> New York, NY 10036

BYTE

> 70 Main St.
> Peterborough, NH 03458

Data Based Advisor

4010 Morena Blvd., Suite 200
San Diego, CA 92117

Database Programming and Design

500 Howard St.
San Francisco, CA 94105

Datamation

275 Washington St.
Newton, MA 02158

DBMS

501 Galveston Dr.
Redwood City, CA 94063

IEEE Software

IEEE Computer Society
10662 Los Vaqueros Circle
Los Alamitos, CA 90720

InfoDB

P.O. Box 20651
San Jose, CA 95160

Info World

1060 Marsh Rd.
Suite C-200
Menlo Park, CA 94301

PC

One Park Ave.
New York, NY 10016

PC World

501 Howard St.
San Francisco, CA 94107

Software

1900 West Park Drive
Westborough Office Park
Westborough, MA 01581

Systems Integration

275 Washington St.
Newton, MA 02158

Newsletters

Compass   [Clipper]

    Reference Pages
    P.O. Box 1436
    Coeur d'Alene, ID 83814

Database Review

    P.O. Box 20651
    San Jose, CA 95160

.dBf

    Pinnacle Publishing Inc.
    28621 Pacific Highway S.
    P.O. Box 8099
    Federal Way, WA 98003

D.O.S.S.   [Clipper]

    Four Seasons Publishing Co., Inc.
    P.O. Box 20025
    New York, NY 10017

foxtalk   [FoxBASE+]

    Pinnacle Publishing Inc.
    28621 Pacific Highway S.
    P.O. Box 8099
    Federal Way, WA 98003

Pinter FoxBASE Letter

    1015 Fremont St.
    Menlo Park, CA 94025

Reference: Clipper

    Pinnacle Publishing Inc.
    28621 Pacific Highway S.
    P.O. Box 8099
    Federal Way, WA 98003

R:VIEW   [R:BASE]

    Pinnacle Publishing Inc.
    28621 Pacific Highway S.
    P.O. Box 8099
    Federal Way, WA 98003

SmarTimes   [SmartWare]

    Pinnacle Publishing Inc.
    28621 Pacific Highway S.
    P.O. Box 8099
    Federal Way, WA 98003

APPENDIX G
MISSPELLINGS AND CORRECT SPELLINGS

Misspelling	Correct spelling
accownt	account
acess	access
ackcess	access
acknoledge	acknowledge
acknowlege	acknowledge
acronim	acronym
adaptor	adapter
administrater	administrator
adress	address
afferant	afferent
alfabetic	alphabetic
algorhythm	algorithm
algorithum	algorithm
alphibetic	alphabetic
apend	append
archatecture	architecture
arckitecture	architecture
asending	ascending
assemblor	assembler
atribute	attribute
avrage	average
binery	binary
Boolian	Boolean
capobility	capability
cash	cache
collishun	collision
comit	commit
compatability	compatibility
concatination	concatenation
concurrancy	concurrency
consistancy	consistency
derect	direct

Misspelling	Correct spelling
describtor	descriptor
descripter	descriptor
desending	descending
desine	design
dicshunary	dictionary
dinamic	dynamic
dipendence	dependence
directery	directory
dumension	dimension
efferant	efferent
ekspert	expert
encript	encrypt
encypher	encipher
enviornment	environment
enviroment	environment
exturnel	external
faren	foreign
feald	field
filtar	filter
foren	foreign
gloabal	global
heterogenius	heterogeneous
imige	image
indipendance	independence
infarmation	information
inheritence	inheritance
inquirey	inquiry
inturpreter	interpreter
knowlege	knowledge
kwerey	query
labil	label
labul	label
layor	layer
licence	license
locol	local
lok	lock

Misspelling	Correct spelling
manditory	mandatory
modil	model
modual	module
modufy	modify
moniter	monitor
murge	merge
navagation	navigation
nemeric	numeric
newmeric	numeric
noad	node
operater	operator
paralel	parallel
persistance	persistence
processer	processor
que	queue
queary	query
randim	random
recievable	receivable
redundent	redundant
reposatory	repository
rilation	relation
sekwential	sequential
sinchronous	synchronous
skrean	screen
skroal	scroll
sintax	syntax
statik	static
struckture	structure
superviser	supervisor
synchronus	synchronous
termenal	terminal
tipe	type
tranzaction	transaction
vallidate	validate
vurchual	virtual
windo	window

APPENDIX H
dBASE COMMANDS AND MEANINGS

Commands are in both dBASE III PLUS and dBASE IV, unless otherwise noted.

Command	Meaning
&&	Lets user add comments at end of program line
*	Lets user add comment lines by themselves
!/RUN	Executes an operating system command
?/??	? displays a value on the next line; ?? displays the value on the same line
??? (dBASE IV)	Sends control codes to printer
@ ("AT")	Indicates position coordinates on screen or printer
ACCEPT	Lets user enter character data into a memory variable
ACTIVATE MENU (dBASE IV)	Activates defined pad menu
ACTIVATE POPUP (dBASE IV)	Activates defined popup menu
ACTIVATE SCREEN (dBASE IV)	Disables active window, restores full screen output
ACTIVATE WINDOW (dBASE IV)	Activates defined window
APPEND	Adds a new record to end of database
APPEND FROM	Adds record from another database
APPEND MEMO (dBASE IV)	Adds text file to memo field in current record
ASSIST	Switches from line control to menu control
AVERAGE	Computes arithmetic mean of numeric expressions
BEGIN/END TRANSACTION (dBASE IV)	Treats series of operations as a logical unit
BROWSE	Allows interactive record editing and adding
CALCULATE (dBASE IV)	Computes functions in one pass through a file
[C]CALL	Executes a routine written in another language
CANCEL	Stops execution of a program file
CASE	Indicates a branching point at a true condition
CHANGE/EDIT	Allows full-screen editing of database fields
CLEAR	Erases screen
CLEAR ALL	Releases all memory variables and arrays, closes open database files; selects default work area; closes index, format, and memo files; rejects current @...GET commands
CLEAR FIELDS	Releases field lists created with SET FIELDS TO

Command	Meaning
CLEAR GETS	Cancels pending GET statements
CLEAR MEMORY	Releases memory variables
CLEAR MENUS (dBASE IV)	Erases bar menus and removes them from memory
CLEAR POPUPS (dBASE IV)	Erases popup menus and removes them from memory
CLEAR TYPEAHEAD	Empties keyboard typeahead buffer
CLEAR WINDOWS (dBASE IV)	Erases all windows
CLOSE	Closes alternate, database, format, index, and procedure files
COMPILE (dBASE IV)	Converts source program into executable form
CONTINUE	Continues record-by-record search, using previous LOCATE command
CONVERT (dBASE IV)	Adds internal field _DBASELOCK
COPY FILE	Duplicates a closed file
COPY INDEXES (dBASE IV)	Copies index files into a multiple index file
COPY MEMO (dBASE IV)	Copies text from the current record's memo field to a text file
COPY STRUCTURE	Copies the active database's structure to a new file
COPY ...STRUCTURE EXTENDED	Creates new database containing information about current database's structure
COPY TAG (dBASE IV)	Copies a multiple index file TAG into an index file
COPY TO	Moves data to a new file
COUNT	Counts number of records within a given scope
CREATE	Starts interactive program to define structure of new database
CREATE...FROM	Produces new database file using a STRUCTURE EXTENDED file
CREATE LABEL	Generates mailing labels
DEACTIVATE MENU/POPUP/WINDOW (dBASE IV)	Deactivates and erases a menu, popup, window, or group of windows
DEBUG (dBASE IV)	Executes specified program or procedure under control of interactive debugger
DECLARE (dBASE IV)	Activates an array
DEFINE BAR (dBASE IV)	Defines selection item in a popup menu
DEFINE BOX (dBASE IV)	Prints boxes in reports
DEFINE MENU (dBASE IV)	Initializes horizontal PAD menu
DEFINE PAD (dBASE IV)	Defines a single selection item in a pad menu
DEFINE POPUP (dBASE IV)	Adds a popup menu definition to memory

Command	Meaning
DEFINE WINDOW (dBASE IV)	Creates a window definition
DELETE	Marks records to be removed from active database
DELETE FILE	Deletes a file
DELETE TAG (dBASE IV)	Erases TAGs from multiple index file or closes index files
DIR/DIRECTORY	Displays information about files on designated drive
DISPLAY*	Selects records for viewing or printing
DISPLAY FILES	Lists names of files on given drive and directory
DISPLAY HISTORY	Shows latest commands in order
DISPLAY MEMORY	Displays information about active memory variables
DISPLAY STATUS	Displays information about open files, function key assignments, and SET commands
DISPLAY STRUCTURE	Shows database name, record number, last update, bytes per record, and fields of each record
DISPLAY USERS (dBASE IV)	Shows assigned workstation names of users logged in
DO	Executes a program file or a procedure
DOCASE...CASE...OTHERWISE ...ENDCASE	Starts decisionmaking structure that selects action to execute from a list
DO WHILE...ENDDO	Repeats program statements as long as a condition holds
EDIT	Allows full-screen editing of fields
EJECT	Sends form feed character to printer
ENDPRINTJOB (dBASE IV)	Marks end of a PRINTJOB construct
ENDTEXT	Marks end of an unformatted text block set off by TEXT
END TRANSACTION (dBASE IV)	Terminates transaction logging initiated by BEGIN TRANSACTION
ELSE	Indicates alternate execution with a false IF condition
ENDCASE	Ends a DOCASE structure
ENDDO	Ends a DOWHILE structure
ENDIF	Ends an IF structure
ENDSCAN (dBASE IV)	Ends a SCAN structure
ERASE	Same as DELETE FILE
EXIT	Terminates DO WHILE/ENDDO loop, passing control to first statement after ENDDO
EXPORT	Copies open database file to foreign format

Command	Meaning
FIND	Does fast search in indexed file using character string or numeric argument
FUNCTION (dBASE IV)	Marks beginning of user defined function (UDF)
GET	Displays variable; accepts input when activated with READ
GO	Moves record pointer
HELP	Displays help screen or menu
IF...ELSE...ENDIF	Evaluates an expression; performs one action if result is true, another if it is false
IMPORT	Creates database file from foreign file format
INDEX	Reorders database in numeric, character, or date order, according to a key, by creating an index file
INPUT	Prompts user to enter data into a memory variable
INSERT	Adds a record just after the current one
JOIN	Merges records from two databases
LABEL FORM	Prints mailing labels using file created with CREATE/MODIFY LABEL
LIST*	Selects records for viewing or printing
LIST FILES	Lists names of files on specified disk drive and directory
LIST HISTORY	Shows latest commands in order
LIST MEMORY	Displays information about active memory variables
LIST STATUS	Displays information about open files, function key assignments, and SET commands
LIST STRUCTURE	Shows database name, record number, last update, bytes per record, and fields of each record
LIST USERS (dBASE IV)	Shows assigned workstation names of users logged in
LOAD	Puts a binary program in memory for CALL to execute
LOCATE	Searches database file for record satisfying criteria
LOGOUT (dBASE IV)	Ends a session, presents login screen
LOOP	Returns program control to top of DO WHILE...ENDDO loop
MODIFY	Invokes interactive program to change label forms, query files, report forms, screen files, database files, or view files
MODIFY COMMAND	Calls up full-screen program editor
MOVE WINDOW (dBASE IV)	Moves a window

Command	Meaning
NOTE/*/&&	Permits addition of program documentation
ON ERROR/ON ESCAPE/ ON KEY	Executes a command on a condition
ON PAD (dBASE IV)	Activates popup when cursor bar is moved to specified menu pad
ON PAGE (dBASE IV)	Executes a command when a PRINTJOB reaches a specified line number
ON READERROR (dBASE IV)	Executes a commmand when user enters invalid data in input field
ON SELECTION PAD (dBASE IV)	Executes a command when user presses Enter (Return) for pad menu selection
ON SELECTION POPUP (dBASE IV)	Executes a command when user presses Enter (Return) for popup menu selection
OTHERWISE	Indicates alternative action in CASE structure when no CASE applies
PACK	Purges deleted records from active database file
PARAMETERS	Subprogram command to receive items sent by calling program and give them local variable names
PLAY MACRO (dBASE IV)	Replays a macro
PRINTJOB ...ENDPRINT JOB (dBASE IV)	Identifies a program section as a report, invoking print controls
PRIVATE	Permits creation of memory variables in a subprogram with same names as PUBLIC variables or ones declared in calling program
PROCEDURE	Marks beginning of a program in a procedure file
PROTECT (dBASE IV)	Invokes security setup program
PUBLIC	Makes memory variables accessible anywhere in a program
QUIT	Ends a session
READ	Permits editing of memory variables or fields displayed with an @ ...GET statement
RECALL	Removes deletion marks from records in active file
REINDEX	Rebuilds active indexes
RELEASE	Erases variables from memory
RELEASE MENUS/POP-UPS/WINDOW (dBASE IV)	Erases specified bar menus, popup menus, or windows from screen and memory
RELEASE MODULE	Removes LOADed assembly language module from memory
RENAME	Changes name of a disk file

Command	Meaning
REPLACE	Replaces specified field or fields with values of specified expressions
REPORT FORM	Generates a report using a form created by the report generator
RESET (dBASE IV)	Sets integrity tag in a database file to false
RESTORE	Retrieves variables SAVEd in a memory file
RESTORE MACROS (dBASE IV)	Loads keyboard macros from file into memory
RESTORE WINDOW (dBASE IV)	Loads window definitions from file into memory
RESUME	Continues execution of program paused by SUSPEND
RETRY	Returns control to caller from subprogram, re-executes line that called it
RETURN	Ends program execution, returns control to caller
ROLLBACK (dBASE IV)	Reverses changes made to records during transaction
RUN/!	Executes operating system commands or other applications from within a program
SAVE	Stores memory variables in a disk file
SAVE MACROS (dBASE IV)	Saves keyboard macros from memory in macro file
SAVE WINDOW (dBASE IV)	Saves window definitions from memory in a disk file
SCAN...ENDSCAN (dBASE IV)	Repeats program statements in-between while skipping through database records
SEEK	Searches indexed database for matching key
SELECT	Chooses a work area
SET	Displays menu for controlling system attributes
SET ALTERNATE	Redirects line-oriented screen output to ASCII file
SET AUTOSAVE (dBASE IV)	Determines whether a disk write occurs after each update to a record
SET BELL	Toggles computer bell ON or OFF during data entry
SET BLOCKSIZE (dBASE IV)	Changes disk storage block size of memo fields and multiple index files
SET BORDER (dBASE IV)	Changes default window and popup borders, and boxes created by @...TO
SET CARRY	Determines whether data from previous record is copied to one newly added by APPEND, BROWSE, or INSERT
SET CATALOG	Keeps a record of open files

Command	Meaning
SET CENTURY	Allows the input of four-digit years in data fields
SET CLOCK (dBASE IV)	Displays a clock, sets it to specified coordinates, or deactivates it
SET COLOR	Switches between color and monochrome displays
SET COLOR TO	Changes screen color or video attributes
SET CONFIRM	Determines whether user must press Enter (Return) when entering data into input field
SET CONSOLE	Determines whether messages, reports, or listings appear on screen
SET CURRENCY (dBASE IV)	Controls currency symbol in PICTURE and FUNCTION numeric output
SET DATE	Sets convention used for displaying dates
SET DEBUG	Prints line-by-line history of a program's execution when SET ECHO is ON
SET DECIMALS	Determines number of decimal places in mathematical functions and calculations
SET DEFAULT	Sets disk drive for data and program files
SET DELETED	Controls whether records marked for deletion remain visible
SET DELIMITERS	Determines whether delimiters appear around data entry areas
SET DESIGN (dBASE IV)	Controls access to design mode in which end users are restricted from creating and modifying databases, reports, and other objects
SET DEVICE	Determines whether output from @...SAY commands is sent to screen or printer
SET DISPLAY (dBASE IV)	Selects type of graphics display card
SET DOHISTORY (dBASE III PLUS)	Determines whether program file commands are recorded in history buffer
SET ECHO	Controls whether to display command lines as executed
SET ENCRYPTION (dBASE IV)	Determines whether files created by COPY, JOIN, and TOTAL are encrypted
SET ESCAPE	Controls Esc key's effect on program execution
SET EXACT	Determines how to compare character strings
SET EXCLUSIVE	Determines whether database files are opened in shared or reserved mode
SET FIELDS	Controls whether all or selected fields are accessible in database files
SET FILTER	Makes visible only records for which the condition is true

Command	Meaning
SET FIXED (dBASE III PLUS)	Determines whether to display the number of decimal places specified by SET DECIMALS
SET FORMAT	Opens specified format file
SET FUNCTION	Programs function keys
SET HEADING	Controls display of FIELD titles for AVERAGE, DISPLAY, LIST, and SUM
SET HELP	Controls whether help message appears after incorrect command entry
SET HISTORY	Saves typed commands in buffer
SET HOURS (dBASE IV)	Determines whether clock displays 12- or 24-hour time
SET INDEX TO	Opens index files
SET INSTRUCT (dBASE IV)	Controls display of instruction boxes
SET INTENSITY	Controls whether input fields appear in standard or enhanced video
SET LOCK (dBASE IV)	Determines whether some commands initiate automatic file locking
SET MARGIN	Sets left printer margin
SET MARK (dBASE IV)	Defines separator used in date displays
SET MEMOWIDTH	Controls width of memo field output
SET MENU (dBASE III PLUS)	Determines whether a menu of cursor control keys appears during full-screen operations
SET MESSAGE	Defines a string to be centered on screen line 24
SET NEAR (dBASE IV)	Controls "closest match" SEEKing and FINDing
SET ODOMETER	Controls update interval during execution of commands that display a record count
SET ORDER	Designates a master index from list of open index files
SET PATH	Specifies directory trees to be searched for files not in current directory
SET POINT (dBASE IV)	Replaces decimal point with another symbol in numeric output
SET PRECISION (dBASE IV)	Specifies degree of numeric accuracy in operations using BCD (type N) data
SET PRINT	Directs all output, except @...SAYs, to the printer
SET PRINTER	Directs printed output to specified DOS device
SET PROCEDURE	Opens a PROCEDURE file, loading its PROCEDUREs into memory
SET REFRESH (dBASE IV)	Determines frequency of screen update during BROWSE and EDIT to reflect changes by other LAN users

Command	Meaning
SET RELATION	Links databases
SET REPROCESS (dBASE IV)	Determines number of retries of a record- or file-locking operation in multiuser applications
SET SAFETY	Warns when an operation or command will destroy a file by overwriting it
SET SCOREBOARD	Controls whether system messages appear on line 0 when STATUS is SET OFF
SET SEPARATOR (dBASE IV)	Specifies numeric separator character in PICTURE template output
SET SKIP (dBASE IV)	Lets user define a one-to-many relation in related files
SET SPACE (dBASE IV)	Determines whether expressions displayed with ? and ?? are separated by a space
SET SQL (dBASE IV)	Switches between Structured Query Language mode and normal dBASE data handling commands
SET STATUS	Controls status bar displayed on screen line 22
SET STEP	Pauses program execution after each statement to help in debugging
SET TALK	Controls whether certain commands echo results on screen during execution
SET TITLE	Controls file title prompt when a CATALOG is active
SET TRAP (dBASE IV)	Controls activation of debugger in case of program error
SET TYPEAHEAD	Changes size of keyboard typeahead buffer
SET UNIQUE	Determines whether index file will include records with duplicate keys
SET VIEW	Opens view file created with CREATE/MODIFY VIEW or CREATE VIEW FROM ENVIRONMENT
SET WINDOW (dBASE IV)	Lets user specify window for editing memo fields in APPEND, BROWSE, CHANGE, EDIT, and GET/READ
SHOW MENU/POPUP (dBASE IV)	Displays specified menu or popup without activating it
SKIP	Moves pointer in active database file by a specified number of records
SORT	Copies active database file to new file, arranging records in alphabetical, chronological, or numerical order
STORE	Assigns values to memory variables

Command	Meaning
SUM	Sums numeric fields or expressions incorporating them
SUSPEND	Pauses execution of program, leaving environment attributes intact
TEXT	Displays unformatted block of text
TOTAL	Sums numeric fields for groups of records with same keys, and sends results to summary database file
TYPE	Lists contents of text file
UNLOCK	Releases current record and file locks on active database, in multiuser systems
UPDATE	Replaces fields in records of current database with data from other databases
USE	Opens database file
WAIT	Pauses program execution until user presses a key
ZAP	Removes all records from active database

*DISPLAY pauses when the screen fills, awaiting user action; LIST does not pause. Otherwise, the two commands are the same.

Source: Kalman, D. *The dBASE Language Handbook*. San Marcos, CA: Microtrend Books, 1989.

APPENDIX I
ABBREVIATIONS AND ACRONYMS

ACL	access control list
ACM	Association for Computing Machinery
ADC	analog-to-digital converter
ADP	automatic data processing
ALGOL	ALGOrithmic Language
ANSI	American National Standards Institute
API	Applications Programming Interface
APP	Applications Portability Profile
APPC	advanced program-to-program communications
APSE	Ada Program Support Environment
ASCII	American Standard Code for Information Interchange
BASIC	Beginner's All-purpose Symbolic Instruction Code
BCNF	Boyce/Codd normal form
BIOS	Basic Input/Output System
bit	binary digit
BNF	Backus-Naur form
bps	bits per second
BSD	Berkeley Software Distribution (UNIX)
CA	collision avoidance
CACM	Communications of the Association for Computing Machinery
CAD	computer aided design
CAD/CAM	computer aided design/computer aided manufacturing
CAE	computer aided engineering
CAM	computer aided manufacturing
CAS	communication application specification
CASE	computer aided software engineering
CCEP	Commercial COMSEC Endorsement Program
CD	collision detection
CD-ROM	compact disk read-only memory
CGA	color/graphics adapter
CICS	Customer Information Control System (IBM)
CIM	computer integrated manufacturing

CISC	complex instruction set computer
CLOS	Common Lisp Object System
CM	configuration management
COBOL	COmmon Business Oriented Language
CODASYL	Conference On DAta SYstems Languages
cps	characters per second
CPU	central processing unit
CRC	cyclic redundancy check
CSMA	carrier sense multiple access
CSMA/CA	carrier sense multiple access/collision avoidance
CSMA/CD	carrier sense multiple access/collision detection
DA	database administrator *or* desk accessory
DAC	digital-to-analog converter
DBMS	database management system
DBTG	CODASYL Data Base Task Group
DDL	data definition language *or* data description language
DES	Data Encryption Standard
DFD	data flow diagram
DIF	Data Interchange Format
DML	data manipulation language
DOS	Disk Operating System (refers to MS-DOS when discussing PCs)
dpi	dots per inch
DSS	decision support system
e-mail	electronic mail
EAN	European Article Number
EBCDIC	Extended Binary Coded Decimal Interchange Code
EDI	electronic (business) data interchange
EDIF	electronic design interchange format
EGA	enhanced graphics adapter
EIS	executive information system
ER	entity/relationship
ESA	Enterprise Systems Architecture
FIFO	first-in, first-out
5NF	fifth normal form
FLOPS	FLoating point Operations Per Second

FORTRAN	FORmula TRANslation language
4GL	fourth generation language
GIS	geographic information system
GOSIP	(U.S.) Government Open Systems Interconnections Profile
GUI	graphical user interface
HDLC	high-level data link control
hex	hexadecimal
HIPO	Hierarchy plus Input-Process-Output
IAN	International Article Number
ID	identification
IDMS	Integrated Database Management System
IDMS/R	Integrated Database Management System/Relational
IEEE	Institute of Electrical and Electronics Engineers
IGES	Initial Graphics Exchange Specification
I/O	input/output
IP	Internet Protocol
IRDS	Information Resource Dictionary System
IS	information systems
ISAM	indexed sequential access method
ISDN	Integrated Services Digital Network
ISO	International Standards Organization
ISO/OSI	International Standards Organization/Open Systems Interconnection
JAN	Japanese Article Number
KAPSE	Kernel Ada Program Support Environment
KEE	Knowledge Engineering Environment
LAN	local area network
LIFO	last-in, first-out
LISP	LISt Processing language
LU 6.2	Logical Unit 6.2
MAP	Manufacturing Automation Protocol
MAP/TOP	Manufacturing Automation Protocol/Technical and Office Protocol
MAPSE	Minimal Ada Program Support Environment
max	maximum
MDA	monochrome display adapter
memvar	memory variable

min	minimum
MIPS	million instructions per second
MIS	management information system
modem	modulator/demodulator
MS-DOS	Microsoft Disk Operating System (also called PC-DOS)
MUMPS	Massachusetts General Hospital Utility Multi-Programming System
MVS	Multiple Virtual Storage
MVS/ESA	Multiple Virtual Storage, Enterprise System Architecture
MVS/XA	Multiple Virtual Storage, Extended Architecture
NBS	(U.S.) National Bureau of Standards
NCSC	(U.S.) National Computer Security Center
NDL	Network Database Language
NIST	(U.S.) National Institute of Standards and Technology
NPL	nonprocedural language
NSA	(U.S.) National Security Agency
OCR	optical character recognition
OLTP	on-line transaction processing
1NF	first normal form
op code	operation code
OS	operating system
PAD	packet assembler/disassembler
PC	personal computer (usually, specifically IBM and compatible models)
PDES	Product Data Exchange Specification
PJ/NF	projection-join normal form
POS	point-of-sale
POSIX	Portable Operating System *and* UNIX
PSDN	packet-switched data network
PS/2	Personal System/2 (IBM)
QBE	Query-By-Example *or* query by example
QMF	Query Management Facility
RAM	random-access (read/write) memory
RAMP	risk analysis and management program
RGB	red-green-blue
RISC	reduced instruction set computer
ROM	read-only memory

RVM	reference validation mechanism
SAA	Systems Application Architecture
SDLC	Synchronous Data Link Control
SGML	Standardized General Markup Language
SMFA	system management functional area
SNA	Systems Network Architecture
SPARC	Scalable Processor ARChitecture
SQL	Structured Query Language
TCB	trusted computing base
TCP	Transmission Control Program
TCP/IP	Transmission Control Program/Internet Program
TDI	trusted database interpretation
TDR	time domain reflectometer
3NF	third normal form
TIFF	Tagged Image File Format
TIGER	topographically integrated geographic encoding and referencing system
TOP	Technical and Office Protocol
TSR	terminate and stay resident
2NF	second normal form
UDF	user-defined function
UPC	Universal Product Code *or* Uniform Product Code
VGA	video graphics array *or* video graphics adapter
VM	Virtual Machine (IBM operating system)
VMS	Virtual Memory System (DEC)
VSAM	virtual storage access method
VTAM	virtual telecommunications access method
WAN	wide area network
WORM	write once, read many
WPC	World Product Code
WYSIWYG	What You See Is What You Get
XCMD	external command
XFCN	external function

APPENDIX J
STRUCTURED QUERY LANGUAGE (SQL)
COMMANDS

Command   **Meaning**

DATA DEFINITION LANGUAGE

    CREATE   Create a schema, table, or virtual (view) table
    DROP*   Delete a schema, table, or virtual (view) table

DATA MANIPULATION LANGUAGE

    CLOSE   Close a cursor
    DECLARE   Define a cursor
    DELETE   Delete a row
    FETCH   Position cursor on next table row and retrieve values from it
    INSERT   Create new rows
    OPEN   Open a cursor
    SELECT   Retrieves values from specified rows
    UPDATE   Change data in a row

DATA CONTROL LANGUAGE

    GRANT   Define specified access privileges to a database
    REVOKE*   Remove specified access privileges to a database

*Not in American National Standard X3.135-1986.

Reader Comments
Database Dictionary

This book has been edited, the edited material reviewed, and the program matter tested and checked for accuracy; but bugs find their way into books as well as software. Please take a few minutes and tell us if you have found any errors, and give us your general comments regarding the quality of this book. Your time and attention will help us improve this and future products.

Did you find any mistakes? _____

_____

_____

Is this book complete? (If not, what should be added?)_____

_____

_____

What do you like about this book? _____

_____

_____

What do you not like about this book? _____

_____

_____

What other books would you like to see developed?_____

_____

_____

Other comments:_____

_____

_____

If you would like to be notified of new editions of this and/or other books that may be of interest to you, please complete the following:

Name_____

Address: _____

City/State/Zip_____

Mail to: **Microtrend™ Books**
Slawson Communications, Inc.
165 Vallecitos de Oro
San Marcos, CA 92069-1436

From the Lance A. Leventhal Data Based Advisor Series...
The first dictionary specifically for PC database users and specialists.

Database Dictionary

The Database Dictionary

Ellen Thro

NOW AVAILABLE ON DISK

The disk version of the Dictionary provides for ready access to definitions and cross-references. It may be activated as a pop-up under keyboard control from within an application (such as a word processor or database). Users can scroll through the text, obtain help, or save information via simple menus and key controls.

The Dictionary can be used with any editor or word processor. It is available for IBM and compatible computers with at least 256K memory under MS-DOS 2.0 and above.

A README.DOC file explains how to use the Dictionary. The package includes a printed instruction book.

To order, send $49.95, plus $3 for shipping and handling, to:

> Slawson Communications, Inc.
> 165 Vallecitos de Oro
> San Marcos, CA 92069

Or order by phone:
(800) SLAWSON or (619) 744-2299 (weekdays 8 A.M. - 5 P.M. Pacific Time).
FAX (619) 744-0424

"Rick Spence has taken on the formidable challenge of writing the definitive Clipper text."—**Brian Russel, Nantucket Corporation**

The **DATA BASED ADVISOR®** Series
Lance A. Leventhal, Ph.D., Series Director

Clipper® Programming Guide

by Rick Spence

Nantucket's Clipper compiler for dBASE programs is one of the most popular productivity tools in the database world. Rick Spence, co-developer of Clipper and expert columnist in *Data Based Advisor* and *Reference: Clipper* magazines, provides an up-to-date description of how to use Clipper effectively. He includes many examples drawn from actual applications and extensive discussions of arrays, user interfaces, query methods, memo fields, direct file access, networking, and file structures. He also explains the details of how to interface C programs to Clipper and presents complete sample programs for hot key management, mouse interfaces, and serial communications. The book starts where the manual leaves off; it provides new and advanced material, not duplication. As Brian Russell of Nantucket Corporation states in his foreword, "...no other author could explain Clipper so succinctly..."

Special Features of the book are:

■ Up-to-date coverage of Clipper

■ Extensive description of C programming for Clipper

■ Detailed procedures and examples for using Clipper on local area networks

■ Description of advanced query techniques involving multiple databases and multiple relations

■ Many new functions, tips, hints, and warnings derived from the author's extensive experience as both a developer and user of Clipper

■ Uses modern programming techniques throughout—all examples are modular, well-structured, and well documented.

■ All Clipper and C code in the book is also available on disk.

$24.95, ISBN 0-915391-31-7, 680 pages, 7 x 9, trade paperback, illustrations.

Available from your favorite book or computer store or use the order form in this book.

Slawson Communications • 165 Vallecitos de Oro • San Marcos, CA • 92069-1436

"Paul Heiser is the Peter Norton of the dBASE world, and the author of its bible, *Salvaging Damaged dBASE Files.*" —**Dennis Dykstra, *PC World* Magazine**

The **DATA BASED ADVISOR®** Series
Lance A. Leventhal, Ph.D., Series Director

Salvaging Damaged dBASE®
Files

SECOND EDITION

by Paul Heiser

In this new, totally revised edition, Paul Heiser covers dBASE IV and describes how to use DEBUG, Norton Utilities, IBM's Disk Repair, Westlake Data's DiskMinder, Mace Software's dBFix, and his own dSALVAGE and dSALVAGE Professional.

Thousands benefitted from the first edition of *Salvaging Damaged dBASE Files*. Here are even more proven methods for dealing with all types of dBASE file damage. You can overcome such problems as spurious data (including non-printing characters), extra end-of-file markers, nulls, damaged or destroyed file headers, displacement, damaged file allocation tables, and cross-linking. You can recover all or most of your data after power loss, improper disk handling, and file or format mixups. Heiser provides systematic procedures with step-by-step descriptions that even a beginner can follow. This is the book for you if you're a dBASE user who depends on database information. Don't wait until a disaster happens.

Paul W. Heiser is a well-known database authority and the author of several previous dBASE books. He has been working with dBASE products for many years in a variety of applications. His company also provides specialized software for file recovery. His dSALVAGE product received *PC World's* Best Buy Award in May 1989.

$24.95, ISBN 0-915391-33-3, 400 pages, 7 x 9, trade paperback, illustrations

Available from your favorite book or computer store or use the order form on the next page.

Slawson Communications • 165 Vallecitos de Oro • San Marcos, CA • 92069-1436

ORDER FORM

Thank you for purchasing this Microtrend™ book. To order additional copies of this book or any of our other titles, please complete the form below. Or call 1-800-SLAWSON.

Name_____

Address_____

City_____ State_____ Zip_____

Qty	Title	Price Each		Total	

Dept. SDDB

Subtotal	

U.S. SHIPPING
Books are shipped UPS except where a post office box is given as a delivery address.

Sales Tax: CA residents add 7.25%	
Shipping charge: $3.00 per book	
TOTAL	

FORM OF PAYMENT

☐ Visa ☐ MasterCard ☐ Check

Card #: | | | | | | | | | | | | | | | | | | |

Expiration date: _____

Signature: _____ Date_____

Mail this order form to:

Microtrend™ Books
Slawson Communications, Inc.
165 Vallecitos de Oro
San Marcos, CA 92069-1436

619/744-2299

BUSINESS REPLY MAIL

FIRST CLASS MAIL   PERMIT NO. 77   Escondido, CA

Postage will be paid by addressee

DATA BASED
ADVISOR®

The Database Management Systems Magazine

Box 3735
Escondido, CA 92025-9895

NO POSTAGE
NECESSARY
IF MAILED
IN THE
UNITED STATES

BUSINESS REPLY MAIL

FIRST CLASS MAIL   PERMIT NO. 77   Escondido, CA

Postage will be paid by addressee

DATA BASED
ADVISOR®

The Database Management Systems Magazine

Box 3735
Escondido, CA 92025-9895